Oral Art Forms and their Passage into Writing

Oral Art Forms
and their Passage into Writing

Edited by
Else Mundal and
Jonas Wellendorf

Museum Tusculanum Press
University of Copenhagen 2008

Else Mundal and Jonas Wellendorf (eds.):
Oral Art Forms and their Passage into Writing

© Museum Tusculanum Press and the authors, 2008
Consultant: Ivan Boserup
Composition by Jonas Wellendorf
Cover by Pernille Sys Hansen
Set in Adobe Garamond
Printed in Denmark by AKA Print
ISBN 978 87 635 0504 8

Cover illustration: fol. 182v (Herr Bligger von Steinach)
from the manuscript Codex Manesse (Cod. Pal. germ. 848)
© Universitätsbibliothek Heidelberg

This book is published with the financial support from
Bergen Universitetsfond

Museum Tusculanum Press
Njalsgade 126
DK-2300 Copenhagen S
www.mtp.dk

Contents

Introduction

ELSE MUNDAL

THE ARTICLES IN this book deal with oral art forms and their passage into writing in different cultures. They build on papers presented at a conference organised by the Centre for Medieval Studies at the University of Bergen in June 2004.

The oral art forms of the past can be studied only through later written records. It is in many cases difficult to know how representative a written form of a text is of the earlier oral form – or forms. There are also differences from one genre to another both regarding how much one oral performance could differ from another and how much the written form could differ from an oral performance. It is obvious that some oral genres had a form which did not allow much variation from one performance to the other. The most typical example of this is the Old Norse skaldic poetry. There is general agreement among scholars that skaldic poetry was memorised poetry, not improvised. The performer should – in principle – be able to recite the stanzas as he had learned them using the same words every time he or she performed; and when a skaldic stanza was written down, it would have been written down as it was recited word-for-word, or if the scribe knew the stanza himself, he would have written it down exactly as he would have recited it. In this case the oral text is extremely stable compared to other oral texts, and the written form would not add anything new to the oral form – what is new is that the written medium provided a safe-keeping for the text outside the human mind. The written skaldic stanzas give us in many ways direct access to the oral forms behind. There are, however, also important aspects of oral skaldic poetry which the written form does not give much information about, for instance aspects related to performance.

At the other end of the scale we have written texts which have no equivalents or close parallels on the oral stage, but which at least to some extent build on an oral tradition and adopt some of its content as well as its compositional and stylistic features. In this case it is more difficult to draw conclusions about the oral art forms behind the written texts. However, the marks the oral tradition has left on the written text may provide us with some information about the previous oral forms which again may form a basis for theories about the oral forms behind the written texts and about their relation to each other. The sagas of Icelanders are typical texts of this kind. In cases where Latin texts build on oral tradition in the vernacular, the relation between the oral tradition and the written form is even more complicated.

Most oral art forms are to be found somewhere on a scale between the skaldic poetry where the written form in principle should reflect older oral forms rather closely, and medieval written prose texts which give vague and uncertain information about the oral tradition upon which the written texts build. Old Norse Eddic poetry, Old English poetry, Homeric epic, Serbian epic songs and medieval ballads, to mention some genres from different European cultures, are genres which were less stable in oral tradition than skaldic poetry and the relation between the first written form and the oral form(s) on which the written form was built was also less predictable than in skaldic poetry. There is, however, reason to believe that there are great differences among these genres regarding where they fit in between memorised literature, of which skaldic poetry is the most typical example, and improvised literature which was more or less reshaped in every oral performance. The Eddic poetry is – according to most scholars – to be seen as essentially memorised oral literature, although it must have been more open for improvisation and changes than skaldic poetry. Old English oral poetry on the other hand was probably even more open for changes in oral tradition than the Nordic Eddic type. We know from modern times that Serbian oral songs could change considerably from one performance to the other, and the differences between versions of ballads written down in the nineteenth century and those recorded earlier were often great.

The articles of this book focus on oral art forms of all the different types mentioned above, and investigate literature belonging to different genres and areas.

The first three articles in the book all deal with saga literature, especially the sagas of Icelanders. Theodore M. Andersson tries to establish what is possible to deduce about the oral stories which the authors of saga literature had to build upon. He concludes that the style of the written sagas is likely to be largely oral, but the shape of any given saga must have been exclusively determined by the saga writer. The saga writer had, however, different types of narrative found in oral tradition to build upon, for instance biographical traditions, genealogical traditions, regional traditions about important events in a particular district, and traditions attached to landmarks, place names, and so on. Andersson suggests three types of overall organisation that the saga authors could choose from to create their stories: he could choose a biographical structure, he could write a sort of district chronicle, or he could be guided by the feud structure.

As opposed to Theodore M. Andersson, Gísli Sigurðsson finds the Old Norse texts unhelpful on their own when it comes to considering the nature of oral art forms in the Middle Ages. According to him, a more promising approach to envisaging the Old Norse oral background can be arrived at by drawing on the contemporary field studies from a variety of oral cultures.

In the third article Tommy Danielsson discusses the possibility of an oral background for one particular saga of Icelanders, *Gísla saga Súrssonar*. The beginning of this saga exists in two rather different versions. The question raised by Danielsson is whether the long *S*-version may point towards an oral background to a higher degree than the shorter *M*-version.

In the fourth article Minna Skafte Jensen discusses the oral-formulaic theory in the light of three living traditions, two from India and one from Egypt. These oral traditions are especially interesting in connection with this theory as they confirm that oral epic can be of considerable length, even longer than the *Iliad* and the *Odyssey*. The flexibility of the long oral narrative is also confirmed. However, the comparison of different oral cultures shows that it varies how carefully passages will be memorised from one genre and tradition to another.

The fifth and the sixth articles concentrate on the relationship between vernacular tradition and Latin prose. Lars Boje Mortensen follows the writing process from a collection of material in the vernacular to the finished Latin text. He focuses on the various elements of this process, interviewing and note-taking, draft-writing, and finally the copying of the text into codex form. The conclusion is that the passage into writing entailed two major stages, one from interview to draft notes of various sorts, another from drafts to the calligraphed parchment book. These two stages should not only be separated due to their technical and practical implications, but it is equally important that the boundary surrounding the book format was charged with connotations of sacred writing and therefore more difficult to cross.

Anna Adamska presents some of the results of the long-term research project undertaken in Utrecht concerning the passage from orality to literate behaviour and literate mentalities in medieval Western society. In her article she focuses on the transition from memory to written record in East Central Europe. She emphasises that the passage from oral vernacular to written Latin and the passage from oral vernacular to written vernacular were two very different phenomena.

In the seventh article Sonja Petrović investigates the oral and the written art forms in Serbian medieval literature. In the Serbian culture oral and written art forms coexisted for centuries, and Petrović demonstrates by means of examples the complexity of the contacts between the oral and the written forms.

The topic of the eighth article is the Old English poem *Beowulf*. Graham D. Caie asks what this old poem tells us about oral forms. *Beowulf* no doubt contains formulas and stylistic features which are typical of orally composed poems. Caie shows, however, that works which we know were written compositions share identical formulas. The use of formulas should therefore not be confused with oral composition.

The ninth and the tenth articles deal with Scandinavian medieval ballads. This genre could in many cases go from oral to written form, and back again. Olav Solberg argues that the so-called *Eufemiavisorna*, 'Eufemia's lays' (composed shortly after 1300), borrowed formulas and expressions from the ballad genre which had been introduced in Norway only 15–20 years earlier, and many of these formulas were still in use when ballads were recorded in the nineteenth century. This shows that the ballad style was stable even though its contents changed. Solberg also argues that when it comes to the question of how formulas were used, unlike the Yugoslavian singers who recomposed the poems by means of formulas at every performance, the Scandinavian ballad singers memorised the ballads. The formulas, however, helped the singers to learn the ballads by heart.

Jonas Wellendorf focuses on one ballad, the *Draumkvæde*. This is a ballad which was obviously composed directly or indirectly on the basis of vision literature. There are, however, some important differences concerning the content and motifs between all the different versions of the ballad on one hand, and the visionary literature on the other. Wellendorf's explanation of these differences is that the poem at the time of its composition would have kept itself largely within the confines of the accepted visionary framework. However, as time passed, the genre of visions went out of fashion, and the ballad was open for changes to fit a new and different context.

In the eleventh article Bernt Øyvind Thorvaldsen investigates the relationship between text and context in texts which include verses of Eddic form. The written text is considered to represent a special kind of performance. In his discussion of the relationship between the oral form and the written performance Thorvaldsen pays special attention to non-verbal aspects, the interactions of participants, and the social aspects of art forms. How an oral art form and its context can be understood is discussed on the basis of three different texts in which the Eddic form is used. These examples show that the performance perspective, when applied to oral art forms, indicates that orality and literacy must be viewed as integrated aspects of expression, not as antipodes of two basically different communicative cultures.

The twelfth article deals with skaldic poetry, and the question raised by Bergsveinn Birgisson is: what have we lost by writing? Bergsveinn Birgisson argues that in the old poems from the time before the arrival of writing and Christianity we find reflections of a way of thinking that is different from the one manifested in the later skaldic poetry. This archaic mentality which, according to Bergsveinn Birgisson, is typical of the old, pre-Christian oral culture, is easily seen in the metaphors, or in the Old Norse *kenningar*, which create pictures that mirror another mentality, way of thinking and aesthetics than in the later written culture.

The topic of the thirteenth article, written by Guðrún Nordal, is the dialogue between audience and text as exemplified by *Njáls saga*. In some of the manuscripts of this saga written only a few decades after the saga was composed, there are added a number of skaldic stanzas which were obviously inspired by the prose text of the saga. As Nordal sees it, the audience in the fourteenth century has here put its stamp on the narrative by enriching the prose with new skaldic stanzas. This points to a lively interaction between the written and the oral culture. The written text is not stable, but is open to changes that aim to satisfy the tastes of the listening audience.

In the penultimate article Ljubiša Rajić discusses the mixing of *oratio recta* and *oratio obliqua*. This style element, which is called *oratio tecta*, has been seen as characteristic of literacy when used in Old Norse prose, and as characteristic of orality when used in folk-stories in the Balkan area. Rajić is inclined to regard the switching between *oratio recta* and *oratio obliqua* as more typical for speech than writing. The fact that this style element has been judged differently within different cultures could also be a reminder that there may be great differences from one culture to another concerning what should be regarded as hallmarks of orality and literacy.

The last article, written by Else Mundal, compares two versions of the Eddic poem *Vǫluspá* in order to try to decide whether the different versions of the poem are the result of oral or scribal variation. The answer to this question has great consequences for the view of the stability of oral Eddic tradition. If the different versions of this poem are the result of oral variation, which the comparison seems to indicate, Eddic stanzas changed little in oral tradition, and the genre is much closer to memorised poetry than to improvised.

It is the wish of the editors and the authors that the articles in this book focusing on different oral art forms from different geographical areas and from different periods of time will stimulate the scholarly discussion of the many interesting questions connected to the oral art forms of the past.

From Tradition to Literature in the Sagas

Theodore M. Andersson

T HE PROBLEM OF how oral tradition may have passed into the written sagas of medieval Iceland and our assessment of the form in which the stories were transmitted orally continue to defy our best efforts at achieving a consensus. The puzzle may seem surprising because there is a great abundance of material at our disposal, more than enough, it would seem, to underpin a reasonable hypothesis. Unlike the Homerists, we are not confronted with two finished poems and a great dearth of auxiliary information. Despite their shortage of first-hand evidence the Homerists manage in fact to sound much more confident about the oral antecedents of Homer than do the Norsists, with their stock of half a hundred texts and a number of references to saga telling. One crucial difference is that the Homerists have been able to enlist the international fund of oral-formulaic analogies in their cause, whereas no such general theory is available for prose narrative.

Perhaps if we had a clearer sense of saga chronology we would be able to make better progress. If we knew precisely, or even approximately, which sagas were written first, we might surmise that they lie closer to the oral substratum and we might then measure the gradual transition from oral style to written style, but the dating of the sagas has become, if anything, more difficult in recent years. Sagas that were once considered early by consensus have now been assigned much later dates.[1] In this area too the Homerists demonstrate an almost carefree certitude while the Norsists can find almost no common ground.[2] About all they agree on is that there must have been some sort of oral transmission before the sagas were written down.

Over the decades, however, the assessments of this transmission have differed widely. The Norwegian historians of the nineteenth century believed that it was a fixed tradition, and that view persisted as late as Andreas Heusler's final statement in 1941.[3] But by 1941 this doctrine had already been overtaken by the more inventionist views of Icelandic scholars beginning with Björn Magnússon

---

[1] On *Fóstbrœðra saga* see Jónas Kristjánsson 1972. On *Heiðarvíga saga* and *Bjarnar saga Hítdœlakappa* see Bjarni Guðnason 1993; Bjarni Guðnason 1994.

[2] See Vésteinn Ólason 1998, 21: "The uncertainties of dating [the sagas] make it a hazardous venture to speculate about any kind of development during the thirteenth century."

[3] Heusler 1941, 208–213.

Ólsen and culminating in the Íslenzk fornrit introductions from the 1930s down to the 1950s. Walter Baetke's monograph from 1956 carried the view that the sagas are contrived fictions a step further.[4] The issue is an old one and was once a contentious one, but in the latter part of the twentieth century it no longer generated the same interest that it had excited earlier in the century. The waning interest is illustrated by two books written from diametrically opposed standpoints in 1976. Óskar Halldórsson wrote a small but pioneering book on *Hrafnkels saga* from the traditionalist perspective, and Rolf Heller wrote a large, compendious book on *Laxdæla saga* from the inventionist perspective.[5] By all rights that perfectly symmetrical opposition should have revived the debate and inspired a new round of inquiry, but it did not.

Ten years later in 1986 Carol Clover wrote a paper in which she tried to find a compromise between the traditionalist and inventionist extremes.[6] She argued that the long stories could have been known to the Icelandic audience in outline (a phenomenon she called the "immanent saga"), but she went on to say that such longer tales were not realized as complete narratives or performed in recitation until they were written down. Rather, the Icelanders told shorter stories, as is customary in most prose traditions around the world. These shorter stories were ultimately elaborated by writers in such a way as to produce long saga texts. There seems to have been no direct response to Clover's argument until my own paper of 2002, in which I offered arguments for believing that there may have been long oral stories as well as short ones.[7]

At the end of the twentieth century it therefore appeared that the classical problem of saga transmission had fallen into abeyance. Then quite suddenly in 2002 there appeared three substantial and quite radical books on the subject, two by Tommy Danielsson and one by Gísli Sigurðsson.[8] Gísli concentrated on the sagas from the East Fjord district in Iceland and studied the ways in which they both coincide and diverge from one another. He concluded that the relationship between somewhat differing accounts of the same story is not literary but is based on a fluid oral tradition that could be set down differently by different writers. Tommy Danielsson focused on the most famous of the East Fjord sagas, *Hrafnkels saga*, and concluded that it is not a literary creation, as Sigurður Nordal had argued in 1940, but rather a traditional story about a regional dispute. In his second volume he surveyed some of the kings' saga material and emphasized again the importance of the oral traditions that gave rise to the kings' sagas.

There is clearly much common ground in the books by Gísli Sigurðsson and Tommy Danielsson. Both of these scholars attribute an important formative role to the oral tradition. On the other hand, both believe that there are

---

[4] The whole debate has been reviewed most recently by DANIELSSON 2002a, 231–277.

[5] ÓSKAR HALLDÓRSSON 1976 and HELLER 1976. With an almost prophetic sense that the debate had reached a preliminary plateau, MUNDAL 1977 also chose this year to summarize it in *Sagadebatt*.

[6] CLOVER 1986.

[7] ANDERSSON 2002.

[8] DANIELSSON 2002a,b; GÍSLI SIGURÐSSON 2002. The latter is now available in English translation in GÍSLI SIGURÐSSON 2004. I have reviewed these books in ANDERSSON 2004.

real limitations to what we can say about the nature of the oral tradition. Gísli Sigurðsson believes that the tradition was so radically transformed in the written texts that these texts no longer reveal anything about the prior tradition.[9] Tommy Danielsson stresses that the interaction between oral story and written text, an interaction running in both directions, was so great over such a long period of time that it has become impossible to separate oral and literary layers in the written sagas.[10] This cautious assessment has the effect of producing a real paradox; just as the oral transmission seems to become more palpable and a more important element in our thinking, it seems also to vanish from our field of vision and become less accessible to scrutiny. We are told in effect that there was an extensive and well-developed oral tradition, but that we are not in a position to describe it. I find myself reluctant to subscribe to this resignation and believe that we can, after all, say something about the underlying oral tradition.

We might do well at the outset to remind ourselves of the famous passages on oral storytelling. Apart from the wedding at Reykjahólar in 1119, the most familiar of these passages is an Icelander's recital of Haraldr harðráði's adventures in the very presence of the king himself.[11] We may recall that the storyteller is quite nervous at the prospect of telling the story because he fears the king's reaction, but at the conclusion of the story the king compliments him on the strict accuracy of his recital. Truth is therefore an important consideration. In this case the story is about contemporary adventures learned by the teller from an eyewitness. Some approximation of the truth is therefore possible. The truth also looms large in another episode, at the end of *Njáls saga*, when Njáll's avengers overhear a version of the burning of his house that is false. In this case the teller pays the price for his falsehoods by losing his head. People who listened to such accounts were clearly preoccupied with the truth. They expected the truth and could be imagined to resort to violent correctives.[12]

It goes without saying that saga authors in the thirteenth century could not reproduce anything resembling the truth from the Saga Age, but they and their listeners must have thought they could. We must therefore ask what it means that the sagas were thought to be in some manner truthful. Perhaps it means that teller and audience thought that a facsimile of the truth was possible because they assumed that the story had been handed down in an unbroken transmission from the time of the events. They believed that the tradition was maintained as a reservoir of truth. That must mean that there was a certain stability in the tradition and that tellers were reluctant to deviate too far from what was construed as an accepted version.

The idea of truth is perhaps also suggested by the famous reference to *lygisǫgur* at Reykjahólar.[13] Here we learn that the saga of Hrómundr Gripsson

---

[9] Gísli Sigurðsson 2002, 39, 51, 325–327; 2004, 37, 48, 328–330.
[10] Danielsson 2002a, 304.
[11] *Morkinskinna* 199–200.
[12] On the transition from truth to fiction see Meulengracht Sørensen 2001.
[13] *Þorgils saga ok Hafliða* 22.

had been told to King Sverrir and that he had reacted by saying that such *lygisǫgur* were amusing. Perhaps we will not be overinterpreting this passage if we understand it to mean that King Sverrir *even* liked fictional sagas, though of course truthful sagas might normally be preferred. In other words, the term *lygisǫgur* implies the existence of true sagas.

Aside from the issue of truth, there is a second important issue that emerges from the Icelander's recital at King Haraldr's court. Andreas Heusler was the first to look at the story closely and to extract from it conclusions about the nature of the oral tradition.[14] The king directs and articulates the story in such a way that it runs through the twelve days of Christmas in twelve successive installments. Heusler thought that each installment lasted about fifteen minutes, so that the whole story took about three hours. Heinrich Matthias Heinrichs thought that was an underestimate,[15] and I believe it is a radical underestimate. We should remember that Heusler believed the written sagas to be memorized and therefore of essentially the same length as the oral sagas. He would instinctively have made the performance time at Haraldr's court approximate the reading time of the equivalent passage in *Morkinskinna* as closely as possible. But it defies reason to imagine that King Haraldr's court would have come to a complete standstill once a day for twelve days in succession to listen to a fifteen-minute episode. I am more inclined to believe that the recital may have gone on for an hour or two. It was, after all, an official court entertainment.

That story sessions could have been of considerable duration is confirmed by other episodes, not only the one in *Njáls saga* but also a well-known record of storytelling at the end of *Fóstbrœðra saga*. Here, as elsewhere, storytelling is an official occasion, this time at a thingmeeting in Greenland. The teller is provided with a special seat and everyone gathers around to hear the story. It is about the fall of Þorgeirr Hávarsson and is told by one of his killers. The story is judged to be very entertaining, so much so that one of the listeners comes to the thingbooth of Þorgeirr's foster brother Þormóðr Bersason to let him know that he is missing a really good story. Such an absence from the site of the storytelling might in itself take fifteen minutes, but the absent listener seems not at all concerned about losing the thread of the story or any of the excitement. Again, the implication is that the recitation is of relatively long duration, far longer than the equivalent passage on Þorgeirr's death in *Fóstbrœðra saga*, a passage that occupies five half-pages in the *ÍF* edition and includes some of Þormóðr's later stanzas that would not have been part of the oral story version.[16] What does this say about the relationship between oral delivery and the written saga? It suggests that what we have in the written sagas is a substantial abbreviation of the oral forerunner, in other words that there is not much similarity between the oral story and the written saga. What remains in the written sagas must be no more than an epitome of the underlying oral tale, a literary encapsulation of what went before.

---

[14] Heusler 1941, 205.
[15] Heinrichs 1975, 230.
[16] *Fóstbrœðra saga* 206–211.

So far I would conclude that the oral stories were, barring evidence to the contrary, considered to be true, or at least traditional, and that the stories were extensive and capable of being told at some length. But of course there would have been shorter stories as well. The most palpable evidence of short stories is found in the *þættir*, which seem clearly not to be abridged but are focused so sharply and told so pointedly that they must derive from equally lean and economical oral narratives. How old such stories might be is a matter of guesswork, but there is already a collection of some sixteen *þættir* in *Morkinskinna* from ca. 1220. If Ármann Jakobsson is right that they belong to the original redaction, we may surmise that they were in circulation at least as early as the twelfth century.[17] Because they are so short and pointed, the written versions may resemble the oral versions more closely than in the case of the longer sagas. Even we moderns can retell a *þáttr* without too much difficulty. We might also consider what influence these small, carefully crafted, and stylistically refined stories may have exerted on the longer written sagas.

Indeed, it is not sufficient to ask whether the oral stories were long, short, or both. We must also ask whether they were merely informational or stylistically heightened and dramatically shaped, like the *þættir*. Some sagas (I think of *Orkneyinga saga* or *Eyrbyggja saga* or the Vinland sagas) are less dramatic than others, but there is evidence that the oral stories must in some cases have been quite dramatic and suspenseful. In the first place, it is clear from the storytelling incidents that the stories were considered to be entertaining and held the attention of large audiences. It is also clear from both *þættir* and written sagas that dialogue was an important part of the traditional technique. The percentage of direct speech in the sagas rarely falls below 20% and ranges as high as 31% in *Laxdæla saga*, 39% in *Hænsa-Þóris saga* and *Njáls saga*, 44% in *Ljósvetninga saga*, and 47% in *Bandamanna saga*.[18]

There is a further reason for believing that there were dramatized oral stories. The sagas from an early period, that is, the sagas set in the Saga Age, are distinctly more dramatic than the later sagas, notably those collected in *Sturlunga saga*. It has been duly noted that the sagas in the Sturlung collection have their dramatic moments, for example the prelude to the Battle of Ǫrlygsstaðir in *Íslendinga saga*, but despite the occasional exception the difference in overall drama between the classical sagas and the contemporary sagas is quite manifest. The difference has generally been explained through the supposition that the classical sagas passed through a sort of storytelling filter at the oral stage and were thus transformed into streamlined narratives, while the contemporary sagas experienced no such narrative refinement and remained at a more chronicle-like stage.[19] This explanation seems altogether satisfactory, although there were contemporary sagas that imitated oral style and traditional sagas that imitated chronicle style.

---

[17] ÁRMANN JAKOBSSON 2002, 51–53.
[18] NETTER 1935, 17–18.
[19] LIESTØL 1930, 6–14.

If we look at the earliest sagas, we can see how these styles combine in a somewhat awkward way. Oddr Snorrason's *Óláfs saga Tryggvasonar* begins well enough because the initial chapters are based on an orderly written model, but the saga soon lapses into a loose concatenation of incidents with no real story line.[20] It is only the concluding account of the Battle of Svǫlðr that is dramatically articulated and bears the marks of a highly developed storytelling art. *The Oldest Saga of Saint Olaf*, which can be extrapolated from *The Legendary Saga*, is an even looser agglomeration of episodes often based on clusters of skaldic stanzas. In these early sagas the practices of oral storytelling have not yet been effectively harnessed.

What does that tell us about the underlying oral tradition? It may suggest that much of the oral material was transmitted in fragmented and episodic form. Only occasionally had the narrative been articulated in story form, as in the description of the Battle of Svǫlðr. In other words, the narrative was often passed down not in neatly composed sagas but in random bits and pieces. The oral transmissions were not necessarily fixed but were multifarious and could be collected and recorded in various combinations.

There were nonetheless highly developed storytelling skills, as the young Icelander's performance at King Haraldr's court makes clear. These oral skills were transferred to the writing stage in a remarkably short time. If our dating is reliable, there was a fully elaborated written saga style already in place in the 1220s, in *The Saga of King Magnús and King Haraldr* from *Morkinskinna* and in *Egils saga*. How did the transfer from oral style to written style come about? The saga authors could of course have been content with the loose anecdotal form that we find in the early Olaf sagas. At least one of them was. I refer to *Reykdœla saga*, a saga characterized by serial composition, repetitive phrasing, and a low percentage of direct speech (6%). But as time went on, other saga authors embraced a dramatic style borrowed, I surmise, from the best storytellers. Good examples of this new style might be *Fóstbrœðra saga*, *Heiðarvíga saga*, *Ljósvetninga saga*, and *Þorgils saga ok Hafliða*, although the dating of all these sagas is in dispute.

To recapitulate the main points so far, the sagas were considered to be truthful, that is to say, they were considered to stand in a narrative continuity descended from some original truth. The written sagas probably represent an abbreviated version of very extensive traditions cultivated orally in various forms. The storytelling based on these traditions could be random and episodic or, in the hands of a skilled teller, the stories could be dramatic and narratively compelling. The saga writers could use both the episodic transmissions and the fully articulated stories, but the best of these writers took over the dramatic form from the skilled storytellers. The fullness of the traditions and the variety in the form of transmission suggest that the stories were not fixed but fluid, not binding on the writer but merely available for recasting in a form chosen by the writers.

---

[20] I argue this view in ANDERSSON 2003, 6–14.

That brings us to the main point. Ever since the nineteenth century there has been an assumption that a written saga is a replication of an equivalent oral saga, though there has been much disagreement about how exact the replication is. This assumption is evident from the fact that much of the early twentieth-century debate was centered on differing redactions of one and the same saga, notably *Bandamanna saga* and *Ljósvetninga saga*. The question was whether the differing redactions were oral variants or literary variants. Even in so close a correspondence as exists in the *M* and *K* redactions of *Bandamanna saga* Heusler detected oral variants, and Liestøl did not contradict him.[21] More recently Hallvard Magerøy studied both cases in great detail and concluded that both are instances of literary variation.[22] I think it quite unlikely that anyone today would disagree with him.

In the meantime Gísli Sigurðsson has shifted the ground significantly by concentrating on differing versions in different sagas rather than differing redactions of the same saga. His approach reveals flexible traditions cast differently by different authors, not fixed traditions. The metaphor used by Tommy Danielsson to convey such flexibility is "det muntliga havet" (the open sea of orality).[23] This term suggests again that there were no fixed traditions, only an ebb and flow of open-ended stories. Thus there would have been no identifiable *Hallfreðar saga*, no *Egils saga*, no hypothetical *Snorra saga goða*, only a variety of stories about all these characters.

Gísli Sigurðsson and Tommy Danielsson are reluctant to write about the exact nature of the oral transmissions, but I believe we need not be quite so hesitant. The extant saga literature is so extensive that I think it safe to assume that types of narrative that are ubiquitous in the written literature would also have had some presence in the oral stories. Let me therefore suggest the kind of narrative I think would have been found in the oral tradition.

There must have been something akin to biographical traditions, or at least something that was biographical enough to be converted into biographical form. Such biographical traditions are the backbone of the kings' sagas, the skald sagas, and a number of sagas in the Sturlung collection. There must have been stories about pagan apparitions, ghosts, revenants, sorcerers, and magic spells because these matters surface again and again in a variety of sagas, in which they have no particular function and are unlikely to have been invented for literary effect.

There must have been genealogical traditions of an extent and complexity that is difficult for modern readers to imagine. It is not possible that all the names and relationships in the sagas could have been extracted or hypothesized from *Landnámabók* or similar genealogical records. Nor can they all have been invented, a procedure that would stand in opposition to the generally shared expectation that the oral stories were truthful, that is, rooted in traditions deriving from some ultimate reality. There must have been regional traditions

---

[21] Liestøl 1930, 47–48.
[22] Magerøy 1956, 1957.
[23] Danielsson 2002b, 385–395.

focused on the events and political interactions in a particular district. We find this political core in all the sagas, whether it be the classical sagas or the contemporary sagas. In particular there must have been traditions about lawsuits and litigation, the sort of focus that Tommy Danielsson has emphasized as the background for *Hrafnkels saga*.[24]

Finally, there must have been traditions attached to particular landmarks, place names, and residences. These traditions do not add much to the narrative substance of the sagas, but they recur in almost all the sagas as incidental information. They too must therefore have been lodged in the oral stories. All of these matters would have been conveyed in the oral transmissions, but not in any particular form or combination. They could have been assembled and recombined in countless different forms depending on the aim of the storyteller or saga writer. If the sagas had been fixed, the aim or intention would have been to some extent inherent in the tradition and would have been somewhat similar from one saga to another. But the sagas are sufficiently diverse that it seems more likely that it was the individual author who lent a particular thrust to the narrative.

With a considerable degree of oversimplification, I will suggest just three types of overall organization that the saga authors could choose from in order to determine the thrust of their stories. They could choose a biographical structure, an option that produced all the kings' sagas, all the bishops' sagas, and the sagas we refer to as skald sagas. It also produced the outlaw sagas (*Gísla saga*, *Grettis saga*, and *Harðar saga Grímkelssonar*) and several sagas in the Sturlung collection (*Sturlu saga*, *Guðmundar saga dýra*, *Þórðar saga kakala*, and *Þorgils saga skarða*).

A second option was to organize the saga as a sort of district chronicle. Among the classical sagas this option is represented by such texts as *Eyrbyggja saga*, *Laxdœla saga*, *Ljósvetninga saga*, *Reykdœla saga*, *Vatnsdœla saga*, and *Víga-Glúms saga*. In the Sturlung complex the obvious example is *Íslendinga saga*, and we might add such peripheral texts as *Færeyinga saga* and *Orkneyinga saga*. A third option for the author was to be guided by the feud or conflict principle that must have been at the center of many oral stories and is found in *Droplaugarsona saga*, *Heiðarvíga saga*, *Hrafnkels saga*, *Hœnsa-Þóris saga*, *Njáls saga*, or *Vápnfirðinga saga*. The conflict pattern is also central in several of the regional sagas, for example *Ljósvetninga saga*, *Reykdœla saga*, or, in the Sturlung collection, *Þorgils saga ok Hafliða*.

Thus we can identify something like an overall structure in many of the sagas, but nowhere do we find a pure form. There are no pure biographies among the classical sagas, no pure district chronicles, and no pure feud sagas. Thus *Egils saga* is predominantly biographical but also regional and agonistic. *Ljósvetninga saga* is regional and agonistic in equal parts. *Eyrbyggja saga* is regional but also biographical in its account of Snorri goði's dealings. *Laxdœla saga* is regional and agonistic, but it concludes with a biographical focus on Guðrún Ósvífrsdóttir. The emphasis, or the combination of emphases, was surely an option exercised by the saga author, but we may assume that it was a

---

[24] DANIELSSON 2002a, 282.

matter of choice for the antecedent storytellers as well. Each teller must have made individual decisions on styles of presentation as well as the selection of particular incidents.

These choices could have been almost infinitely variable. I see no reason to believe that a given written saga corresponded to a particular oral story. Indeed, I believe this is the fundamental principle in the studies of Gísli Sigurðsson and Tommy Danielsson. There would have been no *Egils saga* before there was a written *Egils saga*, but there would presumably have been dozens of stories about Egill's life, perhaps even summaries of his life. There would have been supernatural stories about shape-shifting, magic, and berserks immune to steel. There would have been genealogical traditions about settlement and intermarriage in Borgarfjǫrðr and the neighboring districts. There would have been regional stories about contentious dealings in Borgarfjǫrðr, for example Þorsteinn Egilsson's dispute with Steinarr Ǫnundarson, which figures at the end of the written saga. There would have been stories about Egill's legal claims and lawsuits. There would have been stories about his duels and conflicts with royalty. There would have been traditions about places, the place where Skalla-Grímr fetched up a great stone from the fjord to serve as an anvil, or the place where Egill hid his chests of silver at the end of his life. And there would of course have been stories about Egill's poetry. But none of these stories and traditions would have been in anything like the biographical structure we now have in our written *Egils saga Skallagrímssonar*.

I conclude with a final recapitulation of what I think we might deduce about the oral stories that circulated before, and no doubt after, there were written sagas. These stories were thought to be true, although this may only mean that they were thought to be about real people and to have been passed down in relatively stable form from the time of the actual events. The stories could be short, as in the *þættir*, or they could be told at some length for a relatively large gathering of people, as an official entertainment. In other words, the stories were not predetermined or fixed but were flexible; the form they took depended on the occasion and the skill of the teller.

The stories were not necessarily in dramatic style, but they must often have been so because they were considered entertaining and because the written sagas more often than not reflect a dramatic style. It is unlikely that the subject matter of the oral stories was very different from the subject matter of the written sagas. The oral stories were presumably also about supernatural matters, the lives of Icelandic ancestors, the legal and contentious dealings of these ancestors, district interactions, and places to which important events were attached. This does not, however, mean that there was any precise correlation between a written saga and an antecedent oral story. The writer of a saga chose freely among the available traditions and determined the structure of the saga as a whole, whether that structure was to be in chronicle or regional form, in biographical form, in the form of a feud story, or in any combination of these forms. The *style* of the written sagas is likely to be largely oral, but the *shape* of any given saga, the final product as a whole, must have been the exclusive determination of the saga writer.

Bibliography

Primary sources

Fóstbrœðra saga, eds. Björn K. Þórólfsson and Guðni Jónsson in *Vestfirðinga sǫgur*, Íslenzk fornrit 6, 119–276. Reykjavík 1943.
Morkinskinna, ed. Finnur Jónsson. STUAGNL 53. København 1932.
Þorgils saga ok Hafliða, ed. Örnólfur Thorsson in *Sturlunga saga* I: 7–46. Reykjavík 1988.

Secondary sources

ANDERSSON, Theodore M. 2002: "The long prose form in medieval Iceland." *JEGP*, 101 380–411.
———— 2003: *Oddr Snorrason: The Saga of Olaf Tryggvason, Islandica*, vol. 52. Ithaca.
———— 2004: "Five saga books for a new century: A review essay." *JEGP*, 103 505–527.
ÁRMANN JAKOBSSON 2002: *Staður í nýjum heimi: Konungasagan Morkinskinna.* Reykjavík.
BJARNI GUÐNASON 1993: *Túlkun Heiðarvígasögu, Studia Islandica*, vol. 50. Reykjavík.
———— 1994: "Aldur og einkenni Bjarnarsögu Hítdœlakappa." In Gísli Sigurðsson, Guðrún Kvaran & Sigurgeir Steingrímsson (eds.) *Sagnaþing helgað Jónasi Kristjánssyni sjötugum 10. apríl 1994*, vol. 1, pp. 69–85, Reykjavík.
CLOVER, Carol J. 1986: "The long prose form." *Arkiv för nordisk filologi*, 101 10–39.
DANIELSSON, Tommy 2002a: *Hrafnkels saga eller Fallet med den undflyende traditionen.* Hedemora.
———— 2002b: *Sagorna om Norges kungar: Från Magnús góði till Magnús Erlingsson.* Hedemora.
GÍSLI SIGURÐSSON 2002: *Túlkun Íslendingasagna í ljósi munnlegrar hefðar: Tilgáta um aðferð.* Reykjavík.
———— 2004: *The Medieval Icelandic Saga and Oral Tradition: A Discourse on Method, Publications of the Milman Parry Collection of Oral Literature*, vol. 2. Cambridge, Mass.
HEINRICHS, Heinrich Matthias 1975: "Die Geschichte vom Sagakundigen Isländer (Íslendings þáttr sǫgufróða): Ein Beitrag zur Sagaforschung." In Helmut Arntzen, Bernd Balzer & Rainer Wagner (eds.) *Literaturwissenschaft und Geschichtsphilosophie: Festschrift für Wilhelm Emrich*, Berlin.
HELLER, Rolf 1976: *Die Laxdœla saga. Die literarische Schöpfung eines Isländers des 13. Jahrhunderts, Abhandlungen der Sächsischen Akademie der Wissenschaften zu Leipzig, philol.-hist. Kl.*, vol. 65,1. Berlin.
HEUSLER, Andreas 1941: *Die altgermanische Dichtung.* Potsdam, 2. ed.
JÓNAS KRISTJÁNSSON 1972: *Um Fóstbrœðra sögu.* Reykjavík.
LIESTØL, Knut 1930: *The Origin of the Icelandic Family Sagas.* Oslo, transl. A. G. Jayne.

MAGERØY, Hallvard 1956: *Sertekstproblemet i Ljósvetningasaga, Avhandlinger utgitt av Det Norske Videnskaps-Akademi i Oslo, II, hist-phil. Kl.*, vol. 2. Oslo.

———— 1957: *Studiar i Bandamanna saga, Bibliotheca Arnamagnæana*, vol. 18. Copenhagen.

MEULENGRACHT SØRENSEN, Preben 2001: "'Græder du nu Skarpheðinn?' Nogle betragtninger over form og etik." In *At fortælle historien: Studier i den gamle nordiske litteratur*, pp. 241–248, Trieste.

MUNDAL, Else 1977: *Sagadebatt*. Oslo.

NETTER, Irmgard 1935: *Die direkte Rede in den Isländersagas*. Leipzig.

ÓSKAR HALLDÓRSSON 1976: *Uppruni og þema Hrafnkels sögu*. Reykjavík.

VÉSTEINN ÓLASON 1998: *Dialogues with the Viking Age: Narration and Representation in the Sagas of the Icelanders*. Reykjavík.

Orality Harnessed: How to Read Written Sagas from an Oral Culture?

Gísli Sigurðsson

O UR KNOWLEDGE OF orality and its part in the transmission of stories and poems has changed beyond recognition from the times in the nineteenth and early twentieth centuries when scholars in the field of Scandinavian studies first started giving serious consideration to the oral tradition behind the Icelandic sagas, edda poems and skaldic verse.[1] More than anything else, all ideas needed complete revision in the wake of the advances made by Milman Parry and Albert B. Lord which came to the attention of the wider scholarly world with the publication of Lord's *The Singer of Tales* in 1960. Around the same time a spate of other research saw the light of day dealing with various societies that preserved and transmitted knowledge, stories and poems without recourse to the written word. These advances prompted various scholars in the fields of classics and medieval studies to follow the methods of Parry and Lord and attempt to apply information from living oral cultures to the conditions that were thought to have prevailed at the times when ancient texts were first taken from men's lips and set down in written form.[2]

Much of this work involved the investigation of formulas and themes, features which were held to be primary characteristics of oral poetry and among the main tools used by oral storytellers and poets in the creation of their work. It soon became clear, however, that formulas were not restricted to oral poetry; they were indeed common in oral verse, but could equally be the product of the pen and the written poet.[3] Gradually people began to lose confidence in the notion that formula research provided an infallible guide to whether a particular text was of oral origin or not. However, this observation of the workings of oral tradition under real conditions generated another, much more important, conclusion: namely, that much of what older scholars had believed about oral tradition was simply not true – unfounded preconceptions such as that texts were typically preserved word for word in oral tradition, or that oral performance

---

[1] ANDERSSON 1964; MUNDAL 1977; 1993; DANIELSSON 2002.
[2] FOLEY 1988.
[3] BENSON 1966.

was incompatible with artistic sophistication. Similarly, the whole matter of the historicity of oral tradition was shown to be much more complicated and problematical than had previously been thought: oral traditions could not be raided unquestioningly as sources of historically reliable information, as "romantically" inclined scholars had believed; but neither were the sceptics right in assuming that it was impossible for memories to survive in some form for two or three hundred years passed on by word of mouth.[4]

These fundamental findings demanded an entire re-evaluation of all our ideas about ancient texts which might be rooted in oral preservation, a change so radical as to merit comparison with the revolution in the natural sciences that came with Darwin's ideas about evolution. It became necessary to rethink, from the bottom up, exactly how it was possible, and how it was not possible, to talk about ancient texts. But rather than face up to, and require others to face up to, the revolution that was bubbling away under the surface, many scholars chose (and choose) to take up arms in defence of established positions with enormous vehemence, either rejecting outright the credibility of the information on oral tradition which has now become available or, at the very least, denying that it had any relevance to the ancient societies they were interested in, in which conditions, they claimed, had been entirely different from those among the "primitive" peoples that were being put forward for comparison.[5] Others preferred simply to turn a blind eye to the new research into oral culture, acting as if it had simply not taken place, and there was therefore no need to take its findings into account in their work.[6] As a result, a deep and unbridgeable chasm has developed between scholars, with one group continuing to talk about the old texts as if nothing has happened[7] and the other struggling to come to terms with the implications of a putative oral tradition behind the texts.[8]

It seems fair to ask what exactly those of us who deal with medieval texts ought to be doing with them.[9] Are we looking for historical truth, plain and simple? Or should we be focusing merely on the history of sources, particular manuscripts and documents? Or the history of literary genres and/or medieval ideas? Or should we be trying to confront culture, literature and history in the Middle Ages as a single and integrated subject of enquiry? The tendency of many scholars to immerse themselves in only one of the aspects mentioned above has at times resulted in their failing to see their own area of research as just one small fragment of the overall picture that scholarship is trying to draw up at any time. By studying a text with only its manuscript history in mind, or merely as a representative of a particular literary genre, we lay ourselves open to the danger of our research revolving around itself alone and our losing sight of the essential point that lies behind it: the culture that shaped the text, the

[4] HEINRICHS 1976; GÍSLI SIGURÐSSON 2004, 42.
[5] GREEN 1990; LORD 1995, 187.
[6] ÁRMANN JAKOBSSON 2002; TULINIUS 2004; SVERRIR JAKOBSSON 2005.
[7] See SVEINBJÖRN RAFNSSON 1999.
[8] MUNDAL 1990; FOLEY 1991; 2002 ; GÍSLI SIGURÐSSON 2004.
[9] SCHAEFER 1993.

meaning of the text and the function it fulfilled in the lives of the people that knew it.[10]

In addition, the source value of one and the same text can vary greatly depending on which area of scholarship is looking at it – though each claims to be dealing with human life and conditions in its own way. Historians tend to look only for what texts can tell us about the "reality" outside the text, i.e. life itself and the actual events that we like to believe happened in some sort of way in the real world. The literary specialist can afford largely to ignore these kinds of considerations and concentrate on the artistic features and narrative devices that form part of the "author's" arsenal. To the anthropologist, it is enough to view the text as offering a general mirror of human life, customs and practices, without special reference to specific persons and events. The philologist and palaeographer is intent on word forms, orthography, letter forms, common errors in manuscripts of the "same" text and similar physical attributes. Which raises the question: But what does the medievalist do? Surely their job should take in all these things, not each individually, but all together and in unison.

Consider, for example, the picture we have of writing in twelfth century Iceland. An obvious starting point presents itself, the well-known passage from *The First Grammatical Treatise* in which, describing the literary activity of the time, the author says that people have now begun "to write and read, as is now the custom in this country too, both laws and genealogies, or exegetical writings, as well as the erudite lore that Ari Þorgilsson has set down in books with reason and intelligence".[11] When scholars attempt to construct a literary history of the times on the basis of sources like this, they almost invariably operate on the assumption that one written text preceded another – which is perfectly understandable if all you are thinking about is the written texts *per se*; they then try to explain the reasons why the text was written, and how one text went on to influence others. The problem here is that this is a highly self-referential, even solipsistic, way of working, that in the worst case runs the risk of losing all contact with anything remotely connected to the real world.

If we assume, as we must, that the texts that have come down to us from the Middle Ages existed against the background of an oral narrative and poetical tradition, we need to understand that the writing of the text was a creative process very different from what goes on nowadays when someone produces a piece of writing. As a general rule, many stories and poems of a similar kind had existed on people's lips before the extant text came to be written. People had particular ideas about the past, then just as now, and passed these ideas on, one to another, in the form of oral narratives. People's world view was bound up in and given shape by stories, for instance their ideas about the gods and other supernatural powers, without the existence of printed books with maps and tables in them; there were laws in force and court rulings were made on the basis of them even though there were no books with numbered clauses for lawmen to use as citations; people carried out their religion observances, recited their

---

[10] Corbett 1992.
[11] Cf. Hreinn Benediktsson 1972, 208.

genealogies, passed on navigational information and acquired knowledge of distant lands, astronomy, poetics and rhetoric without ever once setting eyes on written textbooks on these subjects. Knowledge in these areas was preserved by word of mouth and passed on in an organised fashion at the oral stage, because organised education in a culture is in no way dependent on the existence of teaching books.[12]

Medieval studies conducted without taking into account or showing any familiarity with research into oral societies can hardly claim to shed much light on society and culture in the Middle Ages. Such studies can, at best, deal with the sources we still possess from the Middle Ages as viewed through essentially modern eyes. Knowledge and learning in an oral society was not, any more than in modern societies, public property and there for all and sundry to use; rather, it was preserved and passed on by specific, specially trained individuals who had consciously devoted themselves to this learning and to whom society turned for knowledge of it. The sagas tell us that young boys were expected to learn the law and did this by spending time with legal experts who acted as their tutors; from Snorri's *Edda* it is quite clear that systematic thinking about the art and practice of poetry was part of the training of the skalds, and anyway it is unthinkable that so highly developed an art form as the *dróttkvætt* could have flourished without the kind of formal training that leads to professionalism.[13] Genealogy was central to defining people's rights and obligations within society, not just as regards their duty of vengeance but also in matters of inheritance and maintenance, and so one may suppose that acquiring proficiency in such matters bore practical dividends beyond any mere academic curiosity. As in all oral societies, rhetoric was a necessity of life, since people's power and influence depended in large part on their ability to talk others over to their point of view.[14]

However much we accept that all this learning was highly regarded and that those who controlled it were held in high esteem, it is just as important to realise that the body of oral knowledge was protean and ever-changing, subject to the external circumstances at any given time, to the individuals who maintained it and passed it on, to the prevailing political and social conditions, to its audience, etc. etc. An immediate consequence of individuals and societies preserving their records of former times in oral form is that this knowledge undergoes constant renewal. It is both ancient and modern at the same time, not one or the other. This key point has particular relevance to modern studies that aim to sift the heathen from the Christian in ancient Scandinavian texts: in such cases, the answer is without doubt much more often "both" rather than "one or the other".[15]

Another thing we need to be awake to is the fact that everybody is different and people were affected by their environment in how they presented their

[12] Gísli Sigurðsson 2004, 53–66.
[13] Gísli Sigurðsson 2004, 6–17.
[14] Gísli Sigurðsson 2004, 53–66.
[15] Gísli Sigurðsson 2004, 22–32.

poems and stories. Very often oral tradition exhibits a strong tendency, whether conscious or otherwise, to uphold the ideology of the ruling forces within a society. But it also provides scope for criticism and divergent ideas and points of view, and it is by no means certain that a written tradition has the ability to reflect this variety. In the case of early Icelandic culture, the written tradition was considerably more exclusive than the oral, the preserve of the Church and a very limited number of powerful magnates. Because of the very strength of the oral tradition as a medium for ideas, one would expect that, in order to introduce a new idea and get it accepted, it would have been necessary to clothe it in the colours of the tradition. As is well known, the medieval Church spread its message through use of the traditional narrative and poetical forms that it found in different places. A fine example of this occurs in the Icelandic poem *Merlínusspá*, where the original prose is rendered into verse in the style of the edda poems, in particular *Vǫluspá*. As an illustration of how the advances in oral studies of recent decades have passed many scholars completely by, I might here cite the example of the historian Sveinbjörn Rafnsson, who in an article published in 1999 put forward the view that the "author" of *Vǫluspá* had modelled his poem on *Merlínusspá*; with even the most cursory familiarity with oral tradition it is difficult to see how Rafnsson could allow himself to come out with quite such an improbable assertion.[16]

The tradition acts as a repository for people's experience of life and ethical outlook. Stories and poems pass on these ideas, teaching rising generations how to conduct themselves within society, instructing them in what is right and what is wrong in human interaction and in how public life operates. The sagas of Icelanders (family sagas) are deeply preoccupied with passing on accepted precepts of social behaviour, particularly regarding the resolution of feuds through the offices of the law, as well as preserving a great deal of practical knowledge on matters such as land use, route descriptions and everyday information relevant to the immediate surroundings of the people we may suppose told these stories. The sagas present ideas about the proper conduct of chieftains and their followers; they can serve to instil men with courage in the face of conflict;[17] and in the case of the myths and their cosmology, provide them with an understanding of the universe itself, the settings of myths where, according to Snorri's *Edda*, the gods have their dwellings. All these things are aspects of the primary function of narrative art, to bring order to chaos and give it shape within the bounds of systematic thought.

An almost universal feature of oral societies is the telling of stories and performing of poems about gods and heroes, about famous chieftains and the founders and originators of various objects and institutions. People learn and assimilate the tradition that passes this material on from generation to generation. All knowledge, laws and rules in oral societies depend on the tradition being maintained, ensuring that the thread is never broken. Much of this remains entirely unaffected by the arrival of writing. The art of telling

---

[16] Gísli Sigurðsson 2004, 47.
[17] Gísli Sigurðsson 1998, xxxvii–xxxviii; 2004, 39, 57.

stories, for instance, does not change, nor the art of poetical composition, and the social position of those who have power over these art forms remains strong.

However, the adoption of writing does bring with it a number of very important changes. So far as the Middle Ages are concerned, the most visible effects in the early days lay in the sphere of religion. The new faith spread hand in hand with the book and the written culture that went with it. The book in which God's word was recorded held a central and highly symbolic position in all religious observance and the entire ideology of the Church. Without the Bible, Christianity would hardly have managed to take hold in the way that it did – just as the Qur'an was inextricably linked with the spread of Islam. Literacy and its uses became part of the power system of the clerics. At the initial stage, book learning was of importance only within the Church, but as writing began to spread into other areas of national life the status of individuals and balance of power within other groups of society were disrupted according to their success in mastering the new technology.

People's horizons broadened once books became the medium for stories and information. There was now access to reading material from faraway countries and former ages – material that oral tradition had had no way of supplying. Large anthological codices were produced, providing readers with a wider overview of disparate material than had been possible in the days of oral tradition. Writing thus offered new ways of compiling, preserving and communicating the art of storytelling. The book form also called for more systematic methods of presentation while also giving people an entirely new perspective of time through a chronology that dated events from the birth of Christ. In every area of culture scholars proceeded to present traditional knowledge with reference to the chronology of the Church rather than on the basis of the regnal years of kings or the lives of great leaders and started arranging events in the kind of time order with which we are now familiar. Coincident with this, knowledge started to accumulate: obsolete knowledge was no longer allowed to fade away in silence but continued to exist as letters on the pages of the books in which it was set down. It was there for people to turn to whenever they wanted, even many generations later, to be retrieved in the same words as when it had been recorded. This was something that had not been possible before. And to this was added the new learning and scholarship that the Church had brought with it, swelling the traditional knowledge that society already possessed.

There is a widespread misconception that education and organised training in the acquisition of knowledge in the Middle Ages was restricted to clerical learning. Obviously, this learning was only one part of the "knowledge bank" of society, though in many cases a very prominent one to modern eyes as a result of the ways in which medieval people chose to record their knowledge. In mainland Europe generally, most of the material preserved came from the hands of clerics, the product of monasteries, but the example of Iceland shows that there was plenty more on offer if people had the imagination to apply the techniques of writing to fields outside the confines of the Church and employ it to record the secular and spiritual learning pursued within society at large.

We generally give considerably greater weight to the written word than the spoken, and this has long been the case. Agreements and contracts are endorsed by signature; laws are printed and their inception advertised in the printed media. It is often forgotten that, even today, agreements are perfectly valid though made only by word of mouth, so long as witnesses can be called in to verify them. When researching conditions in the Middle Ages, scholars commonly take the view that the written word was immediately and unconditionally accorded precedence over oral report and the testimony of wise men and women. This is most unlikely, however much emphasis there is among medieval scholars on authoritative sources – *auctoritates* – such as the Bible and Aristotle. So in our own research we need to assume that the word of wise men and women was equally held in high esteem and that many years must have passed before people started trusting books better than such people as repositories of knowledge. The change in attitude that followed the spread of writing took a long time to become universally established and to some extent is still not complete, for even nowadays important announcements are read out before an audience before they can take effect, when technically it should be enough just to distribute the written texts set down on paper.

People in the Middle Ages believed traditional lore to hold genuine records of former times. Later scholars, of course, have had no difficulty identifying innumerable historical errors in this lore and gone on from this to tar everything with the same brush. The tendency has been to "pour the baby out with the bathwater" and reject the testimony of oral sources *en bloc*, rather than face up to the questions they present and that demand solution. In the modern world people like Ari fróði and Snorri Sturluson would find themselves in opposing camps of the Authors' Union, with Ari in the academic wing and Snorri among the creative writers. But if such a society had existed in medieval times, Snorri would probably have felt nonplussed if he had applied membership of the scholars' section too and been turned down. In the light of the comments made above regarding the limited interests of different areas of scholarship, the position now is that many if not most academics seem to take the view that it is perfectly acceptable to disregard entirely any potential source value that the ancient texts they deal with might have: they have enough on their plates analysing these texts for the information they provide on literary history, on the history of the times when they were written, on the history of ideas, on linguistics, orthography, palaeography, etc. Be that as it may, out there in "the real world" there is still genuine interest among the general public as to whether some of what the ancient books say happened may perhaps have really happened in the way they say it did.

For some time now scholarship has avoided any serious attempt to face up to this problem and sought refuge in atomistic subdisciplinary approaches. Within the traditional framework of scholarship, many scholars have simply been daunted by the challenge of struggling with a tradition that was both ever-changing and ancient at the same time, of coming to terms with the idea that it was capable of taking in new material while simultaneously carrying memories from the distant past. This kind of indeterminacy sits uncomfortably in the "either/or" mindset prevalent among academics. It is, for example, possible to demonstrate that, however many doubts we have about individual minor points such as names, dates and events, the overall picture presented by the old texts of the human settlement of the islands of the north Atlantic is pretty much the same as the picture that emerges from archaeological research (without making any claims about exactly what the people were called or what story should be located where). The general information contained in the texts – information that is demonstrably correct – could not have been preserved and found its way onto parchment without there having been an unbroken tradition telling of these events, starting from the time when they happened and continuing all the way down to the time when they were put into writing. The problem is that we simply have no methods for distinguishing what is to be believed from what may be pure fiction.

The dream of scholars that, in cases where it is possible to trace comparable texts in manuscripts of different ages, the older a text is the more it should be trusted may be nothing more than a fond illusion: everything that the oldest text has to say came to it originally from oral tradition, and additional information found in younger manuscripts may well have been put in simply to fill the picture using other material from the same tradition – making it just as reliable, and just as unreliable, in both cases. This basic fact seems to have been lost on scholars who assume, for instance, that information found in *Íslendingabók* or *Landnámabók* is in some way more reliable than that found in younger sagas, when the truth is that all these sources are based on oral tradition. The only way to approach the source value of the old texts is therefore to be completely clear in our minds that they are all reflections of the view of the past that the tradition passed on to the writers of the sagas. What is said and how? And what attitudes do they reveal concerning the people, issues and other subjects they talk about? We cannot simply pick and choose, accepting some things and rejecting others because we find them implausible, since people's experience of reality has always been multifaceted and ever-changing. Things that to modern science might be utterly unthinkable were part of daily life to people in the Middle Ages, and even today are fervently believed by many who do not subscribe to the recognised world view of the university educated classes.

The old texts are notoriously unhelpful on their own when it comes to the questions we would like answers to regarding the nature of oral art forms in the Middle Ages. The information they convey is both very limited and totally unaware of the problems and issues raised by modern scholarship. A much more promising approach to drawing up a credible picture of the oral background of medieval texts is to use contemporary field studies from a variety of oral cultures and look for common features that are traceable to their orality. And here the most distinctive characteristic seems to be variation, i.e. the absence of fixed form. Oral literature is fluid and constantly changing, depending on the performer, the audience and the social settings. We need, of course, to be extremely cautious when trying to use detailed information from one culture to shed light on another, but one principle is beyond dispute: it is impermissible to postulate something for oral art forms of former ages for which we do not possess living examples in the present. The theoretical possibilities are considerably more numerous than the possibilities that can actually be confirmed from contemporary living evidence.

The most fundamental change that comes with writing is that a single performance of an oral "work" becomes fixed. This single performance can then be read again and again with its wording unchanged however many new readers and listeners there are and however much the text is transported between cultures and ages. This change affects how people think about texts: the idea takes hold that there is one "correct", fixed version, and that this is the way things ought to be (which we have no reason to believe was how texts were generally viewed in earlier times, other than in very exceptional circumstances, particularly in ritual use, where great care may have been taken to preserve and perform texts verbatim). We know of course that it is perfectly possible to learn, memorise and recite long texts verbatim, verse or prose. But this only shows that this is a feasible possibility rather than in any way normal practice, and anyway only applies once it has become the custom to fix texts in writing and the idea of a fixed and definitive text has taken hold within a culture.

In an oral society, just as in a literate one, the artistic form affects and shapes what is told and how it is told. The content is, to a large extent, determined by the form. The form thus plays a central role in deciding the kind of picture that a work draws up of the reality it refers to. But there is no hard and fast line dividing oral art forms from written ones: it is perfectly possible for a literate person in a society that is still largely oral to take existing oral forms and adapt them to the new possibilities, to create new forms of art and learning that look both back to preliterate times and forward to the new world, the world of the book. Literature – written literature – can yield a rich harvest when those who hold the quill have the knowledge and imagination to harness a living tradition of oral stories and poems and perfect the process of reshaping and reinterpretation that is necessary to convert them from one medium to another, from orality to vellum manuscript.

Translated by Nicholas Jones

Bibliography

ANDERSSON, Theodore M. 1964: *The Problem of Icelandic Saga Origins: A Historical Survey*. Yale.

ÁRMANN JAKOBSSON 2002: *Staður í nýjum heimi: Konungasagan Morkinskinna*. Reykjavík.

BENSON, Larry D. 1966: "The literary character of Anglo-Saxon formulaic poetry." *PMLA*, 81 334–341.

CORBETT, Noel 1992: "What's new in philology." *Romance Philology*, 46 (1) 29–39.

DANIELSSON, Tommy 2002: *Hrafnkels saga eller Fallet med den undflyende traditionen*. Hedemora.

FOLEY, John Miles 1988: *The Theory of Oral Composition: History and Methodology*. Bloomington.

——— 1991: *Immanent Art: From Structure to Meaning in Traditional Oral Epic*. Bloomington.

——— 2002: *How to Read an Oral Poem*. Urbana, Chicago.

GÍSLI SIGURÐSSON (ed.) 1998: *Eddukvæði*. Reykjavík.

GÍSLI SIGURÐSSON 2004: *The Medieval Icelandic Saga and Oral Tradition: A Discourse on Method, Publications of the Milman Parry Collection of Oral Literature*, vol. 2. Cambridge, Mass.

GREEN, D. H. 1990: "Orality and reading: The state of research in medieval studies." *Speculum*, 65 (2) 267–280.

HEINRICHS, Heinrich Matthias 1976: "Mündlichkeit und Schriftlichkeit: Ein Problem der Sagaforschung." *Jahrbuch für Internationale Germanistik. Series A*, 2 114–133.

HREINN BENEDIKTSSON (ed.) 1972: *The First Grammatical Treatise, University of Iceland Publications in Linguistics*, vol. 1. Reykjavík.

LORD, Albert B. 1960: *The Singer of Tales, Harvard Studies in Comparative Literature*, vol. 24. Cambridge, Mass.

——— 1995: *The Singer Resumes the Tale*. Ithaca, edited by Mary Louise Lord.

MUNDAL, Else 1977: *Sagadebatt*. Oslo.

——— 1990: "Den norrøne episke tradisjon." In Øivind Andersen & Thomas Hägg (eds.) *Hellas og Norge: Kontakt, Komparasjon, Kontrast*, pp. 65–80, Bergen.

——— 1993: "Bookprose/Freeprose theory." In Phillip Pulsiano (ed.) *Medieval Scandinavia: An Encyclopedia*, pp. 52–53, New York.

SCHAEFER, Ursula 1993: "Alterities: On methodology in medieval literary studies." *Oral Tradition*, 8 (1).

SVEINBJÖRN RAFNSSON 1999: "*Merlínusspá* og *Völuspá* í sögulegu samhengi." *Skírnir*, 173 377–419.

SVERRIR JAKOBSSON 2005: *Við og veröldin: Heimsmynd Íslendinga 1100–1400*. Reykjavík.

TULINIUS, Torfi 2004: *Skáldið í skriftinni: Snorri Sturluson og* Egils saga. Reykjavík.

On the Possibility of an Oral Background for *Gísla saga Súrssonar*

Tommy Danielsson

T HERE ARE TWO versions of the Norwegian introduction to *Gísla saga*. The shorter text, called the *M*-version, is preferred in the modern editions, and the longer one, the *S*-version, has often been considered derivative and late. The prelude tells of conflicts in two generations in Súrnadalr on the west coast of Norway, and after this introduction *M* and *S* differ only in details.

In 1964, Theodore Andersson reviewed the problem of the *M*- and *S*-versions and concluded that the considerable variations between the texts could not be oral – one reason being that the sequence of events is the same in *M* and *S* – and he maintained that "it is impossible to escape from an element of conscious alteration on the part of S".[1] Consequently, when examining the prelude in 1969 among some remaining ambiguities in *Gísla saga*, he did not consider *S* at all.[2]

Since then, the view of *S* has changed, at least to some degree. Hartmut Röhn has pointed out that *S* should be understood in the light of the literary tastes of the fourteenth century instead of being dismissed in a normative manner as non-classical. The interpolations should not be regarded as 'Fremdkörper' and not be looked upon as compositional shortcomings.[3] Alan Berger has been highly critical of the second chapter of *M*, including the praise of it by commentators like Holtsmark and Andersson. Berger finds the chapter morally distasteful and prefers the *S*-version. He regards *M* as some kind of abbreviation and suggests that *S* should be taken more seriously. On the other hand, Berger finds it impossible to decide whether *S* "preserves a style of saga-writing antedating the classical style, or whether it is a post-classical expansion".[4] In the same year as Röhn and Berger published their findings, Guðni Kolbeinsson and Jónas Kristjánsson tried to show that the *S*-version reflects the original in a better way than *M* – even though they also give

---

[1] ANDERSSON 1964, 145.
[2] ANDERSSON 1969, 12–18.
[3] RÖHN 1979, 112–113.
[4] BERGER 1979, 163–168.

examples of the opposite.[5] This argumentation has been developed by Alfred Jakobsen who concludes that first *M* has abbreviated an original text, and then it has supplied some characteristics of its own.[6] Recently, Þorður Ingi Guðjónsson has penetrated the problem in depth and reached about the same conclusions.[7]

However, all of these critics postulate a first original text and a following evolution of scribal versions. Here, I will try to argue a different standpoint. Therefore, I will not focus on the scribal connections between *M* and *S* in the prelude or elsewhere, and I will not try to decide which of the versions is the best preparation for the main story. Instead, I will ask whether *S* might point towards an oral background to a higher degree than *M*. Also, I will ask whether passages can be found in the rest of the saga – where only one version is available – that, in any way, analogically point towards the tradition. And all of these speculations are, of course, made possible by the new foregrounding of the *S*-version.

Naturally, this means that I believe in the existence of an oral saga and good story-tellers – because bad story-tellers would have been rejected by their audience. Furthermore, I believe that the basis for remembering was the course of events itself – a movie in the head – and I believe that the mastery of form was what singled out the good teller from the bad. As to when the oral saga was somehow written down by scribes, or the tradition was exploited by scribes, I believe that orality was, as a rule, corrupted in the process of being transferred into the new medium. It was haunted by abbreviation, by faulty memory and reconstructions and by the overall impossibility of transference. Consequently, I believe that it was the story-teller and not the scribe who was the real artist; this not, however, prohibiting the written text from becoming a work of art for us to enjoy more than we probably would have with a more faithful transcription.

To begin with, I will focus on two passages in the prelude, one in each of the two generations described. In the first a berserk challenges a man called Ari to a fight or else give up his wife Ingibjǫrg. Ari is killed, whereupon his brother Gísli – in fact, our Gísli's uncle – takes up the challenge and kills the berserk with a sword lent to him by Ingibjǫrg's thrall, Kolr. Gísli then refuses to return the sword, which leads to a confrontation in which both Kolr and Gísli are killed. All this is told in a straightforward and temperate way by the *M*-version, except for one thing: it indicates that Ingibjǫrg liked Gísli better than she did Ari (3–6). The *S*-version presents the same course of events, but is detailed in quite another way, especially regarding the dialogue. Direct – not reported – speech is used throughout the scenes, and everything is dramatized (5–14). If one is used to the laconic style of the sagas one might think *S* lacking, but if one tries to imagine a performance by a professional story-teller, *S* seems to be much more authentic than *M*.

[5] GUÐNI KOLBEINSSON & JÓNAS KRISTJÁNSSON 1979, 161–162.
[6] JAKOBSEN 1979a, 280–284; 1979b, 268–279.
[7] VÉSTEINN ÓLASON & ÞÓRÐUR INGI GUÐJÓNSSON 2000, 113–118.

One may get a feeling that *S* comes close to the actual telling and that an oral performance of *M* would come to nothing. In other words, *M* points towards an oral saga that might resemble *S*. Notice also that the indication of Ingibjǫrg's erotic preferences is missing in *S*, and that *M*'s short notation stands quite in isolation, just as something said in passing – maybe as a foreshadowing of Ásgerðr's (or Þórdís's) amorous affairs. And if one gets the feeling in *M* that Ingibjǫrg withholds the sword until it is time for Gísli to use it, nothing of the sort is the case in *S*. Here, it seems that the distressed Ingibjǫrg suddenly remembers Kolr when Gísli interferes. She fears that Gísli's undertaking will be hopeless if he does not get help from others, and she *thinks* that Kolr has a good sword even if he himself slanders it. Note also that Kolr is of noble birth in *S* and is therefore a person whose words cannot be easily dismissed. In other words, the narration of *S* is quite coherent, while the narration of *M* seems somewhat problematic even if it is short.

All of this is even more the case in the second passage, taking place in the next generation, when Gísli – our Gísli – on loose grounds kills his sister Þórdís's lover in the presence of his brother, Þorkell, who is a close friend of the lover in question. When Þorkell gets angry, Gísli jokes with him and bids him to calm down, whereupon Þorkell seeks out a friend of the lover and incites him, on the one hand to take revenge, and on the other to try to marry Þórdís himself. I think Alan Berger is quite right in questioning this whole course of events.[8] Gísli's action and his attempts to calm Þorkell down, as well as Þorkell's reaction, are exceptional, especially as some time later, after Gísli's killing of the friend of the lover, Þorkell's and Gísli's relationship is said to have improved (6–9). In the extremely detailed account of *S*, nothing is left in the dark, but unfortunately a lacuna breaks off the text just after the killing of the lover. The lover is repeatedly warned to stop visiting Þórdís, and Gísli is repeatedly egged on by his father, so the slaying does not come as a surprise. Þorkell criticizes the deed and he leaves home feeling ill at ease, but he does not take any measures (15–16, 20–27). Thus, it is possible to draw the same conclusions as we did for the first passage. It might be said that *M* foreshadows the complicated relations between Gísli, Þorkell and Þórdís, but that at the same time it complicates matters so much that we need another text in order to grasp the actual situation. And that text might be thought of as an oral saga, to some degree represented by the *S*-version. *M* points towards orality by being confused, and *S* gives us a glimpse of that orality by being so easy to imagine in actual performance.

I will now give some examples from *Gísla saga* of scenes where perhaps the oral saga was more specific and clear than the written text as it had more tools at its disposal. If my assumption is right, the teller was more of an expert of his material than the scribe. He could modulate his voice and use his body to communicate what would otherwise be ambivalent and obscure.

At the spring assembly, before all the conflicts start, Gísli and his companions are sitting drinking while all the others are at court doing whatever they

8 Berger 1979, 163–164.

are there to do. A man named Arnórr, a chatterbox, enters their booth and criticizes them, as it seems, in the name of the community. Gísli responds, the men go to the court and Þorgrímr, Gísli's brother-in-law, offers assistance in extremely hyperbolic words. One of the chieftains answers that the cases being decided are insignificant, "but we will call on you if we need your help". The next sentence emphasizes that people thought Gísli and his men worthy and dignified (20–21).

There is a lot of tension in this sequence, and it is quite hard to handle it in a meaningful way. Gísli and his men are being criticized – *and* they are being admired. They are offering help – *and* they are being dismissed. It might be said that the chatterbox is just chattering, but when he once again enters the booth with gossip, he is telling the truth about the sage Gestr's prophecies of the future for Gísli, Þorkell, Þorgrímr and Vésteinn. Nothing is explained in depth, and we might regard the passage as typical of the suppressed and objective saga-style. The writer simply tells what he sees from his camera-eye position, but he does not spell out in full what goes on below the surface. Together with the audience, we must think and interpret for ourselves. We must decide the status of Arnórr, what people really think, and whether the chieftain at the court is being ironical or not.

But there is another possibility. Maybe in the oral performance all was crystal-clear, for what had the oral story-teller to win by being obscure? The passage offers a multitude of opportunities for performing, and there must have been an obvious reason for telling it. Something important, something worth telling, tragic or comic, was communicated to the audience, and, we can only guess what that something was because the written text does not provide enough clues. The teller could enact Arnórr's chatter, Gísli's sudden awareness, Þorgrímr's pomposity and the chieftain's irony. And he could use more and different words than those that found their way to the parchment. The writer tried to transcribe, and maybe he thought he was successful, but when the scenes were complicated and had double meanings he was in for an impossible quest. Consequently, the text of the scribe points towards more complete versions and – in my opinion – these versions must have been oral.

In a famous episode, where Gísli and Vésteinn are abroad in Denmark and about to part company Gísli makes a coin that can be taken apart and gives one of the pieces to Vésteinn as a token. The pieces are to be sent as a warning if one of their lives is in danger. Of course this happens, even if the warning is in vain and comes too late.

There is nothing to criticize here. But in the moment just before, when Vésteinn asks Gísli permission to travel to England, Gísli makes him promise never to leave Iceland in the future without consulting him (28). This should also, just as the coin, have a meaning. But the promise leads to nothing. Why? Of course, Gísli's words might be viewed simply as some kind of courtesy phrase, but then again, maybe they point towards something that was part of another – oral – story. Maybe the promise was vital, and maybe it tied Vésteinn's hands at some crucial moment and thereby influenced the deadly course of events.

The scene where Þorkell discovers the infidelity of his wife, Ásgerðr, with Vésteinn is detailed and has an oral character, but the end is somewhat problematic (30–34). I am referring to the passage where Ásgerðr disarms Þorkell and by threatening him with a humiliating divorce forces him to make room for her in the bed; and soon they become reconciled "as if nothing had happened". This is surprising, to say the least, in the light of what soon will happen. Vésteinn will be murdered in bed, and even though we cannot be sure of who committed the deed, the motive must be adultery. Why then pretend that all was well between Þorkell and Ásgerðr, and why does Ásgerðr disappear from the story altogether? Maybe something is missing here, and maybe the oral story-teller had more to say about these complications.

The slayings of Vésteinn and Þorgrímr are, of course, well-known climaxes in *Gísla saga*, and here the problems have been discussed in depth by various critics. The effect of not mentioning the identity of Vésteinn's killer has been admired and has led to speculations (43–44).[9] But the question is whether it is conceivable that an oral teller really got away with such a strategy, or whether the effect is only possible in writing. If the teller is present, one can question him, and the answer "I don't know" will not be accepted. Furthermore, the fact that the *S*-version mentions Þorgrímr as the killer – just as *M* does in the chapter heading – cannot be wholly dismissed.[10]

As to the identity of Þorgrímr's killer, we need never be left in the dark, but problems exist nevertheless (52–54). On his way to the scene of the crime, Gísli enters the cow shed at Sæból and ties the cattle's tails together, but nothing is said of the consequences. One can of course imagine what a story-teller could do with this. Also, the written text has difficulties in describing what really took place after the slaying. First, it is said in many words that everyone was intoxicated and could not act in any useful way. But in spite of this, Eyjólfr takes the lead and proposes some sound advice: "Light the lights and block the doors!" But as no one is found, they all think that someone inside is the killer. It looks as if the text tries to erase the course of events that it itself proposes. The tied cattle's tails foreshadow a pursuit that Eyólfr's words poignantly deny. Could it be that the scribe found reasons not to relate the sequence of the oral saga that told – perhaps in too comical a way – of the chase through the cow shed?

When Bǫrkr arrives from across Breiðafjǫrðr to summon Gísli for the slaying of Þorgrímr, Þorkell, Gísli's brother, is in his company, and Þorkell's main intension is obviously to warn Gísli (63–65). As the men get closer to Gísli's farm, Þorkell excuses himself and says that he has a debt to collect on one of the farms nearby. He rides ahead and when he reaches the farm in question he borrows a horse, leaving his own standing grazing outside the house. He orders the farmer's wife to tell the men when they arrive that he is inside counting the silver. Then he seeks out Gísli, tells him what is happening, and after that returns to Bǫrkr and his following from behind, slowing down their pace.

[9] See ANDERSSON 1969, 18–28 for a survey.
[10] *Membrana deperdita* 32.

The guile of the horse outside the farm is a blind motif leading to nothing, and the reason might be that the scribe refrained from relating a passage told by the oral teller. All that is left is a slight trace pointing to orality. Besides, the sequence is still more confused. The meeting of Þorkell and Gísli is interrupted by the start of a new chapter, and by the confusing statement that Bǫrkr announces the case and Gísli sells his land. And when Bǫrkr, immediately thereafter, discovers Gísli and chases him, Þorkell has completely vanished from the face of the earth. In my view, all these events – including the slaying of Þórðr, the thrall, and the wounding of Gísli – were told in a much more consequential and continuous way by the oral saga-teller, a way that the scribe was unable to recall and therefore could not disentangle.

The passages mentioned are perhaps the most clear-cut instances in the *Gísla saga* where the handling of an oral saga tradition might be a tool to explain the existing text. But of course, many more sequences might be discussed in much the same way. The meeting of Gísli and Þorkell after the slaying of Vésteinn, when Þorkell repeatedly makes inquiries of Auðr's reaction, is interesting, but here the incorporation of several skaldic verses complicates matters (46–48). Also, the ensuing first ball games, where Þorkell incites Gísli to confront Þorgrímr, seem to require a more detailed context in order to be fully understood, a context that may have been delivered in the oral saga (49–50).

Supposedly, the oral saga was digressive by nature, and the performance of the individual episodes must have mattered a lot. The excellence in dramatizing the individual events must have made all the difference between the good and the not-so-good oral teller. Of course, this is also the case in the written saga, but here there are limits. Being trained as we latecomers are in the tradition of the novel, we often prefer texts that function as wholes, where every situation and every phrase can be related to the structure of the text in its entirety. And this is just what the saga of Gísli has been most praised for. Because the saga is short, there is an economy of text, and very few incidents diverge in a noteworthy way from the main story-line. However, one example of divergence is the Norwegian prelude. Franz Seewald had some problems with it, but, on the other hand, matters have been settled by Anne Holtsmark, Peter Foote and Theodore Andersson. According to Holtsmark, the family traditions at the beginning set the tone for the drama of Gísli; Foote maintains that the prelude defines the central characters; and Andersson is of the opinion that the introduction suggests several capital themes in the story, including the "pattern of resentment".[11] The prelude foreshadows and motivates all that is to come. This kind of thinking also characterizes Thomas Bredsdorff's discussion in *Kaos og kærlighed*, and it can now be taken for granted.[12]

I have no objections here, but maybe the discussion overemphasizes the importance of the overall structure. As I said before, I am convinced that the prelude was part of the oral saga – even if I also think that the *S*-version points

[11] ANDERSSON 1969, 12–18; FOOTE 1963, 107; SEEWALD 1934, 52; HOLTSMARK 1951, 33–34.
[12] BREDSDORFF 1971, 67–81.

more clearly in that direction – but maybe we are told of the incidents more for their own sake, and their own drama, than because of that which was to come. The written version, especially *M*, reduced this effect by abbreviation and thereby made way for the structural judgements of the critics of today. But this also means that, even in the times of the saga, the awareness of the whole was never totally absent.

Another episode that has been criticized as digressive – this leading to attempts to integrate it – is Þorgrímr's killing of the Norwegian salesmen (24–26). In the episode Þorgrímr bought timber from the two traders, but when his son was sent to stack it, conflict arose and the son was killed. The Norwegians tried to get away, but Þorgrímr caught up with them as they took a rest after riding all night and killed them after first rousing them from sleep. All of this seems to have nothing to do with the main course of events, but here also, solutions have been found.[13] Either, as Seewald thought, Þorgrímr is implicated by the deed as the slayer of Vésteinn, or, as suggested by Andersson, the episode demonstrates that Þorgrímr, being a hero of the right stuff, does not kill sleeping men, even if the consequences are to his disadvantage. The man who kills Vésteinn, on the other hand, does not consider this procedure necessary. Still, it must be remembered that Vésteinn in fact was awake, even if the spear was in his breast before he knew what was happening, but the same can be said about Gísli's killing of Þorgrímr – Gísli does wake him up, but, seemingly, just as a matter of form. No fight ensues, and Þorgrímr has no chance to react.

I find it hard to believe that the saga-man intended these connections. In relation to the whole, the episode of the Norwegian traders is a digression, and there probably were more like it in the oral saga. In the tradition, Þorgrímr slew these men in quite a remarkable way, and therefore it was worth telling about; the episode was *sǫguleg* in its own right, and there are no ambiguities in the saga on the matter. It is said that "[t]his done, Þorgrímr returned home and became renowned as a result of this expedition". Þorgrímr is established as a great hero because of things he did and because he was a great man, they are worth telling about. But when a scribe, like the *M*-scribe, took it upon himself to turn a long oral saga into a short written one, most of these kinds of digressions disappeared.

Also, the episode of the sorceress Auðbjǫrg and her son, Þorsteinn, (and the subsequent deaths of Auðbjǫrg and her brother, Þorgrímr nefr) digresses to some extent (57–60). Þorgrímr nefr plays an important part in the main action: he forges the fragments of the sword Grásíða into the spear that kills Vésteinn and Þorgrímr and his magical rites stop Gísli from getting help from the chieftains of Iceland. Þorsteinn, on the other hand, is Gísli's companion in the second ball games where he succeeds in knocking down Bǫrkr. But after that the story goes astray. Þorsteinn quarrels with a certain Bergr about what happened at the games and receives a blow from him without the opportunity of revenge, the consequence being that Auðbjǫrg conjures up a snowstorm

---

[13] Seewald 1934, 8; Andersson 1969, 22–23.

leading to an avalanche that buries Bergr's farm. This, in turn, occassions Bǫrkr to stone Auðbjǫrg to death, and immediately thereafter Gísli does the same to Þorgrímr nefr. The passage is curious, to say the least, and it is not easy to speculate on its origins. But maybe we can discern a strategy typical of the oral forerunners, namely, composition by association, or by some kind of 'reality principle'. From the central action one is led to events of minor importance for the story, but remarkable in the context of reality. After all, Bergr was killed by sorcery, and a sorcerer and a sorceress were executed by the heroes of the saga. One digresses when suddenly one discovers side-tracks worth telling.

Of course, Gísli's outlawry brings about lots of opportunities for incorporating material; one does not even need to digress, but simply add stories of Gísli's adventures, and of how he just about escaped his pursuers. If anything, it is noteworthy how few such stories there are, and it can be supposed that the oral saga had many more, and that the section in question was highly unstable and subject to change, depending on the development of the saga and the preferences of the individual tellers. And it can be observed, as expected, that some of the most scenic and detailed parts are to be found in the outlawry section.

Some of the more famous passages of *Gísla saga* – among these the events leading up to the slaying of Vésteinn (39–42) – have been regarded as particularly effective because of their construction. Here, the inflexible ticking of fate's clock is combined with reticence on important issues, all of which makes us, to some degree, fellow creators. Nothing is spelled out in detail and the imagination of the reader is called forth. But the question is where this very notable effect stems from. Does it stem from the ability of the writer to create suspense by careful construction and by the detailed arrangement of rhetorical devices? Or does it stem from the ability of the oral teller to tell exciting parts of sagas in thrilling ways?

When Þorgrímr and Þorkell invite important people to the winter night's feast, Gísli, in vain, tries to warn off Vésteinn, sending him his part of the divided coin; but by bad luck the messengers miss him and only catch up with him when it is too late to turn back. Now the text becomes really portentous. Vésteinn rides on, approaching Haukadalr by way of three stations, and thrice he is warned by various persons to be on his guard. Moreover, the moon is shining, and the horse's bells tinkle provokingly. As he passes Sæból, he is hurried on by the servant boy, Geirmundr, who, likewise, tries to distract the suspicious working woman Rannveig. But Rannveig tells Þorgrímr that maybe it was Vésteinn who just rode by and she is sent to Hóll to make sure. Rannveig, however, is dismissed by Gísli and Auðr as she is unable to ask straight questions. All of this is very effective, but at the same time extremely confusing, as the following morning Vésteinn makes no secret of his whereabouts, but instead, by way of Gísli, offers some splendid gifts to Þorkell at Sæból. Some commentators have spotted orality here because of the triad of warnings, and in my view, the art of the oral teller is what gives the sequence significance.[14] But it is hard to escape the feeling that something is missing, or that the written text misses some important point. As it seems the climax of it all is Rannveig's confusion when returning to Sæból. Maybe, the oral story-teller was able to get away with this by an elaborate performance, but I find it more probable that something is astray here. A build-up that leads to nothing is only confusing. There is a parallel, of course, when Gísli's servant girl, Guðríðr, is sent to Sæból the morning after Vésteinn's death to check out things, but this too can only be made obvious by way of elaborate dramatization.

As mentioned above, one could say that all of this is intentional, like the concealed identity of Vésteinn's slayer, but I am not so sure. There are, in fact, moments when the text spells out the meaning, becoming almost overly obvious. For example, after the slaying of Þorkell the text tells us that people thought that Gestr had conspired with Vésteinn's sons. We are also told that Gísli's attackers had seen the trail in the rime, and that Þorgrímr nefr forgot the islands when he put his spells on Gísli. As novel-trained readers we would have figured these things out without the text's help, and we might have preferred the silence as part of the effect. But maybe we are mistaken. For the oral story-teller, it would be quite natural to add some reminders now and then as the story went on becoming more and more complicated.

Thus far, I have tried to pin down the oral forerunners by the traces of their absence, but the question, too, is whether parts of *Gísla saga* can be said to bear pronounced oral stamps of their own. If we imagine the oral story-teller as an extremely talented presenter who uses words and body language to bring out lively events and confrontations, then we are bound to focus on sections in the written sagas that are detailed and exhaustive – sections in which the action is really depicted to bring out the scenes in full, and in which the dialogues bring out more than just the summing-up or the point of the story. The clever teller of anecdotes, as we know him, is clever simply because of the capacity to delay and postpone that which is to come.

Now, it can be noticed that some parts of the *Gísla saga* are both detailed and somewhat out of style, especially if we try to read the text as a tragedy of sorts. Twice Gísli changes places with persons of some insignificance – with a thrall and with a fool – and both times we get very close to the events (64–65, 82–83). Equally detailed is the burlesque account of Gísli taking refuge under the mattress of the extremely shrewish wife of the farmer Refr (86–88). The conversation between Ásgerðr and Auðr, which was overheard by Þorkell, also takes on a life of its own, outgrowing the importance of the main story-line (30–32).

In fact, the relation between scenic elaboration and what we would regard as essential episodes is quite weak. Thus, the length of the episode of Alfdís, the shrew, surpasses even Gísli's slaying of Þorgrímr. Could it be that these sequences also point towards the oral saga, and that the scribe included some of them because they made such a great impression that they stuck in his memory

---

[14] PRINZ 1935, 147–148.

and were quite easy to recall with pen in hand? In other words – could it be that the oral saga was poignantly scenic in character, much more so, even, than the written counterparts indicate?

A couple of incidents in the thirteenth century have been connected to the *Gísla saga* in various ways and have been used to date the conception of the written saga. Thus, it is said that the spear Grásíða, which Gísli owned, was used on two occasions, in 1221 and 1238.[15] Furthermore, Hrafn Sveinbjarnarson was a chieftain who lived near Geirþjófsfjǫrðr, where Gísli lived during his outlawry, and where Hrafn was killed in 1213.[16] He had many connections; the circle around him has been mentioned as a background to the saga, and the sister of his main enemy has been compared to Gísli's sister, Þórdís. A saga about Hrafn was written in around 1230.

Likewise Aron Hjǫrleifsson was sheltered by Hrafn's sons and lived for three years, starting in 1222, in outlawry in Geirþjófsfjǫrðr. Aron's destiny is described in Sturla Þórðarson's *Íslendinga saga* and in a separate *Arons saga*, possibly composed as late as in the middle of the fourteenth century.[17] Some isolated overlappings in the texts on Aron and Gísli have been mentioned by Peter Foote, Rolf Heller and Aðalgeir Kristjánsson. The idea is either that Aron's outlawry – he being the most famous outlaw of his century – influenced the author of *Gísla saga* and even gave the impetus to its conception, or, that *Gísla saga* influenced Sturla and the late *Arons saga*.[18]

If, on the other hand, we postulate an ongoing oral saga which has been continuously told (at least in the West Fjords), the situation becomes really interesting. In this case, history and tradition came to life when Aron suddenly showed up. And if so, what, can we imagine, happened? Presumably, if the tradition was strong, the probability of 'loans' in either direction was low. People knew about Gísli and they would have been suspicious of transferences, but if, over time, one of the traditions subsided, things would have been different. However, *Gísla saga* was soon written down and fixed, and thereby, the possibilities of loans into the Aron-tradition were still more blocked.

But if the saga of Gísli was the work of an author, intent even on commenting on his own times, it seems almost unavoidable for him to be influenced by Aron's fate in obvious ways. This is clearly not the case, for the similarities are indeed insignificant, and it has taken some time for them to be observed at all. Taken out of their context they might seem impressive, but when one reads the text, they completely disappear. It is a wonder that Sturla and the writer of *Arons saga* did not make more use of *Gísla saga* to straighten up their account, when, at the same time, they bothered to mention those small details at all. In my view, the only explanation is that the Gísli-tradition was too strong. Sturla based his stories of Aron on relatively short-lived, and thereby quite unstructured, oral

---

[15] Holtsmark 1951, 10–13.
[16] Foote 1963, 131–133.
[17] Porter 1993, 21–22.
[18] Foote 1963, 130–131; Heller 1966, 59–62; Aðalgeir Kristjánsson 1965, 150–157.

traditions, weakened, as well, by the emerging tradition of writing. Is it perhaps too daring to think that he, with a glint in his eye, made some intertextual references to Gísli, but on the whole stuck to the 'truth'?

Incidentally, *Arons saga* might be an interesting case in other ways. If it is true that it was written down around 1350, with nothing preceding it except the passages in *Íslendinga saga*, one might wonder whether it was based on some kind of oral saga. More than a century had elapsed since the events, and the tradition, referring to Andersson, should have done its work by then – and maybe it had.[19] *Arons saga* is good and bad at the same time. It is disorderly in many ways, but some of the scenes do make a vivid impression. Perhaps the saga might be used as a measure of the condition of the orality after the ultimate onset of writing?

Of course, I find it self-evident that the Gísli-tradition was influenced by contemporary events and contemporary views all along. Consequently, the main reason for Aron's fate not to make an imprint was the emergence of the written saga. Therefore, other Arons might have made impressions and then disappeared, just like many other more abstract fashions of the day. This leads us to the problem of the verses. Gísli's dream-verses about the good and the bad dream-woman have attracted much attention through the years, and some of the reached conclusions must be regarded as final.

If one believes in a saga-author, that author cannot have written all of the verses by himself because there are too many discrepancies between prose and verse. One usually does not misunderstand one's own wordings to such a high degree. Likewise, all the verses cannot have been composed by Gísli, or by someone in the tenth century, for Peter Foote and others have convincingly shown that many of the stanzas belong to a twelfth-century skaldic tradition, characterized by antiquarian interests and Christian apocalyptic themes.[20] Accordingly, some verses might be very old, some might belong to the twelfth century, and some might even have been composed in the thirteenth century. If we believe in an oral tradition, and if we do not believe that the scribe alone was responsible for bringing the verses into the saga, then the tradition incorporated stanzas during its entire existence. Maybe the fact that Gísli was renowned for his verses – and that some of the verses were included in the oral saga from the beginning – together with other favourable circumstances, led to an easy entry into the saga for skaldic poetry. And this is of course fundamental – the oral saga evolved over time and absorbed ideas and conceptions, and it was exposed to continual change.

Lars Lönnroth has recently argued that *Gísla saga* is not just a meticulous, realistic report of events: all of this "may in the long run be trivial and unimportant compared to the question of what ultimately happens to Gísli's soul". But Lönnroth also underlines that "this metaphysical perspective is not allowed

---

[19] ANDERSSON 2002, 410–411.
[20] FOOTE 1963, 113–123.

to dominate the foreground of the story". It is only glimpsed now and then in the verses.[21]

I whole-heartedly agree. But, of course, the metaphysical perspective Lönnroth is talking about was not there from the beginning, and, in my view, neither was it created by a thirteenth-century author. It was added to the tradition somewhere along the line, and, as always, it altered the oral saga in important ways.

The questions I have been asking about the presumptive oral saga can, of course, never be answered with any certainty. Perhaps there was no saga before it was written down, and perhaps the underlying traditions were just scattered and broken fragments assembled by scribes or authors or writers and put into position in the framework and context of a written genre. But this is also just an assumption. In my opinion, the discussion must be kept alive as long as we do not know anything for certain – i.e., probably forever. The relations of the written artefacts must be examined, of course, but speculations upon lost written versions should, at least not automatically be preferred to speculations on an oral saga tradition. Both must be taken into account, and there should never be a demand on limiting our attention to that which *is* (the written, preserved saga-texts) at the expense of that which is lost (the oral tradition and the lost texts).

One way of getting a glimpse of the tradition might be to open our eyes to the vestiges and traces that might have left their imprints on the preserved manuscripts. Therefore, we should be on guard towards our own responses when reading sagas. Some of the qualities we perceive might seem qualities only to *our* minds, due to our experiences of the novel and to our aesthetic demands on fictional literary texts. Maybe we ought to look beyond these and see the oral story-teller and his audience at the moment of telling, trying to pin down that which might be regarded as worth telling. Maybe the good scribe was not as good and smart and calculating as we sometimes find him to be. Maybe he was just struggling with the impossible task of putting onto parchment the fascinating stories of the greatest story-tellers in his surroundings. In that case, the only possible outcome was failure, but failure might turn into success when the audience shifted and was substituted by readers in times to come – just as success might sometimes turn into failure. To sum up, the manners of saga-telling that made *Gísla saga* interesting to listen to and easy to remember for those who told it, need not be the same as those that make us appreciate the written saga of Gísli.

---

[21] LÖNNROTH 2002, 462–463.

Bibliography

Primary sources

Arons saga Hjǫrleifssonar, ed. Jón Jóhannesson in *Sturlunga saga* II: 237–278. Reykjavík 1946.

Gísla saga Súrssonar, ed. Björn K. Þórólfsson in *Vestfirðinga sǫgur*, Íslenzk fornrit 6, 1–118. Reykjavík 1943.

Membrana deperdita, ed. A. Loth. Editiones Arnamagnæanæ A 5. København 1960.

Secondary sources

AÐALGEIR KRISTJÁNSSON 1965: "Gísla saga og samtíð höfundra." *Skírnir*, 139 148–158.

ANDERSSON, Theodore M. 1964: *The Problem of Icelandic Saga Origins: A Historical Survey.* Yale.

——— 1969: "Some ambiguities in *Gísla saga*: A balance sheet." *BONIS*, 1968 7–42.

——— 2002: "The long prose form in medieval Iceland." *JEGP*, 101 380–411.

BERGER, Alan 1979: "Text and sex in Gísla saga." *Gripla*, 3 163–168.

BREDSDORFF, Thomas 1971: *Kaos og kærlighed.* København.

FOOTE, Peter 1963: "An essay on the Saga of Gisli and its Icelandic background." In *The Saga of Gisli* (Trans. G. Johnston). Toronto.

GUÐNI KOLBEINSSON & JÓNAS KRISTJÁNSSON 1979: "Gerðir Gíslasögu." *Gripla*, 3 128–162.

HELLER, Rolf 1966: "Aron Hjörleifssohn und Gisli Surssohn." *Arkiv för nordisk filologi*, 81 57–63.

HOLTSMARK, Anne 1951: *Studies in Gísla saga.* Oslo.

JAKOBSEN, Alfred 1979a: "Noen merknader til Gísla saga Súrssonar." *Gripla*, 5 280–288.

——— 1979b: "Nytt lys over Gísla saga Súrssonar." *Gripla*, 5 265–279.

LÖNNROTH, Lars 2002: "Dreams in the sagas." *Scandinavian Studies*, 74 455–464.

PORTER, John 1993: "Arons saga Hjörleifssonar." In Phillip Pulsiano (ed.) *Medieval Scandinavia: An Encyclopedia*, pp. 21–22, New York.

PRINZ, Reinhard 1935: *Die Schöpfung der Gísla saga Súrssonar.* Breslau.

RÖHN, Hartmut 1979: "Der Einleitungsteil der Gísla Saga Súrssonar: Ein Vergleich der beiden Versionen." *Arkiv för nordisk filologi*, 94 95–113.

SEEWALD, Franz 1934: *Die Gisla Saga Surssonar: Untersuchungen.* Göttingen.

VÉSTEINN ÓLASON & ÞÓRÐUR INGI GUÐJÓNSSON 2000: "Sammenhængen mellem tolkninger og tekstversioner af *Gísla saga*." In Kristinn Jóhannesson, Karl G. Johansson & Lars Lönnroth (eds.) *Den fornnordiska texten i filologisk och litteraturvetenskaplig belysning, Gothenburg Old Norse Studies*, vol. 2, pp. 96–120, Göteborg.

The Oral-Formulaic Theory Revisited

MINNA SKAFTE JENSEN

THREE QUARTERS OF a century have passed since Milman Parry published his doctoral thesis. What began as an analysis of Homeric formulaic diction developed into an ambitious theory about oral poetry in general and oral epic in particular. After the publication of Albert B. Lord's *The Singer of Tales* came a period of euphoria in which it seemed that all the old Homeric questions had found their answers, and the theory spread into the other philologies. Next came a period of frustration: scholars tired of simple answers and the theory was widely rejected. In the field of medieval studies an influential paper by Michael Curschmann contested the opinion of Lord that any text is either oral or written, and that transitional texts do not exist. From a background of fieldwork in Sierra Leone and a general knowledge of African oral traditions, Ruth Finnegan criticised the theory for being too rigid. Instead, she stressed the coexistence of written and oral literature in the modern world, and the constant interaction of the two.[1]

In Homeric studies the theory is currently having a comeback and is again eagerly discussed, but in new ways, mainly instigating studies in the social context of early Greek poetry, or used as a key to interpretation. As examples, I point to two recent books that seem especially innovative: Casey Dué's discussion of the kind of intertextuality at work in the Homeric poems and Ruth Scodel's study of the role of the audience.[2]

What has remained relatively unnoticed among philologists is, however, that in the meantime the theory has been adopted by folklorists and anthropologists, and that the amount of oral poetry accessible in descriptions or editions is by now considerable. Great oral traditions still exist in many parts of the modern world and are studied in ways that make them relevant to the understanding of both Homer and other epic poems from earlier periods which have been transmitted to us in writing. Since it is one of the paradoxes of the oral-formulaic theory that it was developed on the basis of a tradition known only in written form, it seems worthwhile to try to assess whether it did actually capture the essentials of orally composed poetry.

---

[1] PARRY 1928a,b (English translation in PARRY 1971, 1–239); LORD 1960; CURSCHMANN 1967; FINNEGAN 1977.
[2] DUÉ 2002; SCODEL 2002.

The oral-formulaic theory in fieldwork

The theory has influenced fieldwork in many respects, both in the methods used and the problems raised.

Because of its focus on the flexibility of epic traditions, scholars have become careful to clarify which performance they are studying, and it is no longer accepted to edit texts conflated from more than one performance or even based on recordings from a multitude of singers. But it is not unusual for scholars to ask singers to produce a special, and often especially long, performance specifically for them; such texts are called 'induced' or 'elicited' oral epics.

Just as interest has gathered around the specific performance, singers have gained individuality in the scholars' eyes. Modern studies and editions regularly inform the reader about the singer in question, his background, education, and role in society. It is also typical of this branch of scholarship that singers are interviewed about their views upon their art, and that such dialogues between artist and scholar are published, at least in selection. Questions concerned with formulas, themes, and orality vs. literacy are central, both for such dialogues and for the analyses which scholars give the recorded texts.

Since this kind of scholarship wants to understand oral art in its genuine form, the question of how the scholar influences the performance becomes of paramount importance. It is, however, a relatively new phenomenon for scholars to be as explicit as Susan Slyomivicz about their own role when recording and editing oral poetry.[3] Sometimes they even neglect stating what they asked for at the beginning of their fieldwork.

Spontaneity and tradition do not interact in the same way in all genres of oral poetry. Therefore, when we want to draw comparisons between oral traditions in the modern world and epic in ancient or medieval times, it is necessary to establish some kind of formal definition. Scholars differ on the issue. I have settled on defining the epic genre as 'a long narrative poem describing historical events'. By 'long' I mean longer than other forms in a community's spectrum of genres; by 'narrative' concerned with action (but description and reflection may occur); by 'poetry' whatever is performed in a style distinguished from daily speech; and by 'historical events' incidents that both singer and audience consider to have actually taken place once upon a time.[4]

I shall present here three living traditions, two from India and one from Egypt. They have been chosen, not because they are closer to Homer than other epic traditions, but because the way they have been described makes them especially interesting in connection with the oral-formulaic theory. Together they also give an impression of the scale of difference that exists among the methodologies of current fieldwork. I will proceed chronologically, in the order in which the studies were published.

---

[3] SLYOMOVICZ 1987, cf. below.
[4] HONKO 1998b, 20–29 has a detailed discussion of how to define the epic form.

The Talminadu *Brothers' Epic*

Brenda Beck studied an epic tradition in the state of Talminadu in South Eastern India.[5] During a period of some years in the mid-1960s she lived as a social anthropologist in a village in the Coimbatore district, where one of the sources of popular entertainment was epic performance. There were local singers, but now and then the village was also visited by professional performers of the same tradition. The subject of the epic is the heroic deeds of two brothers and their sister who, after their death, are given semi-divine status by the gods. The events take place in an undefinable distant past, but in the area in which the singing community lives.

The professional epic singers are itinerant and work in groups. The singing is accompanied by drums. The audiences are mixed: both men and women, adults and children and various castes. The number of nights spent in one performance depends on the interest of audiences. Singers maintain that they can take three months to tell the *Brothers' Story*; the usual event is a narrating over three to four evenings, but it is not uncommon that performance periods are longer, up to two or three weeks.[6] Beck registered a performance sung by E. A. Ramacami that was spread over nineteen evenings between June 23 and September 1, 1965. The total recording time was 44 hours. Except for being present with her tape recorder, the anthropologist did not try to elicit some kind of special performance; this long, continued presentation was a normal way of performing.

In order to facilitate her understanding of the text, Beck asked Mr. Ramacami also to dictate the epic to a scribe, and this was done from June 25 to September 3, 1965. She does not describe the process in detail, but the dates suggest that whenever the singer sung a passage to an audience, he dictated the same passage to the scribe afterwards. The written version is 622 pages, some 11,500 verse lines. Even though the singer considered the two versions to be the same, the written one differed considerably from the performed one.[7] In some cases the order of events was changed and most notably the written version was much shorter than the sung one. Descriptions are left out or abbreviated, and humoristic passages also tend to disappear. In the sung performance there are passages in which audience and singer discuss the events, but these are left out of the written version, too. In Beck's formulation: "[The dictated version] tells one just as much or more about what happened, but less about how things looked and felt".[8]

In addition to these two versions by the same singer she refers to six other texts. Two of them contain just a single passage, the sister's lament at her brothers' death, one of which is a performance by another singer whom Beck registered at a religious festival; the performance lasted twenty minutes. The

---

[5] BECK 1982.

[6] BECK 1982, 85 – Following GENETTE 1980, 25–27, I distinguish between story, narrative and narrating.

[7] BECK 1982, 58–88.

[8] BECK 1982, 67.

other is a manuscript of 27 pages, written in 1930. Next she refers to the epic as she found it in three different paperbacks, printed between 1965 and 1977, and without precise indication of its origin; the text varies from 130 pages, about 4,500 verse lines, to 298 pages, about 9,500 verse lines. Finally, she refers to a radio version from 1966 which gives only a brief outline of the story.[9]

Except for the two above-mentioned versions performed by the same singer, Beck does not state precisely how the various texts are interrelated, presumably because this would be impossible to ascertain. But the general picture is clear enough: the story can be narrated in many ways, in various media to various audiences, and in more or less detail. Also, it is clear from the publishing dates that these specific printed books cannot have been the source of the sung versions; it seems that Beck only began hunting for other versions of the story after attending the performances she recorded in her village. Even so, other printed versions would have been accessible to readers before. Similarly the famous ancient Indian epics, *Mahabharata* and *Ramayana*, were present in various ways. The *Mahabharata* was already translated into Tamil about 1400 AD, and it is recited in various ways at religious festivals or on the radio, it exists in drama and dance and is the basis of films. In her analysis of the *Brothers' Story* Beck often points to various influences from the old epics. But the *Brothers' Story* forms a distinct tradition that does not fit into or relate to the events of the ancient epics.

The Arab *Sirat Bani Hilal*

Susan Slyomovicz and Dwight Reynolds both describe the *Sirat Bani Hilal*, an epic tradition concerned with the immigration of the Bani Hilal tribe from the Arabian peninsula to Northern Africa.[10] This took place during the ninth through twelfth centuries, and ended in two large battles in Tunisia (1153 and 1160) in which the tribe was annihilated. The events are known from written documents, among which is a description by the 14th-century historian Ibn Khaldoun. The protagonists are historical persons documented in other sources, but, according to the scholars, their lives in the epic tradition have little in common with those of the actual persons.[11] The epic tradition is known all over the Arab parts of Northern Africa. The first written manuscripts stem from the end of the eighteenth century, and printed versions are accessible in books. The oral tradition exists, as it seems, on its own conditions, performed by professional singers. Their social status is low, and even though peasants and workers are interested in the stories as the history of their own ancestors, they look down upon the singers and consider them gypsies. Slyomovicz conducted her fieldwork in Upper Egypt, Reynolds in a village in the Nile Delta. In both areas the audiences are male; performance occasions are festive events such as

[9] BECK 1982, 3–4 offers a survey of the versions in schematic form.
[10] SLYOMOVICZ 1987; REYNOLDS 1995.
[11] REYNOLDS 1995, 8–10.

weddings or gatherings of factory workers, but singers also entertain in cafes and marketplaces.

Slyomovicz is careful to describe her own background, her language studies, the way in which she spent a long period working on a lexicon, seated in a friend's cigarette shop in order to gradually become a known figure in the neighbourhood, how she attended the performances of various singers, and how she finally agreed with the singer Awadallah Abd aj-Jalil Ali to accompany him during a longer period.[12] He was an illiterate professional singer, the son and grandson of singers. When performing he accompanied himself on a drum. There were also singers playing a one-stringed violin, the *rabab*, but Awadallah looked down upon them and considered the instrument frivolous. Slyomovicz's purpose was to finally record and publish a specific performance of his, which took place on March 10, 1983. As a result, she was able to present a text with a high degree of precision: she knew when and where it was performed, by whom and to whom, and in her work on the recorded text – transcribing, translating and interpreting – she had the poet-singer at hand and was also able to ask questions of some of those who had been present at the performance. For instance, at a certain point there was some laughing and Slyomovicz did not understand why. When she asked afterwards, it turned out that the singer had related an amorous event in the heroic sphere in such a way that everyone immediately saw a parallel to a scandal in the village connected to the widow of a recently deceased blacksmith.[13]

Reynolds, too, began in Arabic language studies with the purpose of doing epic research. Like Slyomovicz, but unlike Beck, he searched for some time in order to find the best performance milieu for his purpose and ended up in a place called "The Poets' Village", Al-Bakatush. Here a few families specialised in the *Bani Hilal*-Tradition and were called on as entertainers at weddings and other festivities. They accompanied their performance on the *rabab*. Reynolds first visited the village in 1983 and stayed there for longer periods in 1986-88.[14] At the time of his stay there were fourteen active singers in the village. Reynolds was eventually accepted as an apprentice by one of the old singers, taught to play the *rabab*, and also trained in singing the stories. His main intention, he explains, was to find himself a role that was familiar and well-defined in the community, and that gave him a vantage point from which to attend both performances and discussions between singer and audience, as well as conversations among the singers themselves.[15] As indicated in the title of his book, Reynolds was especially interested in the identification he saw between singers and the heroes of which they sing.

The epic consists of some thirty episodes, each of which is a rounded tale meant to be performed during one or a few evenings. The episodes are known under titles, and the singers generally agree on a proper order in which the

---

[12] SLYOMOVICZ 1987, 21–30.
[13] SLYOMOVICZ 1987, 110–111.
[14] REYNOLDS 1995, 36.
[15] REYNOLDS 1995, 42–45.

events follow one another.[16] Reynolds asked the singer Shaykh Biyali Abu Fahmi to do a full performance for him of all the episodes in sequential order, a feat the singer said he had never done before. The performance lasted eleven nights and added up to 32 hours of singing time. However, throughout the following weeks the poet would realise that he had forgotten something, which he then sang to the recorder. With these additions, the poem grew to 37 hours. Afterwards, when the scholar was studying his tapes he found that this induced version tended to give the various episodes in a briefer format than when the singer performed in his usual way; it seems that the fact that the singer knew that he was supposed to give the narrative in its entirety made him choose not to embellish the single details too much.[17] In this case, then, we have an induced epic narrated in chronographic fashion, whereas normally the epic is a cycle of episodes.

The Tulu *Siri Epic*

My last example is the result of many years of fieldwork led by the Finnish folklorist Lauri Honko and involving a team of Indian and Finnish scholars.[18] The epic tradition studied belongs in Karnataka in the South-Western part of India, where a minority of about two million people speak the language Tulu. Honko concentrated his efforts on the singer Gopala Naika, who is also a farmer and the head of a religious community worshipping a certain heroine Siri. The epic in question narrates the story of this heroine and that of her daughter and granddaughters. The dramatic time is the distant past, the places are well-known localities of the area, and the poem tells, among other things, how certain sanctuaries were founded. The epic is mainly performed in two social settings, as entertainment during work in the paddy-field and as a main part of religious festivals, most importantly at the harvest festival. The audience in the field consists of women workers planting rice plants. At the harvest festival, these same women make up the main audience, actively participating in the performance: Gopala Naika first sings for a couple of hours after which he begins asking questions of the women who then impersonate Siri and the other female protagonists of the tale, each relating the specific heroine's story in first-person-format.

Honko visited Naika on several occasions during the 1980s–1990s, and in December 1990 he arranged for a performance of the full story to a small team consisting of his wife, himself, an interpreter and sometimes a few others. The event was recorded with both audio- and video-tape and copied so that versions could be archived in both Helsinki and Mysore. The recording lasted six days, and the total singing time, not counting pauses, was 26 hours.[19] When written out, the elicited poem ran to 15,683 verses, preceded by an invocation of 563

[16] REYNOLDS 1995, 16–19.
[17] REYNOLDS 1995, 41–42.
[18] HONKO 1998a,b.
[19] HONKO 1998b, 270–321.

verses. In printed form, with a parallel translation into English, the recorded poem takes up two solid volumes. A few years earlier the singer had dictated the same poem to an Indian scholar, and the dictated version was 8,538 verses.[20]

In the volume introducing the edition, Honko discusses all kinds of theoretical questions in connection with his fieldwork. Of special importance seems to me his considerations of stability and change in Naika's texts. He maintains that there is a common denominator throughout the many different performances, which he calls the "mental text", a kind of matrix that the singer varies all the time.[21] Another useful concept is the "pool of tradition", which describes the entire complex of stories and techniques that singers share.[22]

Gopala Naika regularly performed to women audiences, and during cult performances the women identified with the heroines in a very direct way. But also in a more general fashion, the epic seems to invite the female audience's identification: not only are the heroines female, but the poem is very much concerned with women's problems – menstruation, pregnancy, childbirth etc. This is, however, an aspect Honko only touches upon very briefly; he is much more interested in the relationship between the poem and the cult.

Conclusions

What can we learn about ancient and medieval epic from such fieldwork? I shall concentrate on only a few main points.

First of all, it is by now well documented that oral epic can be of considerable length. This was known long ago, mentioned for instance by Sir Maurice Bowra in 1952.[23] But scholars have not really taken notice of this, and many readers of Homer still consider the *Iliad* and the *Odyssey* too long to have been orally composed. This view is manifestly wrong. If long oral epics are seldom brought into print, it is not because they do not exist, but because of the difficulties involved in recording, transcribing, translating and publishing, not to mention finding a reading public ready to buy the book. For a young scholar interested in making a career it would be suicide. Honko's project was realised only because he was an authoritative senior scholar and because the Finnish Academy spent generous amounts of money on the project.

Next, the flexibility of long oral narrative is confirmed, and to my knowledge it has been confirmed without exception, during these four decades of fieldwork. Epic singers constantly vary their performance so as to meet the demands of the occasion, and they are ready to meet the special demands of fieldworkers even if these differ from the way the singer normally proceeds. Thus Parry and Lord's concept of composition-in-performance is certainly confirmed.

This is not to say that singers do not memorise. How carefully passages are memorised varies from one genre and tradition to another, but the fact

[20] HONKO 1998b, 15, 276–277.
[21] HONKO 1998b, 92–99.
[22] HONKO 1998b, 66–75.
[23] BOWRA 1952, 354–356.

that memorisation plays an important role in even such flexible texts as those presented here is manifest. Actually, when one studies the texts Parry and Lord themselves published it is clear, I think, that their informants also relied very much on memorising, and the phenomenon ought, perhaps, rather to be termed "recomposition-in-performance".[24]

Singers, nevertheless, maintain that they are not only able to sing the song the same way, word for word and line for line, but that this is actually what they are doing. The ideal is to sing of the events exactly as they happened, with both singers and audiences believing that what moves them is the truth of the story. Another ambition of the singer is to be able to repeat a song verbatim after having heard it only once. Exactly how to interpret this paradoxical difference between what singers say and what they do, may be discussed, but it at least seems clear that the conception of 'sameness' is different in an oral and a written context.

The three oral traditions referred to here all exist in communities in which writing also exists and books are accessible. The *Brothers' Story* in Talminadu and the *Sirat Bani Hilal* in Egypt are relatively easy to acquire in print, whereas the *Siri Epic*, even though it was written before Gopala Naika sang his version to Honko, could not be bought just anywhere. Nevertheless, the poet-singers managed without books, and there is nothing to suggest that they would have felt it helpful to have a book at hand either in preparing or performing their epics.

This, of course, touches upon the question of transitional texts. In *The Singer of Tales* Lord stated that texts were either composed orally or in writing, and that transitional texts did not exist.[25] This was a detail of the theory for which he was severely criticised, to such a degree that towards the end of his life he withdrew his provocative standpoint.[26] But as far as I can see, he had been right in the first place. Of course, part of the problem lies in how the various phenomena are defined; for instance, the poet Petar Petrovic Njegos who was classified as a transitional poet by the aged A. B. Lord, would qualify as a written poet building on an oral tradition according to the principles set forward in *The Singer of Tales*. Lord's original statement, on the contrary, seems to express genuine astonishment at what field experience had taught him: that even though writing was well known and books widespread in the Montenegro singing community he was studying, singers did not find these facilities helpful and did not use them.[27]

In the case of the singers of Al-Bakatush that Reynolds describes, it was not so much books and reading that constituted the cognate medium, the potential inspiration, threat or alternative to traditional oral epic, but cassette tapes and modern types of music. Hosts might prefer to hire a singer with an amplified band to entertain their guests rather than a traditional 'gypsy', and singers might

[24] Cf. SKAFTE JENSEN 1980, 23–25.
[25] LORD 1960, 129.
[26] LORD 1986.
[27] I have discussed the question of transitional texts at some length in SKAFTE JENSEN 1998.

find it more profitable to adapt the traditional art to modern media than to continue performing in the old style.[28] Such hybrids, however, are of little relevance to the study of ancient or medieval epic.[29]

Bibliography

BECK, Brenda E. F. 1982: *The Three Twins: The Telling of a South Indian Folk Epic*. Bloomington, Indiana.

BOWRA, C. M. 1952: *Heroic Poetry*. London.

CURSCHMANN, Michael 1967: "Oral poetry in medieval English, French, and German literature: Some notes on recent research." *Speculum*, 42 36–52.

DUÉ, Casey 2002: *Homeric Variations on a Lament by Briseis*. Lanham.

FINNEGAN, Ruth 1977: *Oral Poetry: Its Nature, Significance and Social Context*. Cambridge.

GENETTE, Gérard 1980: *Narrative Discourse: An Essay in Method*. Ithaca & New York, transl. Jane E. Lewin.

HONKO, Lauri (ed.) 1998a: *The Siri Epic as Performed by Gopola Naika*. Helsinki, in collaboration with Chinnapa Gowda, Anneli Honko and Viveka Rai.

HONKO, Lauri 1998b: *Textualising the Siri Epic*. Helsinki.

LORD, Albert B. 1960: *The Singer of Tales, Harvard Studies in Comparative Literature*, vol. 24. Cambridge, Mass.

———— 1986: "The merging of two worlds: Oral and written poetry as carriers of ancient values." In John Miles Foley (ed.) *Oral Tradition in Literature: Interpretation in Context*, pp. 19–64, Columbia.

PARRY, Milman 1928a: *Essai sur un problème de style homérique*. Paris.

———— 1928b: *L'épithète traditionnelle dans Homère*. Paris.

———— 1971: *The Making of Homeric Verse: The Collected Papers of Milman Parry*. Oxford, edited by Adam Parry.

REYNOLDS, Dwight Fletcher 1995: *Heroic Poets, Poetic Heroes: The Ethnography of Performance in an Arabic Oral Epic Tradition*. Ithaca & London.

SCODEL, Ruth 2002: *Listening to Homer: Tradition, Narrative, and Audience*. Ann Arbor.

SKAFTE JENSEN, Minna 1980: *The Homeric Question and the Oral-Formulaic Theory*. Copenhagen.

———— 1998: "A. B. Lord's concept of transitional texts in relation to the Homeric epics." In Lauri Honko, Jawaharlal Handoo & John Miles Foley (eds.) *The Epic - Oral and Written*, pp. 94–114, Mysore.

SLYOMOVICZ, Susan 1987: *The Merchant of Art: An Egyptian Hilali Oral Epic Poet in Performance*. Berkeley.

The periodical *Oral Tradition* (editor: John Miles Foley) offers articles and sometimes reviews related to the oral-formulaic theory. Its volume 18 (2003) is a collection of brief reports on state-of-the-art under the following headings:

---

[28] REYNOLDS 1995, 95–97, 106.
[29] I am grateful to Jena Habegger for revising my English.

Vol. 18.1: People's Poetry – Japanese – Bible – Performance – Ancient Greek – African – Tibetan and Chinese – Lithuanian – Comparative; Vol. 18.2: Hispanic – Ballad – Celtic – Scandinavian – English – Pan-Asian – Comparative.

On the homepage of *Oral Tradition* (http://www.oraltradition.org) an extended bibliography is to be found in connection with John Miles Foley's *How To Read an Oral Poem* (Urbana: The Illinois University Press 2001).

From Vernacular Interviews to Latin Prose (ca. 600–1200)

Lars Boje Mortensen

Scripta, audita, visa

THE CHRONOLOGICAL CONCEPT 'within living memory' makes intuitive sense in modern as well as in premodern societies. I suppose that Danish and Norwegian are not the only languages in which it is expressed with proverbial and alliterative force ('i mands minde'). If we want to go beyond an intuitive understanding we can use the analysis made by Jan Assmann and call it "Kommunikatives Gedächtnis" which is contrasted to "Kulturelles Gedächtnis". The latter is typically concerned with almost frozen points in the past – often the distant past. In pre-literate societies those mythical points usually lie at a great distance from living memory whereas societies with a certain level of written records are able to bridge, or at least partially fill the gap between the mythical events of cultural foundation and the present. On the other hand the "Kommunikatives Gedächtnis" has an upper limit of approximately eighty years, and a standard lifespan of about forty years.[1]

Similar distinctions were known to medieval historians. When discussing the authorities they built on they usually grouped them as either *scripta*, *audita*, or *visa*, or, as we would put it, written sources, oral sources, and personal experience.[2] Writing was the only reliable access to the distant past and could of course also be used for more recent events. For the period within living memory, namely within the eighty years, writing could be supplemented or substituted with accounts told by older trustworthy members of society. And finally the historian could rely on his own experiences for the most recent events. Let me quote just one example of how such distinctions could be expressed and reflected upon. It is from the meticulous crusading historian William of Tyre who was writing in the Kingdom of Jerusalem around 1180. After the first fifteen books of his work which tell of the background of the Crusades, the establishment of the Kingdom after 1099 and the period up to the death of King Fulk in 1143, William pauses with this reflection:

---

[1] ASSMANN 1992, esp. 48–56.
[2] Cf. GUENÉE 1980, 77–109.

Que de presenti hactenus contexuimus Historia aliorum tantum, quibus prisci temporis plenior adhuc famulabatur memoria, collegimus relatione, unde cum maiore difficultate, quasi aliena mendicantes suffragia, et rei veritatem et gestorum seriem at annorum numerum sumus assequuti, licet fideli, quantum potuimus, hec eadem recitatione scripto mandavimus. Que autem sequuntur deinceps partim nos ipsi fide conspeximus oculata, partim eorum, qui rebus gestis presentes interfuerunt, fida nobis patuit narratione, unde gemino freti adminiculo ea que restant auctore domino facilius fideliusque posterorum mandabimus lectioni.[3]

The events we have described so far in the present History, have been collected from the accounts of other people who still had a full recollection of the distant past. To stick to the truth of the matter, the order of events and the enumeration of the years was fraught with great difficulty by thus begging, as it were, at other people's tables, even if we took down in writing, to the best of our ability, these events through an accurate account. What follows, however, is partly warranted by our own eyes, partly by the trustworthy stories reported to us by those who were present at the events. Leaning in this way on a double support we can – with the help of the Lord – hand over the remainder with greater ease as well as greater credibility to the discretion of our future readers.

Here William discusses the tripartition between written accounts that cover the *priscum tempus* 'olden times', and the eyewitness accounts by the author or by others that cover the approximately most active period within "Kommunikatives Gedächtnis", i.e. of the last forty years. In passing we should pay attention to the obsession with trustworthiness (*fida, fideli, fidelius*) which was of course not determined by allegiance to any scholarly of scientific ideal, but by the deterrent of the consequences of lying and breaking one's word in a society devoted to honour within the peer group, and even more of duplicity in relation to the prospects of eternal salvation. Or to put it more bluntly: it was a matter of great temporal and eternal danger to put lies into prestigious parchment books.[4]

In this paper I want to look at one of the three activities, namely that of contemporary accounts told to the author – or to phrase it in a modern way, that of interviews. The interview itself can hardly be called an art form, but the dialogue between historian and informant must often have been shaped by the kind of work the interview was made for – and those works were full of art. We can put it in terms of classical rhetoric: the process began with *inventio* (the collection of material), went through *dispositio* (structuring) and on to the final stages of *elocutio* (the stylistically elaborated wording); the last phase in

---

[3] WILLELMUS TYRENSIS, *Chronicon*, 16.1.

[4] With reference to William, among others, KERSKEN 2004 analyses the reflections made by medieval historians on the fear of telling the truth about contemporary events in order not to offend commissioners and other potential readers. As a supplement to Kersken's analysis, the other side of the coin, the fear of *not* telling the truth, will be partly thematised here.

our medieval context, the crowning of the *elocutio* and in a certain sense the *memoria* and the *actio* (the memorizing and the deliverance), consisted in the production of a fair copy carefully written on well-prepared parchment. The whole process must have been a complex mechanism between various linguistic, conceptual, and rhetorical levels. Although it is impossible in most cases to really get behind the polished text itself, I shall at least try to adduce some of the evidence we do have of the working conditions of Latin prose writers. I shall first take a look at the interview situation and next at note-taking and draft-writing. Such a fresh look may provide us, finally, with new elements in our on-going search for adequate expressions of orality/literacy-equations.

Interviews

My first example comes from an early Irish author, the Abbot of Iona, Adomnán, who died in 704. In his *Vita Columbae* he traced and authenticated a large number of stories about the founder of the monastery, the Holy Columba who had died almost a century before Adomnán wrote (in 597). In most cases his sources must consequently have been written or second- or third-hand reminiscences, but some of them referred to events after Columba's death when his prophecies and miraculous powers were at work and experienced by people with whom Adomnán had spoken. In the preface he explains:

> Sed ea quae maiorum fideliumque uirorum tradita expertorum cognoui relatione narraturum et sine ulla ambiguitate craxaturum sciat, et uel ex his quae ante nos inserta paginis repperire potuimus, uel ex his quae auditu ab expertis quibusdam fidelibus antiquis sine ulla dubitatione narrantibus diligentius sciscitantes didicimus.[5]

> But let him understand that I shall relate what has come to my knowledge through the tradition passed on by our predecessors, and by trustworthy men who knew the facts; and that I shall set down unequivocally, and either from among those things I have been able to find put in writing before our time, or else from among those that we have learned, after diligent inquiry, by hearing them from the lips of certain informed and trustworthy aged men who related them without any hesitation.

The important phrase here is *diligentius sciscitantes* 'after diligent inquiry'. Adomnán drew on a number of informants both inside and outside the monastery,[6] and he was clearly active during the interviews himself. In most cases Adomnán was socially superior to his informants, although some of the petty kings could count as his peers. As abbot and successor of Columba his authority in taking down the stories he deemed relevant was uncontested. Unfortunately we are not let in on the details of the interviews, but most of them must have been

---

[5] ADOMNÁN, *Vita Columbae*, Secunda praefatio, p. 6–7.
[6] ANDERSON & ANDERSON 1991, lxv–lxviii.

conducted in Old Irish. The Latin end product of Adomnán displays clear influences from the *Life of St Martin* of Sulpicius Severus and especially from the
Latin Bible.[7] I shall return to some elements in this process below, but it should
be mentioned that the monks already led very 'textual' lives and many miracle
and prophecy stories are likely to have influenced the experiences – indeed the
motivation behind the actions and perceptions – long before Adomnán's pen
could twist them in any direction.

Let us proceed to another example where we have better information about
the interview itself. The Danish king Sven Estridsen who died in 1074, was
interviewed by the canon Adam of Bremen who was planning to write the
history of his archiepiscopal see, Hamburg-Bremen. As the Nordic regions fell
within the missionary mandate of Adam's own institution, first-hand information about its history and geography were precious to him. The key passage
about their meeting is the following:

> Novissimis archiepiscopi temporibus, cum ego Bremam venerim,
> audita eiusdem regis sapientia, mox ad eum venire disposui. A quo
> etiam clementissime susceptus, ut omnes, magnam huius libelli
> materiam ex eius ore collegi. Erat enim scientia litterarum eruditus
> et liberalissimus in extraneos, [...]. Cuius veraci et dulcissima
> narratione didici [...] Igitur et ea, quae diximus vel adhuc sumus
> dicturi ex barbaris, omnia relatu illius viri cognovimus.[8]

> Towards the end of the archbishop's reign [Adalbert †1072] I had come
> to Bremen, and when I heard about this king's wisdom I immediately
> decided to pay him a visit. He received me, and everyone else, in the most
> forthcoming manner and I collected rich materials for this little book
> from his very mouth. For he possessed literary learning and was most
> generous towards strangers. [...] Through his truthful and well told story
> I learned [...]. In this way we learned all we have said and will be saying
> about the barbarians from this man's account.

Adam's description is very valuable because we can be certain that he visited
and listened to the king with the express purpose of gathering material for
his book. From the description of Sven's wisdom, literary learning and 'sweet'
rhetoric one could perhaps be tempted to imagine that Sven and Adam held
their conversation in Latin. To my mind, however, that is highly unlikely; first
of all because a long formal training for lay people in this period would have
been highly irregular, secondly because the socially superior individual would
have set the premises for the conversation; furthermore, Sven's literary learning
and wisdom could simply mean that he possessed knowledge stemming from
books – having been informed by clerics, not that he mastered Latin passively
or actively. The description also signals Sven's general receptiveness towards
clerical as well as non-clerical learning. Their conversation was probably held in

---

[7] ANDERSON & ANDERSON 1991, lxvii–lxviii.
[8] ADAM BREMENSIS, *Gesta Hammaburgensis ecclesiae pontificum*, 3.54.

a vernacular language, Adam understanding Danish or Sven speaking German, or, although less likely, perhaps in two languages with an interpreter between them.

The interviewer here was socially inferior and was obviously happy to be granted the interview. But from other passages in Adam's work we learn that he did not simply listen to Sven's monologue. Adam asked questions (*nobis stipulantibus, nobis rogantibus*) and gave emotional responses (*nobis attonitis*, 'we were shocked to hear'); on Adam's insistence Sven elaborated a point (*affirmavit nobis... adiciens*), and in another case he declined to do so (*De quibus cum regem amplius interrogarem: 'Cessa, inquit, fili...'*). Finally it appears that the interview was witnessed by a number of people (*retulit etiam circumstantibus...*).[9]

My third and final example of an interview situation comes from the *Passio et Miracula Olaui*, the legend of St Olav as it was composed around 1170, approximately 140 years after the death of the Norwegian saint king. The passage in question stems from the collection of miracle stories, and thus deals with his posthumous presence as saint, not with his life on earth all those years ago. A boy had recovered his eyesight at a parish church dedicated to St Olav. He then hastened to pay tribute to the saint's main shrine in Trondheim:

> Set quoniam in finibus illis predicti iuuenis nulla habebatur noticia, nudis eius uerbis nulla est fides adhibita. At cum proximo martiris natalicium instaret, inter multitudinem ex diuersis regionibus confluentem assunt eiusdem prouincie honorati uiri predicti iuuenis noticiam profitentes et fideli testimonio relationem eiusdem roborantes.[10]

> But because no one in those parts was acquainted with the aforesaid youth, no one put faith in his words alone. But as Saint Óláfr's day drew near, a multitude gathered from diverse regions, and among them were respected men from his district who acknowledged acquaintance with the aforesaid youth, and confirmed his account with trustworthy testimony.[11]

We do not receive any details about the interviews, but the cleric in charge of taking down miracle reports at the saint's primary shrine no doubt asked questions – as we can gather from the initial rejection of the story. The 'author'

---

[9] Cf. ADAM BREMENSIS, *Gesta Hammaburgensis ecclesiae pontificum* 1.48: Audivi autem ex ore veracissimi regis Danorum Suein, cum nobis stipulantibus numeraret atavos suos: 'Post cladem, inquit, Nortmannicam Heiligonem ...'; 1.54: Aliqua vero recitavit nobis clarissimus rex Danorum ita rogantibus: 'Post Olaph, inquit ...; 2.34–35: Haec parricidae avi pericula Suein rex nobis attonitis exposuit; deinde ad Hericum victorem reflexit narrationem; 2.26: [...] cum recitaret [...] affirmavit nobis [...], adiciens [...]; 3.23: Audivi etiam, cum veracissimus rex Danorum sermocinando eadem replicaret, ...; 2.43: Narravit nobis diu memorandus rex Danorum et qui omnes barbarorum gestas res in memoriam tenuit, ac si scriptae essent, Aldinburg civitatem [...] Multa in hunc modum per diversas Sclavorum provintias tunc facta memorantur, quae scriptorum penuria nunc habentur pro fabulis. De quibus cum regem amplius interrogarem: 'Cessa, inquit, fili. Tantos habemus in Dania vel Sclavania martyres, ut vix possint libro comprehendi.'; II.75: Hoc nobis de se rex ipse narravit [...] Retulit etiam circumstantibus de regio pontificis apparatu ...
[10] *Passio Olaui* p. 109
[11] Translation by KUNIN 2001, 67.

of the miracle reports as we know them is best described as a collective of officials who chose what to believe and what not.[12] In this process they were eager to have tangible evidence before they entered the story as part of the official legend. This interview situation is almost the reverse of the one between Adam and King Sven: the author receives an unsolicited story and is socially superior to the informant. He is sceptical but cannot dismiss anything out of hand. If indeed Olav had cured the boy and the cleric left the story out, he would have committed a dangerous sin of omission.

In these three examples we can see that interviews were part of the authorial process in two different Latin prose genres – the legend of a saint and the history of an ecclesiastical institution. The social relations between interviewer and interviewed cover a range of possible constellations, but there are important similarities as well. In all three cases the interviews were almost certainly conducted in the vernacular with the purpose of moulding the report into an institutionally-backed literary product in Latin.

In the second part of the paper I shall look more closely at the process from interview to final version, addressing first the question of notes and drafts. Were notes usually taken at interviews? Were they taken down immediately in Latin? How were drafts being produced? And what can we learn in more general terms about the relationship between telling stories in the vernacular and writing them down in Latin? Due to the evidence we are not likely to reach comprehensively valid answers, but I believe that it can at least be shown that we ought to focus more on this aspect of Latin literary writing.

Notes and Drafts

Although medieval poets and scholars were no doubt very well trained in the art of memory,[13] this does not preclude that note-taking happened as a matter of fact. Memorising was primarily applied to metrical vernacular compositions or legal formulae or to authoritative Latin writing – prosaic and poetic alike. To imprint prosaic stories told by informants on memory only, could conceivably have taken place to some degree, but the evidence for it, as far as I can see, is not good. On the other hand, the evidence for note-taking (*excipere* is the technical Latin term) and the reworking of various note-based draft versions is, if not overwhelming, at least clear and solid. I shall present a few instances here.

In a Nordic context we have a famous specimen of an autograph, namely the Angers fragment of Saxo Grammaticus' *Gesta Danorum* from around 1200.[14] It is beyond doubt that we are dealing here with the author's alterations and additions, but it is still somewhat misleading to refer to the fragment, as is often

---

[12] Cf. Mortensen 2000 and Mortensen & Mundal 2003.

[13] Carruthers 1990.

[14] Det Kongelige Bibliotek, Ny Kongelige Samling, 869 g 4°; the fragment, consisting of four folios, exists in numerous reproductions, e.g. in facsimile in Bruun 1879 and electronically on the library website (http://www.kb.dk/permalink/2006/manus/525/dan/). It is described by Jørgensen 1926, 403–404 and by Friis-Jensen 2005, with further references.

done, as 'Saxo's draft'. The text is carefully laid out and is already composed in detail. It is instead what might be termed an intermediate fair copy.

The text must often have been more disorderly in the previous stage, without a careful layout of the parchment, such as the unique early medieval draft manuscript (composed during the 990s) of the Frankish historian Richer of Saint-Remi, now in Bamberg.[15] This chaotic assembly of multiform quires and single sheets written in the author's hand in various stages and successive rearrangements (with inconsistencies), brings us closer to the central creative process of composing a text.[16]

Single sheets were often referred to as *schedae* or *schedulae*, a term that is also employed in a number of statements of authorial modesty – "please accept these small sheets", for example[17] – a certain sign connoting that such texts had not yet been taken through all the necessary steps. To illustrate this we can do no better than to cite the Venerable Bede who gives a beautiful description of this in the prologue to his *Life of Saint Cuthbert*:

> [...] quia nec sine certissima exquisitione rerum gestarum aliquid de tanto uiro scribere, nec tandem ea quae scripseram sine subtili examinatione testium indubiorum passim transcribenda quibus-dam dare praesumpsi, quin potius primo diligenter exordium, progressum, et terminum gloriosissimae conuersationis ac uitae illius ab his qui nouerant inuestigans. Quorum etiam nomina in ipso libro aliquotiens ob certum cognitae ueritatis inditium appo-nenda iudicaui, et sic demum ad scedulas manum mittere incipio. At digesto opusculo sed adhuc in scedulis retento, frequenter et reuerentissimo fratri nostro Herefrido presbitero huc aduentanti, et aliis qui diutius cum uiro Dei conuersati uitam illius optime no-uerant, quae scripsi legenda atque ex tempore praestiti retractanda, ac nonnulla ad arbitrium eorum prout uidebantur sedulus emen-daui, sicque ablatis omnibus scrupulorum ambagibus ad purum, certam ueritatis indaginem simplicibus explicitam sermonibus commendare membranulis, atque ad uestrae quoque fraternitatis praesentiam asportare curaui, quatinus uestrae auctoritatis iudicio uel emendarentur falsa, uel probarentur uera esse quae scripta sunt.
>
> Quod cum Domino adiuuante patrarem, et coram senioribus ac doctoribus uestrae congregationis libellus biduo legeretur, ac

---

[15] Bamberg, Staatsbibliothek, Hist. 5. Description in LEITSCHUH & FISCHER 1895, 130–132 and in HOFFMANN 2000. Full facsimile of the manuscript also in Hoffmann's edition after p. 433 (unpaginated).

[16] On the unique status of Richer's manuscript during this early period cf. PETRUCCI 1992, 355. The poor survival of drafts is natural as they must have been discarded as a matter of course, cf. HOLTZ 1992, 329. A recent analysis of Richer's autograph by GLENN 1997 suggests that it includes, in a convoluted manner, three successive draft versions. Cf. HOFFMANN 2000, 8–10. From the late twelfth century and onwards, historians' drafts like Richer's begin to show up more frequently among surviving manuscripts, cf. RIDER 2001, 49.

[17] E.g. the prologue of the Norwegian historian THEODORICUS (c. 1180): *Vestræ igitur excellentiæ potissimum præsentem schedulam examinandam misimus* [...], p. 4. Cf. GARAND 1995, 78.

solertissime per singula ad uestrum pensaretur examen, nullus omnimodis inuentus est sermo qui mutari debuisset, sed cuncta quae scripta erant communi consilio decernebantur absque ulla ambiguitate legenda, et his qui religionis studio uellent ad transcribendum esse tradenda.[18]

... that I have not presumed to write down anything concerning so great a man without the most rigourous investigation of the facts nor, at the end, to hand on what I had written to be copied for general use without the scrupulous examination of credible witnesses. Nay rather, it was only after first diligently investigating the beginning, the progress, and the end of his most glorious life and activity, with the help of those who knew him, that I began at last to set about making notes: and I have decided occasionally to place the names of these my authorities in the book itself, to show clearly how my knowledge of the truth had been gained.

Further, when my little work was arranged, though still kept in the form of notes, I often showed what I had written both to our most reverend brother, the priest Herefrith, when he came hither, and to others who had lived some considerable time with the man of God and were fully conversant with his life, so that they might read and revise it at their leisure; and I diligently amended some things in accordance with their judgement, as seemed good to them. And thus I made it my business to put down on parchment the results of my rigourous investigation of the truth, expressed in simple language quite free from all obscurities and subtleties, and to bring what was written into the presence of your brotherhood, in order that it might be corrected if false, or, if true, approved by the authority of your judgment.

And when I had done this with the help of the Lord, and my little work had been read for two days before the elders and teachers of your congregation and carefully weighed in every detail under your examination, no word of any sort was found which had to be changed, but everything that was written was pronounced by common consent to be, without any question, worthy of being read, and of being delivered to those whose pious zeal moved them to copy it.

We can here follow a bit of the process from interviews to draft. The degree of peer control is remarkable – and a better illustration of early medieval literature as an essentially institutional product would be hard to find. We can also observe the clear distinction of notes – *scedulae* – and the fair copy to be produced by transcribing the notes. Most interesting perhaps is Bede's explanation of his reworked draft – *digesto opusculo sed adhuc in scedulis retento* 'when my little work was arranged, though still kept in the form of notes' – a state perhaps similar to the one we see in Richer's Chronicle autograph.

---

[18] Beda, *Vita sancti Cuthbert*, Praefatio, p. 142–145 (also in *PL* 94, 733B–734); for easier reading I have paragraphed text and translation.

Single sheets of parchment were no doubt often used for notes and drafts, but the main medium for notes was the wax tablet – the *tabula* or *tabella cerata*. As noted by the book historians Rouse and Rouse, virtually everyone who learned to write in the early and high Middle Ages did so by using a wax tablet, and most drafts were also produced in this way.[19] It is impossible to compile any statistics because of a very poor survival rate, but one can indeed take for granted that the Middle Ages was a wax-tablet culture. In passing we can note this medieval background in our literary and philosophical language when we speak of a *tabula rasa* and of literary style – the latter of course deriving from the writing device, the stylus. For note-taking in school and while travelling the wax tablet was superior to single parchment sheets in two ways: one needed only the tablet and the stylus, not ink in addition, and it was reusable. Only with the spread of paper in the late Middle Ages did it meet a serious competitor.

The expediency of wax tablets emerges from a number of literary texts.[20] In the early twelfth century the chronicler Galbert of Brügge explains the tumultuous situation in Brügge after the murder of the Duke of Flanders, Charles the Good in 1127: during the dangers and the confusion he compelled himself to make a record of events, but he found no place where he could write in peace; consequently he jotted down his notes on wax tablets.[21] His contemporary chronicler in Normandy, Orderic Vitalis, tells us of how he satisfied his interest in Saint William whom the troubadours often sang about but whose deeds should be known rather in an "account authenticated by monks" (*relatio autentica, quæ a religiosis doctoribus sollerter est edita*). He was brought such a book, but unfortunately the messenger had to return quickly with it and the cold weather prevented Orderic from copying it. Instead he renders in his account the short version he had taken down on his tablets.[22]

---

[19] Rouse & Rouse 1989, 220.

[20] The basic collection of literary testimonies that refer to drafts and wax tablets was put together by Wattenbach 1896, 51–89. I use a few of them here and supplement with others, partially found with the help of the *Patrologia Latina Database* through lemmata such as *tabula, tabella, cera*, etc. Thorough information on technical aspects and on surviving tablets can be found in Grassmann 1986 & Lalou 1992 and the medieval terminology is treated by Rouse & Rouse 1989. Cf. also Mårtensson 1961 and Huitfeld-Kaas 1886.

[21] Galbertus Brugensis, *De multro Karoli comitis*, 35 p. 81, also *PL* 166, 977B–C; cf. Wattenbach 1896, 72): [...] *et inter tot noctium pericula et tot dierum certamina, cum locum scribendi ego Galbertus non haberem, summam rerum in tabulis notavi, donec aliquando, noctis vel diei expectata pace, ordinarem secundum rerum eventum descriptionem presentem. Et sic secundum quod videtis et legitis in arto positus fidelibus transcripsi. Neque quid singuli agerent prae confusione et infinitate notavi sed hoc solum intenta mente notavi quod in obsidione communi edicto et facto ad pugnam et ejus causam congestum est, atque ad hoc quasi me invitum, ut scripturae commendarem, coegi.* Rider 2001, 29–49 offers a detailed and highly valuable analysis of this passage and of Galbert's working methods – adducing a number of interesting parallels (some of which are the same as here and as in Wattenbach 1896). The result of Rider's analysis supports one of the conclusions below, namely that even in Galbert's case of day-to-day 'reporting' there is no such thing as a spontaneous, unmediated, 'journalistic' report: the selection, organisation and (Latin) conceptualisation is at work from the very beginning and the notes taken down on wax tablets strongly influence the way 'oral sources' are represented in the final version.

[22] Ordericus Vitalis, *Historia ecclesiastica* VI.3, vol. 3, also in *PL* 188, 452B: *Nunc, quia de sancto Guillelmo nobis incidit mentio; libet eius uitam breuiter huic inserere opusculo. Novi quod ipsa raro*

Both Galbert and Orderic refer to the brief and unordered state of their texts; Galbert says *summam rerum in tabulis notavi* 'I made notes of the main points on tablets' and Orderic uses the expression *sicut tabellis tradidi compendiose*, probably intending the summary version but perhaps also referring to notes in shorthand.[23]

But wax tablets were not only used for drafts in emergencies. Let us go back to the seventh century Abbot of Iona, Adomnán, and the fascinating opening paragraph of his work on the topography of the Holy Land, *De locis sanctis*.

> Arculfus, sanctus episcopus gente Gallus diuersorum longe remotorum peritus locorum, uerax index et satis idoneus in Hierusolimitana ciuitate per menses nouem hospitatus et loca sancta cotidianis uisitationibus peragrans, mihi Adomnano haec uniuersa, quae infra craxanda sunt, experimenta diligentius percunctanti et primo in tabulis describenti, fideli et indubitabili narratione dictauit; quae nunc in membranis breui textu scribuntur.[24]

> The holy bishop Arculf, a Gaul by race, versed in divers far-away regions, and a truthful and quite reliable witness, sojourned for nine months in the city of Jerusalem, traversing the holy places in daily visitations. In response to my careful inquiries he dictated to me, Adomnán, this faithful and accurate record of all his experiences which is to be set out below. I first wrote it down on tablets: it will now be written succinctly on parchment.

The Arculf in question had landed by accident in far-away Iona after having completed his journey and was interviewed by Adomnán around 685. They may have shared a vernacular language, but in this case I believe it is equally possible that their talks were held in Latin – an obvious choice for an abbot and a bishop of different origins. Apart from the explicit mention of the transference of text from wax tablets to parchment, it is interesting in our context to follow the way the interview was partly guided by scriptural passages and by the *Onomasticon* of Jerome – a topographical commentary by the church father that Adomnán and Arculf seem to have held in hand while talking about Arculf's travels.[25] The notes from the interview were rewritten mainly in Adomnán's own Latin style with further reliance on biblical and patristic texts. This means that some of the textual inspiration and conceptual framework was already evoked during

inuenitur in hac prouincia et nonnullis placebit de tali uiro relatio ueridica. Hanc etenim Antonius Guentoniensis monachus, nuper detulit; et nobis eam uidere sitientibus ostendit. Vulgo canitur a ioculatoribus de illo cantilena, sed jure preferenda est relatio autentica, quæ a religiosis doctoribus sollerter est edita; et a studiosis lectoribus reuerenter lecta est in communi fratrum audientia. Verum, quia portitor festinabat adire, et brumale gelu me prohibebat scribere; sinceram adbreuiationem sicut tabellis tradidi compendiose, sic nunc satagam summatim commendare, et audacis marchisi famam propagare.

[23] Shorthand can be called *more notariorum* 'by notary method' in as in *PL* 185, 417C: [...] *et quod quisque eorum psallebat, in schedulis more notariorum, tam diligenter excipientes, ut nec minimam syllabam, quantumcumque negligenter prolatam, omitterent.*

[24] ADOMNÁN, *De locis sanctis*, p. 36–37; I added some more commas in the Latin for readability.

[25] Cf. Meehan's Introduction p. 11–18.

the Latin interview itself, and that more of the same was added in the final composition of the work.

The use of notes and the reworking of draft versions on wax tablets or single sheets was probably very widespread, but in the art of Latin prose composition – with all its refinements of choice vocabulary, model authors, prose rhythm, emplotment, etc. – a large part of the hard mental work still remained before the text was finally ready to become (part of) a parchment book.

These factors run together in my final two quotations, of which the first comes from the autobiography of the twelfth-century French author Guibert of Nogent (1053–1124). He relates how, as a young monk, he composed a commentary on Genesis in secret (in defiance of his abbot):

> Opuscula enim mea haec et alia nullis impressa tabulis dictando et scribendo, scribenda etiam pariter commentando, immutabiliter paginis inferebam.[26]

> This little work, as well as others of mine, I took down permanently on the pages as I was composing as well as writing myself, commenting and copying simultaneously, without the use of tablets.

The early-ninth-century bishop of Turin, Claudius, makes a similar statement in a more modest vein, in the preface to his *Commentaries of the Epistles of Paul*:

> Quod vero quaedam minus ordinata quam decet in hoc codice multa reperiuntur, non omnia tribuas imperitiae, sed quaedam propter paupertatem, quaedam ignosce propter corporis infirmitatem et meorum oculorum imbecillitatem, quia non fuerunt in tabellis excepta, vel schedulis digesta, sed ut a me inveniri vel discerni potuerunt, ita hoc affixa codice sunt.[27]

> The many shortcomings to be found in this book should not all be attributed to my ignorance. Some should be pardoned on account of my poverty, some on account of my feeble body and my weak eyes, because

---

[26] GUIBERTUS DE NOVIGENTO, *De vita sua*, 144–145 (*PL* 156, 875D); cf. WATTENBACH 1896, 78 & GARAND 1995, 26–29. Guibert makes the same claim for his stylistically very elaborated *History of the First Crusade, Dei gesta per Francos*, at the end of the prologue, p. 83–84, also in *PL* 156, 684D: *Parcat quoque lector meus sermonis incuriae, indubie sciens quia quae habuerim scribendi, eadem michi fuerint momenta dictandi, nec ceris emendanda diligenter excepi sed uti presto est fede delatrata membranis apposui.* GARAND 1995 provides an in-depth analysis of extant Guibert manuscripts (either autographed or dictated) and a full picture of his working processes, scribal vocabulary, etc. see esp. 26–29 & 71–84. It is taken for granted that Guibert did in fact not use tablets, but composed during writing or dictating directly for the parchment. Regarding the passage quoted above from the autobiography the reading *commutando* for *commentando* is preferred by Garand, that is 'changing' rather than 'commenting' what was about to be written (*scribenda*); there is certainly something odd in having *scribenda* as object; however, those difficulties remain the same whether we choose *commutando* instead of *commentando*. I agree with Labande's translation in taking *scribenda* as the biblical text about to be copied.

[27] CLAUDIUS TAURINENSIS, *Praefatio in catenam super sanctum Matthæum* (*PL* 104, 836C–D).

> the material was fixed in this book as found or made out by me, not as it
> was noted on tablets or reworked on single sheets.

Conclusion

Narrative Latin prose was a medieval art form that was linked to the parchment
book, the codex. There was no way of imagining this art form in the early or
high Middle Ages without involving ideas of authoritative and privileged books
in sacred contexts.[28] Given the primary status of the Scriptures and the Fathers
of the Church, and in the high Middle Ages of some pagan authors as well,
writing in Latin was invariably an intralingual and intertextual game – a very
serious game where honour and salvation were at stake. But it was also an art
form that related directly to oral and vernacular storytelling, often mediated by
interviews.[29]

In the present paper I have tried to put more focus on various elements in
this process, from the interview itself through note-taking and draft-writing on
wax tablets and parchment sheets to the final copying of the text into codex
form.

One point I would like to make regarding the literary aspects of the interview is that while the actual stories told by kings, pilgrims, fellow monks
and others obviously informed and partly shaped the plan of a given literary
work, the emplotment and the disposition, it can be argued, I think, that there
was a feed-back mechanism in place from the plan and idea of a completed
book to the way interviews were conducted. The interviewer was conceptual-
ising and categorising stories while interviewing – Is this an example of the
king's sinful behaviour? – Is this the same sort of miracle that happened to that
other saint? – for example. In this way the latinising and biblisising of 'original'
vernacular stories was not just a filter that was inserted during the process of
literary composition, it was at work already to some extent when the story was
told in a specific way by the informants. I am well aware that this must remain
hypothetical in most cases, but I do think that there is a cautionary tale here
which we should heed before we rashly lump together a number of 'oral sources'
for a Latin work and seem to be confident as to what 'oral sources' really are. We
should pay attention to the fact the interviews and stories were constantly under
literary influence and that authors remembered interviews through notes they
had taken in specific ways. An ideal type illustration could look something like
fig. 1. The first boundary to be crossed is that from the spoken vernacular to
written Latin, where, as I take it, a certain Latin conceptualisation of the stories
was already in place. The notes are then organised, the disposition and the
emplotment are designed – *dispositio* in Roman rhetoric. Further work on the
drafts results in the actual composition – or *elocutio* in rhetorical terms – where
literary models influence language and final emplotment, and where peer group

---

[28] Cf. KELLER 1992.

[29] The complex traffic between vernacular and Latin and between oral and written in the early and
high Middle Ages in Northern Europe is discussed on a more general level in MORTENSEN 2006.

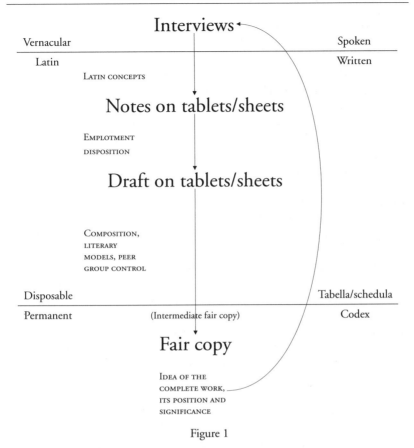

Interviews

Vernacular / Spoken

Latin / Written

LATIN CONCEPTS

Notes on tablets/sheets

EMPLOTMENT
DISPOSITION

Draft on tablets/sheets

COMPOSITION,
LITERARY
MODELS, PEER
GROUP CONTROL

Disposable / Tabella/schedula

Permanent / (Intermediate fair copy) / Codex

Fair copy

IDEA OF THE
COMPLETE WORK,
ITS POSITION AND
SIGNIFICANCE

Figure 1

control reassures the author of the truthfulness of the content. Only then can the second boundary be crossed – the one that leads from the *tabella* or *schedula* to the *codex*, from disposable to permanent writing, from the uncommitted to the dangerous form.

The main point of the present paper is that in contemporary practice this second boundary was perceived as equally or more difficult and consequential than the first one. The transition from orality to literacy could be taken more lightly, as long as the literary mode was a pragmatic and disposable one. The boundary between the pragmatic and the book mode, however, was one that was crossed only with the utmost care.

Bibliography

Primary sources

ADAM BREMENSIS, *Gesta Hammaburgensis ecclesiae pontificum*, ed. B. Schmeidler, Monumenta Germaniae Historica, Scriptores in usu scholarum. Hannover & Leipzig 1917.

ADOMNÁN, *Vita Columbae*, ed. & transl. A. O. Anderson & M. O. Anderson: *Adomnán's Life of Columba*, rev. by M. O. Anderson. Oxford 1991 [1st ed. 1961].

ADOMNÁN, *De locis sanctis*, D. Meehan: *Adomnán's De locis sanctis*, Scriptores Latini Hiberniae vol. III. Dublin 1958.

BEDA, *Vita sancti Cuthbert*, ed. B. Colgrave: *Two Lives of Saint Cuthbert. A Life by an Anonymous Monk of Lindisfarne and Bede's Prose Life*. Cambridge 1940.

CLAUDIUS TAURINENSIS, *Præfatio in catenam super sanctum Matthæum*, PL 104, 833–838.

GALBERTUS BRUGENSIS, *De multro, traditione, et occisione Gloriosi Karoli, comitis Flandriarum*, ed. J. Rider, Corpus Christianorum, Continuatio Mediaevalis 131. Turnhout 1994 (also in *PL* 166, 943–1046).

GUIBERTUS DE NOVIGENTO, *De vita sua sive Monodiae*, ed. E. R. Labande: *Guibert de Nogent: Autobiographie*. Paris 1981 (also in *PL* 156, 837–962).

GUIBERTUS DE NOVIGENTO, *Dei gesta per Francos*, ed. R. B. C. Huygens, Corpus Christianorum, Continuatio Mediaevalis 127 A. Turnhout 1996 (also in *PL* 156, 679–834).

ORDERICUS VITALIS, *Historia ecclesiastica*, ed. M. Chibnall: *The Ecclesiastical History of Orderic Vitalis*, ed. and transl. with introduction and notes by M. C., 6 vols. Oxford 1972–1990.

Passio et Miracula Beati Olaui, edited from a twelfth-century manuscript in the library of Corpus Christi College, Oxford, with an introduction and notes by F. Metcalfe. Oxford 1881 – For translation see KUNIN 2001.

PL – Patrologia Latina, 221 vols., ed. J.-P. Migne. Paris 1844–1865. The *Patrologia Latina Database* is issued by ProQuest Information and Learning Company.

RICHER VON SAINT-REMI, *Historiae*, ed. H. Hoffmann, Monumenta Germaniae Historica, Scriptores tom. 38. Hannover 2000.

THEODORICUS MONACHUS, *Historia de antiquitate regum Norwagiensium*, ed. G. Storm, Monumenta historica Norvegiæ Latine conscripta, p. 1–68. Kristiania 1880.

WILLELMUS TYRENSIS, *Chronicon*, ed. R. B. C. Huygens, Corpus Christianorum, Continuatio Mediaevalis 63–63 A. Turnhout 1986.

Secondary sources

ANDERSON, A. O. & ANDERSON, M. O. (eds.) 1991: *Adomnán's Life of Columba*. Oxford, ed. & trans. [1st ed. 1961, revised by M. O. Anderson].

ASSMANN, Jan 1992: *Das kulturelle Gedächtnis. Schrift, Erinnerung und politische Identität in frühen Hochkulturen*. München.

BRUUN, Christian 1879: *Det i Angers fundne Brudstykke af et Haandskrift af Saxo Grammaticus: Udgivet i fotolithografisk Facsimile.* København.

CARRUTHERS, Mary 1990: *The Book of Memory: A Study of Memory in Medieval Culture, Cambridge Studies in Medieval Literature,* vol. 10. Cambridge.

FRIIS-JENSEN, Karsten 2005: "Indledning." In Karsten Friis-Jensen (ed.) *Saxo Grammaticus: Gesta Danorum Danmarkshistorien,* vol. I, p. 9–32, København: Det Danske Sprog- og Litteraturselskab & Gads Forlag.

GARAND, M. C. 1995: *Guibert of Nogent et ses secrétaires, Corpus Christianorum, Autographa Medii Aevi,* vol. II. Turnhout.

GLENN, Jason 1997: "The composition of Richer's autograph manuscript." *Revue d'histoire des textes,* 27 151–189.

GRASSMANN, Antjekathrin 1986: "Das Wachstafel-Notizbuch des mittelalterlichen Menschen." In H. Steuer (ed.) *Zur Lebensweise in der Stadt um 1200. Ergebnisse der Mittelalterarchäologie. Bericht über ein Kolloquium in Köln vom 31. Januar bis 2. Februar 1984,* p. 223–235, Köln.

GUENÉE, Bernard 1980: *Histoire et culture historique dans l'occident medieval.* Paris.

HOFFMANN, H. (ed.) 2000: *Richer von Saint-Remi: Historiae, Monumenta Germaniae Historica, Scriptores tom.,* vol. 38. Hannover.

HOLTZ, Louis 1992: "Autore, Copista, Anonimo." In G. Cavallo, C. Leonardi & E. Menestò (eds.) *Lo spazio letterario del medioevo. 1., Il medioevo latino,* vol. 1: La produzione del testo, tomo I, p. 325–351, Roma.

HUITFELD-KAAS, H. J. 1886: *En Notitsbog paa Voxtavler fra Middelalderen.* Forhandlinger i Videnskabs Selskabet, Christania.

JØRGENSEN, Ellen 1926: *Catalogus codicum Latinorum Medii Ævi Bibliothecæ Regiæ Hafniensis.* København.

KELLER, Hagen 1992: "Vom ,heiligen Buch' zur ,Buchführung'. Lebensfunktionen der Schrift im Mittelalter." *Frühmittelalterlichen Studien,* 26 1–31.

KERSKEN, Norbert 2004: "Dura enim est conditio historiographorum... Reflexionen mittelalterlicher Chronisten zur Zeitgeschichtsschreibung." In E. Kooper (ed.) *The Medieval Chronicle III. Proceedings of the 3rd International Conference on the Medieval Chronicle Doorn/Utrecht 12–17 July 2004,* p. 61–75, Amsterdam – New York.

KUNIN, Devra 2001: "Passio Olaui." In C. Phelpstead (ed.) *A History of Norway and The Passion and Miracles of the Blessed Óláfr, Viking Society for Northern Research Text Series,* vol. 13, London, transl.

LALOU, Élisabeth 1992: "Inventaire des tablettes médiévales et présentation générale." In É. Lalou (ed.) *Les tablettes à écrire de l'antiquité à l'époque moderne, Bibliologia. Elementa ad librorum studia pertinentia,* vol. 12, p. 233–288, Turnhout.

LEITSCHUH, Friedrich & FISCHER, Hans 1895: *Katalog der Handschriften der Königlichen Bibliothek zu Bamberg,* vol. I,2. Bamberg.

MORTENSEN, Lars Boje 2000: "Olav den helliges mirakler i det 12. årh.: Streng tekstkontrol eller fri fabuleren?" In I. Ekrem, L. B. Mortensen & K. Skovgaard-Petersen (eds.) *Olavslegenden og den latinske historieskrivning i 1100-tallets Norge,* p. 89–107, København.

──── 2006: "Den formative dialog mellem latinsk og folkesproglig litteratur ca 600–1250: Udkast til en dynamisk model." In Else Mundal (ed.) *Reykholt som makt- og lærdomssenter i den islandske og nordiske kontekst*, p. 229–271, Reykholt.

MORTENSEN, Lars Boje & MUNDAL, Else 2003: "Erkebispesetet i Nidaros – arnestad og verkstad for olavslitteraturen." In S. Imsen (ed.) *Ecclesia Nidrosiensis 1153–1537. Søkelys på Nidaroskirkens og Nidarosprovinsens historie*, p. 353–384, Trondheim.

MÅRTENSSON, Anders W. 1961: "Styli og vokstavler." *Kulturen. En årsbok till medlemmarna av Kulturhistoriska föreningen för södra Sverige*, p. 108–141.

PETRUCCI, Armando 1992: "Dalla minuta al manuscritto d'autore." In G. Cavallo, C. Leonardi & E. Menestò (eds.) *Lo spazio letterario del medioevo. 1., Il medioevo latino*, vol. 1: La produzione del testo, tomo I, p. 353–372, Roma.

RIDER, Jeff 2001: *God's Scribe. The Historiographical Art of Galbert of Bruges*. Washington.

ROUSE, Richard H. & ROUSE, Mary 1989: "The vocabulary of wax tablets." In O. Weijers (ed.) *Vocabulaire du livre et de l'écriture au moyen âge*, p. 220–230, Turnhout.

WATTENBACH, Wilhelm 1896: *Das Schriftwesen im Mittelalter*. Leipzig, updated edition, repr. Graz 1958; 1st ed. 1871.

Orality and Literacy in Medieval East Central Europe: Final Prolegomena

Anna Adamska

Introduction

THE COMPLEX RELATIONSHIP between orality and writing in the Middle Ages is the object of intensive study not only by specialists of medieval literature, but also by historians interested in the history of social communication.[1] Within the long-term research project developed in Utrecht in the 1990s, the passage from orality to literate behaviour and literate mentalities in medieval Western society formed the object of a multidimensional investigation.[2] This project covered *inter alia* the introduction and development of written culture in East Central Europe. After eight years of intensive study of literacy in this geographical area, the time for a provisional synthesis is approaching.[3] In this article some of the 'final prolegomena' are presented, especially those that concern the Central European passage "from memory to written record".[4] The articulation of some of the distinct marks of this passage by a historian who is not primarily interested in literary phenomena may be useful from the perspective of the comparative study of orality and literacy in the peripheries of medieval *Latinitas*.[5]

---

[1] The subject of social communication and its media in the Middle Ages already possesses a huge bibliography. See a. o. MOSTERT 1999, 193–318; DEPKAT 2003, 9–48; ROECKELEIN 2001, 5–13; MOSTERT 2005, 29–55. See also BRIGGS & BURKE 2002 and most recently CHINCA & YOUNG 2005, 1–8.

[2] The principal directions of the Utrecht research project have been presented in the volume *New Approaches to Medieval Communication* (1999) and have been developed in following volumes in the series *Utrecht Studies in Medieval Literacy* (see http://www.let.uu.nl/ogc/PPV).

[3] See a. o. ADAMSKA 1999, 165–190; ADAMSKA & MOSTERT 2004, 1–3.

[4] We owe this expression to CLANCHY 1993. The geo-historical term 'East Central Europe' is still subject to discussion (see ADAMSKA & MOSTERT 2004, 2 with bibliographical references). In the Utrecht research project, for several reasons, the choice has been made to concentrate on the medieval kingdoms of Hungary, Bohemia and Poland, within their historical boundaries.

[5] Medieval Scandinavia is, in this respect, a quite natural area for comparison. See a. o. NEDKVITNE 2004.

Historians on the nature of medieval orality

Before presenting the characteristic features of the correlation between orality and literacy in East Central Europe, however, it may be worthwhile to summarise some general historical notions on the subject. Because the relationship between literacy and orality is an extremely complex issue, one has to return to the problem of the terminology and definitions currently used in the field. These problems have considerably influenced the points of view of historians.

Most English language publications concerning anthropology and cultural history consider 'orality' in opposition to 'literacy'. This is especially true of studies dealing with the mechanisms of collective memory and the reconstruction of the past.[6] The question of the ways in which oral tradition worked has first of all occupied (and continues to occupy, as the Bergen symposium proved) the minds of many literary historians and philologists. They often address the oral transmission of literary works.[7] Historians woke up to 'orality' in the 1980s, for instance after reading Walter Ong's publications on the evolution of the media.[8]

Just as in English 'orality' was used in opposition to 'literacy', similarly in German the notion of "Mündlichkeit", influenced by Anglo-Saxon scholarship, was used in opposition to "Schriftlichkeit". This opposition can be followed from the beginning of the 1980s.[9] In a very general sense 'orality' and "Mündlichkeit" (and the French "oralité") refer to oral communication without any recourse to writing. According to an 'extremist' definition, oral culture comprises the sum of all forms of non-written communication, including gestures, smells and flavours.[10]

Whatever the definition, physical contact between the 'sender' and a 'receiver' of a message is in the nature of oral communication: it leads to situations in which a 'receiver' gets a supplementary message through the non-verbal information accompanying an orally delivered text, transmitted by, for example, voice modulation or the behaviour and gestures of the 'sender'. We might be led to conclude that oral communication is therefore 'subjective', and that emotional contact forms an important part of it. To correctly transmit an oral message, it is necessary to use mnemotechnics, which may make use of ritualised formulas. Every change to the contents of the message, whether intentional or not, is thought to form a betrayal of those contents. Because of its repetition of contents, oral culture has often been judged by literate Western scholars as primitive, retarded or barbarian.[11]

We can readily understand what happens when writing is introduced into an oral society. Messages may now be 'cut off' from the physical presence of

---

[6] See a. o. GOODY & WATT 1963, 304–345; STREET 1984; VANSINA 1985; ASSMANN 1992.

[7] This tradition of research has been recently presented by Karl STACKMANN 1999, 398–427.

[8] See especially ONG 1982. For his impact on the study of the history of social communication, see MOSTERT 1999, 24 ff.

[9] MOSTERT 1999, 25 ff.

[10] MOSTERT 1998, 9.

[11] See a. o. STOCK 1983, 12 ff.

'sender' and 'receiver'; with writing the non-verbal information disappears. One may therefore think that written texts make information more 'objective', independent from the here-and-now, and easier to retrieve (and change!) whenever it is deemed appropriate. These principal consequences of the introduction of writing are at the basis of the eighteenth-century paradigm of literacy's superiority over orality.[12]

One can distinguish between different kinds of orality.[13] Among the typologies proposed, the most important distinguishes between 'primary' and 'secondary' orality. Primary oral cultures are those cultures without any contacts at all with the written word – and, according to some, no contact with any other form of the graphic representation of thought either. Such cultures are very rare, and they were certainly absent in the Middle Ages. More often we are dealing with oral cultures that have some ideas about how writing works, but do not themselves use writing because oral ways are sufficient to them.[14] Secondary orality refers to forms of orality which are ultimately dependent on written texts (as, for example, the chanting of the Bible or the 'memorisation' of the Qur'an).

A critical development in the debate on the relationship between orality and written culture among medieval historians has been the gradual realisation of the inadequacy of the traditional opposition. Today we are ever more convinced that the development of literacy did *not* signify utter disaster for orality. We know now that forms of orality and literacy could coexist for a long time.[15] Any medieval society's passage from orality to written culture was a long process with many phases; it should be analysed in its own historical context.

A second important development in research by medieval historians is, that they are finally able to appreciate the efficiency of oral communication, and that – in at least some areas of social life – oral modes were effective until the end of the Middle Ages and beyond.[16]

General lines of the development of literacy in medieval East Central Europe

Medieval East Central Europe forms an extremely interesting area for research on the development of the interrelations between oral and written modes of communication, for two reasons. First, that these countries come late into the fold of Western, Latin Christianity. This happens in the ninth century in Bohemia, and in the tenth century in Poland and Hungary. The countries of East Central Europe adopted the Carolingian cultural model. At least until the thirteenth century, this model was transmitted mainly 'at one remove', through

---

[12] MOSTERT 1998, 4.

[13] See a. o. ONG 1982, 31–77; ZUMTHOR 1987, 18 ff.; BÄUML 1980, 264 ff.

[14] Extremely interesting comparative materials come from the sociological study of illiterates in contemporary Western society. See a. o. KURVERS 2002.

[15] See CLANCHY 1993, 41.

[16] On the continuity of oral forms of law from the early Middle Ages till the end of the *Ancien Régime*, see TÓTH 2000, 147 ff. and MOSTERT in preparation.

the intermediary of German cultural centres. During the Middle Ages, the three countries of East Central Europe developed comparable social and economic structures; this development was accompanied by a permanent cultural exchange of people and ideas. Secondly, these three countries formed (and practically continue to form until today) the eastern border of *Latinitas*. Of course there never was any rigid frontier between the Latin and Orthodox cultural areas, but rather a zone of passage, with a mixture of alphabets and languages.[17]

The introduction of writing was one of the most important consequences of Christianisation.[18] Until then, writing had been virtually unknown to the societies living in the region. The spoken word was the most esteemed form of communication: orality was the norm. If we take this into consideration, we may study the history of medieval East Central Europe as the history of the gradually changing relationship between oral and literate behaviour. In the history of these changes three periods can be distinguished.[19]

In the first period, from the middle of the tenth century (*grosso modo*, the phase of 'formal' Christianisation) until the end of the twelfth century, the use of writing was chiefly limited to religious concerns. The Christian religion could not exist without liturgical books, which in the beginning were imported from the West. From the middle of the eleventh century we can see traces of the activity of local *scriptoria*: those of the important Benedictine monasteries (such as Pannonhalma in Hungary and Břevnov in Bohemia) and also those of the cathedrals (such as Gniezno and Cracow in Poland). The first Central European literary texts appear in this first period; they are clearly associated with the religious sphere. Hagiography of local saints is, until the end of the eleventh century, almost the only literary genre. Only in the twelfth century do the first historiographical texts appear: chronicles presenting the history of a country as the *gesta* of ruling dynasties. One also gets a first glimpse of the practical use of the written word in the twelfth century: in juridical and administrative matters we see *notitiae* and charters being issued and used.

The second phase of the 'literalisation' of East Central Europe covers the thirteenth and fourteenth centuries. The crucial feature of this period is the striking development of pragmatic literacy. While until the end of the twelfth century we can count some dozens of (preserved and produced) charters, shortly after 1200 the number of charters grows by the thousands. This development, comparable to the simultaneous increase of pragmatic literacy in the West,[20] was connected with incisive social and economic changes taking place at the time, especially with urbanisation, which was in large part aided by different versions of the so-called German law. Another significant fact is the successful foundation of the first universities in the region, in Prague (1348) and in Cracow (1364/1400). These universities became intellectual centres whose renown went far beyond Central Europe as a region.

---

[17] See a. o. Łaszkiewicz 2004, 270 ff. An interesting perspective for comparative research has been opened by the monograph of Samuel Franklin 2001 on literacy among the eastern Slavs.

[18] More in Adamska 1999, 169 ff.

[19] The dynamics of this process will be fully described in a separate work (see Adamska in preparation).

[20] See a. o. Britnell 1997, 5 ff.

Finally, the third period of the development of literacy in the area covers the last century of the Middle Ages in the region (which, especially in Hungary and Poland, lasted until well after 1500). It was a period which saw the flourishing of Latin and vernacular literature, and of the use of writing in all domains of daily life. Thanks to a developed school network (especially in Poland and Bohemia), many laymen gained access to the written word. This lay literacy got a new dimension through the introduction of the printed word.

The Central European passage "from memory to written record" seems at first glance to be a 'unidirectional process' which ended in the adoption of writing as the dominant mode of communication. However, as we will see, matters were more complex than that.

From orality to literacy: From spoken vernacular to written Latin

In studying the passage from orality to written culture we deal with very disparate phenomena. One of them is the recording in writing (in Latin) of information about the past and the present, information which had circulated orally (i.e. in the vernacular) before. This phenomenon was typical for the first period in the development of Central European literacy, when, with the one notable exception of Church Slavonic,[21] Latin was the only language of writing. Scholars recognise this, for instance when dealing with the region's historiography.

The first chronicles produced by the three kingdoms in the area were composed *grosso modo* at the same time, at the demand of similar audiences, i.e. the aristocratic lay public of rulers and powerful lords who demanded stories about kings courageous in battle and wise in peacetime. Narratives of this kind are found in the work of an anonymous chronicler, generally known as Gallus Anonymus.[22] In the years 1112–1115/16 he put into writing the oldest history of the Polish dynasty and its patrimony. According to his own testimony,[23] the work, written in rhythmical rhymed prose, was composed at the demand of Michał, chancellor to prince Bolesław III the Wry-mouth. The prince himself had presented the author, who was a foreigner, with most of the necessary information. In this way, the oral traditions of the court were put into writing.[24]

Similar stories of heroism written for an aristocratic lay audience can be found in the oldest Hungarian historiography. Probably around the turn of the eleventh century a series of historiographical notices was written, which are known together as the lost *Gesta*. Traces of these *Gesta* have been identified in

---

[21] During the mission among the Slavs in the later Bohemian lands in the late ninth century, the missionaries Cyril and Methodius elaborated a Glagolitic alphabet suitable for transcribing all dialects of the Slavic language, and for translating the Gospel and important liturgical texts. This written Slavonic language ("Kirchenslawisch") was used in Bohemia until the end of the eleventh century (see ADAMSKA 1999, 172 ff. with bibliographical references).

[22] Still relevant is its edition of Maleczyński (see GALLUS ANONYMUS, *Chronica*). See also the bilingual, Latin-English reprint edition of 2003 (see *Gesta principum Polonorum*).

[23] GALLUS ANONYMUS, *Chronica*, I, Epistola, 1.

[24] For the vast bibliography on this chronicle, see most recently DYMMEL 2004.

later historiographical works. The oldest extant work is the *Gesta Ungarorum Anonymi*, written around 1200.[25]

The first Bohemian historiographical work, the chronicle of the Prague canon Cosmas, was also conceived at the beginning of the twelfth century (ca. 1110–1125). As it is comparable to the Polish and Hungarian works, it can also be considered as a national chronicle, presenting the history of the country and the ruling dynasty of Přemyslides.[26]

Indeed, all historical works mentioned give an official account of the beginning of the nation and the state. They reveal many similarities, both as concerns the high value placed on orally transmitted information about historical events and as concerns the narrative strategies used. All chroniclers of the region struggled with the problem of the translation of concrete historical and social realities into the canon of Latin literary genres and vocabulary. Even more interesting for us is that orality was the natural way of transmitting the historical text to its audience: oral delivery could be helped by the use of rhythmical rhymed prose and by the introduction of dialogues and fictive speeches to animate the narration.[27] All these stategies have been recently called "verschriftete Mündlichkeit" by the Bohemian scholar Marie Bláhová.[28]

Historians dealing with the passage from *vernacular* orality to *Latin* written record also look for valuable evidence elsewhere, such as in sources concerning juridical matters. Especially from the thirteenth and fourteenth centuries onwards, in Hungary, Poland and Bohemia many records of legal investigations have been preserved which had been instigated both by the Church and by secular powers.

First, there are the records of canonization trials, dealing with a new 'wave' of saints from the region (especially women). It was doubtless influenced by new Dominican and Franciscan devotions: St Agnes in Bohemia, Sts Elisabeth and Margaret in Hungary, Sts Hedwig, Stanislas, Hyacinth and Cunegond in Poland.[29] In the procedure developed by the papacy, the crucial element was the interrogation of witnesses in the presence of notaries and interpreters about the miracles performed by the candidates for canonization. The popes ruled that the words of witnesses had to be recorded as faithfully as possible, in the order they had been presented.[30]

We notice similar procedures in investigations of secular matters instigated by the State. From the 1330s onwards, Hungarian kings often demanded inquiries to resolve conflicts about noble status, descent or property. About the same time (in 1320/21 and 1339) a series of trials were held to resolve a serious conflict between the Kingdom of Poland and the Order of the Teutonic

---

[25] The most recent edition dates from 1991 (See *Die "Gesta Hungarorum"*). For the bibliography, see VESZPRÉMY 2004.

[26] COSMAS, *Chronica*. For the rich bibliography, see most recently BLÁHOVÁ 2004.

[27] On this phenomenon in Polish chronicles, see KOROLKO 1993, 130 ff.

[28] BLÁHOVÁ 2004, 329 ff.

[29] See a. o. KLANICZAY 2001.

[30] See VAUCHEZ 1999.

Knights.[31] The records of all these ecclesiastical and secular investigations have one thing in common: they testify to the essential operations of awakening and activating collective memory, and of transforming into written record orally transmitted information about the recent and distant past. They prove that, three hundred years after the introduction of written modes of communication, in Poland and Hungary oral testimony often remained crucial. Traditional historical knowledge, passed on orally from one generation to the next, could cover a period of more than a hundred years. Apparently the transmission of this knowledge had so far taken place mainly within families, and mainly by the males.[32] At the same time, we witness a reorganisation or 'restructuring of the past'[33] which bears the imprint of the interrogators. By the formulation of their questions they put a new structure on the contents of collective memory.

However, this kind of source poses serious problems of interpretation, due to the operations of translation and transcription. The language of the records was Latin, but very few witnesses could express themselves in this language. From the formulary of the trials between Poland and the Order of the Teutonic Knights we know that when a witness was unable to understand Latin, the questions were translated into Polish (or sometimes German). Afterwards, the answers were translated from Polish (or German) into Latin. The question then is, how the double translation and transcription of orally formulated information by educated clerks, in a written protocol, influenced the form of the testimony available to us.

When discussing the passage from oral vernacular to written Latin, one has to remember that it was a 'bi-directional' process as far as the transmission is concerned. A historiographical text, a charter or a written account of the miracles performed by a saint, were most often transmitted to their audience orally, by reading aloud or by melodic recitation.[34]

Unfortunately, direct information about the oral transmission (and simultaneous translation) of Latin texts is far from abundant. Only rarely do we find such clear evidence as in the first Polish chronicle of the so-called Gallus Anonymus, who says that it is a glorious task to recite in schools and in palaces the triumphs and victories of dukes and kings, and that the present work (i.e. the chronicle) must be recited by a true interpreter: *Et sicut vitas sanctorum et passiones religiosum est in ecclesiis predicare, ita gloriosum est in scolis vel in palatiis regum and ducum triumphos vel victorias recitare* [...].[35] And further on: *verio presens opus interpreti recitandum* [*est*].[36]

---

[31] See respectively FÜGEDI 1986, 3 ff.; ADAMSKA 2001, 68 ff.

[32] On the value of testimony dependent on the status of witnesses, see EVERARD 2001, 73–74.

[33] We owe this expression to Patrick GEARY 1994, 134.

[34] The oral transmission of hagiographical texts and charters is ever more receiving the attention of historians (see a. o. VAN EGMOND 1999; ADAMSKA 2005, 289 ff.).

[35] GALLUS ANONYMUS, *Chronica*, III, Epistola, 122.

[36] GALLUS ANONYMUS, *Chronica*, III, Epistola, 122. According to some scholars Gallus's chronicle was, in fact, a text meant for a dramatic performance at the princely court (see TARGOSZ 1980, 154–178).

One may wonder how well-equipped the East Central European vernaculars of the earlier Middle Ages were for expressing the subtleties of Latin vocabulary and syntax. One thing is obvious: no matter how we judge passive and active knowledge of Latin or the efficiency of translation practices,[37] even the greater accessibility of writing matter in Latin in the later Middle Ages never obliterated the practice of translation to gain access to written texts. There would always be those who could only receive the message in their mother tongue.

From orality to literacy: From spoken to written vernacular

The last remark points us towards another aspect of the passage from orality to written record, i.e. from *spoken* to *written* vernaculars. To be more precise: what is important for us today is not so much the translation into the various vernaculars of already existing Latin texts (such as the Bible), as the putting into writing of vernacular texts which so far had been transmitted only orally.

To understand the nature of this passage we have to consider the general question: How do the vernaculars achieve the status of 'writable' and written languages? According to the Italian scholar Armando Petrucci, everywhere in Europe the process of cultural promotion and the conquest of social status by which the vernacular languages passed from being "subsidiary private languages" to languages with a literary public, can be divided into two successive phases.

The first phase was formed by the arrival at what one may call the 'state of writing'. Thus a language, having until then remained merely oral, became recognized as 'writable', and could actually be written by the development of a system of graphic signs for it. It also acquired the textual 'formality' indispensable for writing, even if initially at a rudimentary level only.

The second phase, which is more significant for us, is the conquest by the vernacular languages of the right of 'canonisation in books', by which complex texts in the vernacular become consciously and organically written in book form.[38] In medieval East Central Europe, the evolution of the three dominant vernaculars into 'writable' languages, i.e. Czech, Polish and Hungarian,[39] encountered several problems. First, there was the problem of the adaptation of the Latin alphabet to the specific sounds of these languages, and the fixation of their orthography. It is interesting to see how different graphic solutions were developed in Czech and Polish, which belong to the same western Slavonic linguistic group. Indeed, until the end of the twelfth century they used practically the same language, with the same lexicon and syntax.

To be efficient as written languages, the East Central European vernaculars also needed an adequate vocabulary and a syntax that was flexible and precise enough to 'translate' nuances of Latin if needed.

---

[37] On these problems with regard to East Central Europe, see ADAMSKA forthcomming.

[38] I have been summarizing the arguments presented by PETRUCCI 1995, 175.

[39] For basic information on the chronology of the process, see BIRNBAUM 1999, 384–396. See also ADAMSKA forthcomming.

Probably the hierarchy of genres and practical needs decided that the first texts written in dominant vernaculars of the region[40] concerned religious matters. Consensus has it that secular literature meant for entertainment (e.g. poetry, songs, stories about heroes and historical events) existed almost exclusively in oral form until the fourteenth and fifteenth centuries, especially in Hungary and in Poland. If we try to establish a list of the oldest religious texts written in our vernaculars, all these texts prove problematic in the same way: their dating oscillates by at least a hundred years. There is endless discussion on topics such as the oldest Czech version of the *Kyrie eleison*, the so-called *Hospodyne pomyluj ny*, which has been dated ca. 970, but also ca. 1050. The oldest Polish Marial song, *Bogurodzica*, has been dated ca. 1100, ca. 1250, and ca. 1350. The oldest known Hungarian *Funeral Oration*, called *Halotti Beszééd*, could have been written down ca. 1250, but also ca. 1320.[41] The list of disputed datings could be made much longer. A historian of communication, however, shamelessly leaves these doubts about dating the texts to the experts of historical linguistics and literature.

From a comparative perspective, it is more important that each of the three vernaculars under discussion had a different dynamic of development as a written language. The reasons for this are rather complex, and it is impossible to discuss all of them in this article. We have to limit ourselves to a few examples taken from the kinds of text we could call 'entertainment literature'. This term loomed large in secular literature, comprising as it did court poetry, the *gesta* of local rulers and historiography, the stories of ancient heroes, romances etc.

It was without doubt that Czech became the first language in which this kind of writing could be done. This development was encouraged by a new audience, that of the Bohemian nobility. In the second half of the thirteenth century noblemen received significant political concessions from the rulers. A period of political and economic prosperity was ushered in. This new stability encouraged ambitions to create local centres of court culture, following the model of the royal court of the last Přemyslides and, later, of the Luxembourg dynasty.[42] This new audience is responsible for things like the reception of the literary traditions of Antiquity, which is visible in many translations from Latin into Czech of generally known texts, such as the story of Alexander the Great (*Alexandreida*), the *Historia Apollonii, regis Tyrii* or the *Historia destructionis Troiae*.[43] More relevant for us is the flourishing of Czech lyric court poetry and historiography. Around 1314 the *Chronicle* of Ps.-Dalimil appeared, the first history of the Bohemian lands to be put together in the vernacular.[44] The text was intended for a particular public, specifically the Czech nobility, who were just then trying to establish their own identity in confrontation with, on the one hand, the foreign dynasty of Luxembourgs, and, on the other hand, the

---

[40] We are not going to discuss here the special position of German as a very strong, 'writable', and ambivalent language (see ADAMSKA forthcomming).

[41] See respectively BAUMANN 1978, 56; MICHAŁOWSKA 1995, 278 ff.; MADAS 2004, 315–316.

[42] See: BLÁHOVÁ 1995, 129–133.

[43] See the following editions: *Alexandreida, Próza, Kronika Trojánská*.

[44] Edition: *Staročeská kronika*.

other social groups within Czech society. That the chronicle was versified has led scholars to assume that it had to be transmitted orally and was meant to be learnt by heart.[45]

The role of the audience and its demands in the development of the written vernaculars is clear also in medieval Poland. Here, the rise of secular literature in the vernacular took place almost a hundred years later than in Bohemia. It started at the beginning of the fifteenth century, *mutatis mutandis*, as a consequence of social changes similar to those in the Bohemian lands. Under the rule of the new dynasty of the Jagiellons (from 1385), the Polish nobility received significant privileges, which provided it with economic prosperity and allowed the growth of its cultural interests.[46] From the first half of the fifteenth century we have the first *preserved* written traces of secular poetry in Polish.[47] This poetry had a strongly didactic character. It was intended to teach, to inform (e.g. about recent political events), to help memorise the Church calendar, or the rules of vernacular orthography. Some of these texts, such as those describing good table manners, are comparable to similar texts written everywhere in Europe in the later Middle Ages. They were intended to civilise the manners and daily life of the social elites.[48]

In contrast to Czech and Polish, we have serious problems in following the progress of secular literature in Hungarian. These difficulties result in part from the dramatic dispersion of the Hungarian cultural heritage in the early modern age. In the central and later Middle Ages, Hungary maintained intensive contacts with the West and was receptive to many elements of Western chivalrous culture.[49] However, although there is no lack of scholarly assumptions to the contrary, there are *no* traces whatsoever of the reception of western chivalrous *literature* at the royal court.[50] Another enigma is that there are *no* traces of interest in secular literature on the part of the social group that formed such an important and dynamic public in the other East Central European countries, namely the nobility. Quite the contrary: recent research suggests that the late medieval Hungarian nobility was composed of 'active illiterates': not only did they do without the basic elements of written culture, but they did not feel the need to learn them because they regarded literacy as incompatible with their status as warriors.[51] The importance of the Hungarian epic stories about their nomadic past is well known, as is that of Hungarian vernacular poetry. The problem is that their almost exclusively oral transmission made them inaccessible to modern research.

---

[45] BLÁHOVÁ 1995, 230 ff.

[46] On the social background of these cultural changes, see recently WIESIOŁOWSKI 1997, 714 ff.

[47] They have been edited several times. See most recently *Polska poezja*.

[48] KLANICZAY 2000, 672.

[49] See a. o. KURCZ 1988.

[50] Compare with MADAS 2004.

[51] This radical judgment comes from Pál ENGEL 2001, 223, a leading expert on Hungarian history.

Conclusion

In this article, using the example of medieval East Central Europe, I have tried to show something of the complexities of the passage from 'oral art forms into writing'. It should be clear that this is also an intricate problem for the historian of social communication. We perceive this complexity when we consider the traditional opposition between associated notions, when *oral* = *vernacular* = *lay* is confronted with *written* = *Latin* = *ecclesiastic*. In the development of literacy in the three East Central European countries this schematic opposition is relevant only in the first period of the introduction of written culture. It is disintegrated by the emancipation of the local vernaculars and their elevation to the level of 'writable' and written languages.

I am convinced that another distinction makes more sense: that between the passage from *oral vernacular to written Latin* and the passage from *oral vernacular to written vernacular*, for these are two very different phenomena. It is useful when trying to understand the nature and ways of the transmission of literary texts written in Latin and comparing them with the transmission of vernacular texts. A story or a poem that was written down in Latin, even if it was transmitted to its audience orally by being read aloud, was much more dependent on the material support of writing, which made its form more 'stable'. However, recording in writing, in the vernacular, a song or a poem which we know was previously transmitted orally, raises other problems. Fixing a text in writing does *not* mean that the written version of such a text will form the basis for its future transmission. Quite the contrary: wherever orality provides the main channel of transmission, writing texts down plays only a secondary role.[52] The written version of the text may reflect its genesis, for example as a memory aid for the author. It may also reflect an intermediary phase of its existence, for instance if somebody wished to take notes of a text he had heard. In that case, the written version reflects one of the many possible oral performances of that text. Thus we may assume that, at least for some literary genres, the written version which has been preserved is only one of many existing versions of that text. The written version may be compared to a photograph, recording 'a moment in the life' of an object which has a changeable and dynamic life of its own.

All this suggests that the passage from orality to written culture ought *not* to be perceived as a uni-directional, irreversible process. The complex relationships between these two modes of communication should be studied very carefully, in an interdisciplinary and *transdisciplinary*[53] way.

[52] MICHAŁOWSKA 1995, 336–337.
[53] OEXLE 2003, 243–244.

Bibliography

Primary sources

Alexandreida, ed. Vladimir Vážný. Praha 1963.
COSMAS PRAGENSIS, *Chronica Boemorum*, ed. Bertold Bretholz, MGH SRG NS II. Berlin 1923.
Die "Gesta Hungarorum" des anonymen Notars, ed. Gabriel Silagi & Lázló Veszprémy. Sigmaringen 1991.
GALLUS ANONYMUS, *Chronica et gesta ducum sive principum Polonorum*, ed. Karol Maleczyński, MPH NS II. Kraków 1952.
Gesta principum Polonorum, ed. Paul W. Knoll & Frank Schaer, Central European Medieval Texts III. Budapest 2003.
Kronika Trojánská, ed. Jiři Daňhelka. Praha 1951.
Polska poezja świecka XV wieku, ed. Maciej Włodarski, 4th ed. Wrocław & Warszawa 1997.
Próza českého středověku, ed. Jiři Kolár. Praha 1983.
Staročeská kronika tak řečeného Dalimila, ed. Jiří Daňhelka et al., vol 1–2. Praha 1988.

Secondary sources

ADAMSKA, Anna 1999: "The introduction of writing in Central Europe (Poland, Hungary and Bohemia)." In M. Mostert (ed.) *New Approaches to Medieval Communication*, p. 165–190, Turnhout.
——— 2001: "The kingdom of Poland versus the Teutonic knights: Oral traditions and literate behaviour in the later middle ages." In G. Jaritz & M. Richter (eds.) *Oral History of the Middle Ages. The Spoken Word in Context*, p. 67–78, Krems & Budapest.
——— 2005: "Forschungen an Königsurkunden - über Heinrich Fichtenau hinaus?" *Mitteilungen des Instituts für Österreichisches Geschichtsforschung*, 113 269–292.
——— forthcomming: *Latin and the Vernaculars in East Central Europe from the Point of View of the History of Social Communication*.
——— in preparation: *Landscapes of the Written Word: East Central Europe, ca. 1000 – ca. 1500*.
ADAMSKA, Anna & MOSTERT, Marco 2004: "Preface." In A. Adamska & M. Mostert (eds.) *The Development of Literate Mentalities in East Central Europe*, p. 1–4, Turnhout.
ASSMANN, Jan 1992: *Das kulturelle Gedächtnis. Schrift, Erinnerung und politische Identität in frühen Hochkulturen*. München.
BAUMANN, Winfried 1978: *Die Literatur des Mittelalters in Böhmen*. München & Wien.
BÄUML, Franz H. 1980: "Varieties and consequences of medieval literacy and illiteracy." *Speculum*, p. 237–265.
BIRNBAUM, Henrik 1999: "The vernacular languages of East Central Europe in the medieval period." In B. Nagy & M. Sebok (eds.) *The Man of Many*

Devices, Who Wandered Full Many Ways: Festschrift in Honor of Janos M. Bak, p. 384–396, Budapest.

BLÁHOVÁ, Marie 1995: *Staročeská kronika tak řečeného Dalimila v kontextu středověké historiografie latinského kulturního okruhu a její pramenná hodnota.* Praha.

———— 2004: "Verschriftlichte Mündlichkeit in der Böhmischen Chronik des Domherrn Cosmas von Prag." In A. Adamska & M. Mostert (eds.) *The Development of Literate Mentalities in East Central Europe*, p. 323–342, Turnhout.

BRIGGS, Asa & BURKE, Peter 2002: *A Social History of the Media: From Gutenberg to the Internet.* Cambridge.

BRITNELL, Richard 1997: "Pragmatic literacy in Latin Christendom." In R. Britnell (ed.) *Pragmatic Literacy East and West, 1200–1330*, p. 3–24, Woodbridge.

CHINCA, Mark & YOUNG, Christopher 2005: "Orality and literacy in the Middle Ages: A conjunction and its consequences." In M. Chinca & Ch. Young (eds.) *Orality and Literacy in the Middle Ages. Essays on a Conjunction and its Consequences in Honour of D. H. Green*, p. 1–15, Turnhout.

CLANCHY, Michael T. 1993: *From Memory to Written Record. England 1066–1307.* Oxford, second edition.

DEPKAT, Volker 2003: "Kommunikationsgeschichte zwischen Mediengeschichte und der Geschichte sozialer Kommunikation. Versuch einer konzeptionellen Klärung." In O. Auge (ed.) *Medien der Kommunikation im Mittelalter*, p. 9–48, Weisbaden.

DYMMEL, Piotr 2004: "Traces of oral tradition in the oldest Polish historiography: Gallus Anonymus and Wincenty Kadłubek." In A. Adamska & M. Mostert (eds.) *The Development of Literate Mentalities in East Central Europe*, p. 343–364, Turnhout.

VAN EGMOND, Wolfert 1999: "The audience of early medieval hagiographical texts: Some questions revisited." In M. Mostert (ed.) *New Approaches to Medieval Communication*, p. 42–67, Turnhout.

ENGEL, Pál 2001: *The Realm of St. Stephen: A History of Medieval Hungary, 895–1526.* London & New York.

EVERARD, Judith 2001: "Sworn testimony and memory of the past in Brittany, c. 1100–1250." In E. van Houts (ed.) *Medieval Memories, Men, Women and the Past, 700–1300*, p. 72–91, London & New York.

FRANKLIN, Samuel 2001: *Writing, Society and Culture in Early Rus, c. 950–1300.* Cambridge.

FÜGEDI, Erik 1986: "*Verba volant*: Oral culture and literacy among the medieval Hungarian nobility." In *Kings, Bishops, Nobles and Burghers in Medieval Hungary*, p. 1–25, Aldershot.

GEARY, Patrick J. 1994: *Phantoms of Remembrance. Memory and Oblivion at the End of the First Millenium.* Princeton.

GOODY, Jack & WATT, Ian 1963: "The consequences of literacy." *Comparative Studies in Society and History*, 5 304–345.

KLANICZAY, Gábor 2000: "Everyday life and elites in the later middle ages: The civilised and the barbarian." In P. Linehan & J. Nelson (eds.) *The Medieval World*, p. 671–690, London & New York.

———— 2001: *Holy Rulers and Blessed Princesses: Dynastic Cults in Medieval Central Europe*. Cambridge.

KOROLKO, Mirosław 1993: "Z badań nad retorycznością polskich kronik średniowiecznych (ethopiia – sermocinatio – fikcyjna mowa)." In T. Michałowska (ed.) *Literatura i kultura późnego średniowiecza w Polsce*, p. 125–140, Warszawa.

KURCZ, Ágnes 1988: *Lovagi kultúra Magyararországon a 13–14. században*. Budapest.

KURVERS, Jeanne 2002: *Met ongeletterde ogen. Kennis van taal en schrift van analfabeten*. Amsterdam.

ŁASZKIEWICZ, Hubert 2004: "Le latin et le ruthène face aux langues vernaculaires sur le territoire du Royaume de Pologne et du Grand-Duché de Lithuanie aux XIVe et XVe siècles." In A. Adamska & M. Mostert (eds.) *The Development of Literate Mentalities in East Central Europe*, p. 269–276, Turnhout.

MADAS, Edit 2004: "La naissance de hongrois écrit." In A. Adamska & M. Mostert (eds.) *The Development of Literate Mentalities in East Central Europe*, p. 311–319, Turnhout.

MICHAŁOWSKA, Teresa 1995: *Średniowiecze*. Warszawa.

MOSTERT, Marco 1998: *Oraliteit*. Amsterdam.

———— 1999: "A bibliography of works on medieval communication." In M. Mostert (ed.) *New Approaches to Medieval Communication*, p. 193–318, Turnhout.

———— 2005: "Communication, literacy and the development of early medieval society." In *Communicare e significare nell' alto medioevo*, Settimane di Studio della Fondazione Centro Italiano di Studi sull'alto Medioevo, vol. 52, p. 29–55.

———— in preparation: *Making Court Decisions Known in Medieval Holland*.

NEDKVITNE, Arnved 2004: *The Social Consequences of Literacy in Medieval Scandinavia*. Turnhout.

OEXLE, Otto Gerhard 2003: "Mittelalterforschung in der sich ständig wandelnden Moderne." In H.-W. Goets & J. Jarnut (eds.) *Mediävistik im 21. Jahrhundert. Stand und Perspektiven der internationalen und interdisziplinären Mittelalterforschung*, p. 227–252, München.

ONG, Walter 1982: *Orality and Literacy: The Technologizing of the Word*. London.

PETRUCCI, Armando 1995: "Reading and writing *volgare* in medieval Italy." In *Writers and Readers in Medieval Italy: Studies in the History of Written Culture*, p. 169–235, New Haven & London.

ROECKELEIN, Hedwig 2001: "Kommunikation – Chancen und Grenzen eines mediävistischen Forschungszweiges." *Das Mittelalter*, 6 (1: Kommunikation) 5–13, appeared 2005.

STACKMANN, Karl 1999: "Neue Philologie?" In J. Heinzle & I. Verlag (eds.) *Modernes Mittelalter. Neue Bilder einer populären Epoche*, p. 398–427, Frankfurt a/M. & Leipzig.

STOCK, Brian 1983: *The Implications of Literacy. Written Language and Models of Interpretation in the Eleventh and Twelfth Century*. Princeton.

STREET, Brian 1984: *Literacy in Theory and Practice*. Cambridge.

TARGOSZ, Karolina 1980: "Gesta principum recitata. "Teatr czynów polskich władców" Galla Anonima." *Pamiętnik Teatralny*, 29 141–178.

TÓTH, István 2000: *Literacy and Written Culture in Early Modern Central Europe*. Budapest.

VANSINA, Jan 1985: *Oral Tradition as History*. London.

VAUCHEZ, André 1999: "Les origines et le développement du procès de canonisation (XIIe–XIIIe siècles." In F. J. Felten & N. Jaspert (eds.) *Vita Religiosa im Mittelalter: Festschrift für Kaspar Elm zur 70. Geburtstag*, p. 845–856, Berlin.

VESZPRÉMY, László 2004: "The birth of a structured literacy in Hungary." In A. Adamska & M. Mostert (eds.) *The Development of Literate Mentalities in East Central Europe*, p. 161–181, Turnhout.

WIESIOŁOWSKI, Jacek 1997: "Piśmiennictwo." In B. Geremek (ed.) *Kultura Polski średniowiecznej XIV-XV w.*, p. 669–765, Warszawa.

ZUMTHOR, Paul 1987: *La lettre et la voix. De la littérature médiévale*. Paris.

Oral and Written Art Forms in Serbian Medieval Literature

Sonja Petrović

FROM ITS BEGINNINGS in the common Slavic period in the sixth century up to the Ottoman conquest in the second half of the fifteenth century, Serbian medieval literature was defined by the poetic canons of its epoch and by the universal character of literary endeavour in the Middle Ages. Its poetic and thematic foundations were refined through contact with Byzantine literature and with literatures of surrounding peoples such as other Orthodox Slavic literatures and Latin West European literatures. Normal development of Serbian medieval literature was stunted during the Ottoman rule that lasted from the second half of the fifteenth until the beginning of the nineteenth century. It is understandable why Serbian literature could not follow the line of growth of other European literatures that did not share the same historical path. Although Turkish civilisation had specific influence on Christian Balkan countries, in Serbia medieval literature continued its life almost as in the times of sovereignty, predominantly in the form of hand written manuscripts that were copied in Orthodox monasteries and churches. The climate was very favourable for oral traditional literature and a variety of oral forms was developed to meet the differing needs of the people. The merging of oral and written art forms intensified due to the recurrent migrations that brought about mingling and an interchange of traditions. Independent resistance groups and professional soldiers engaged in the armies of neighbouring Christian states – the Venetian Republic, Austria and Hungary – never really stopped warring against the Ottoman Turks, thus creating by their fight the necessary spirit and poetic material for oral literature to continue its course all the way to the age of Romanticism and the Serbian uprising in 1804. By the second half of the nineteenth century, when bards "learned to write", a range of transitional, semiliterary forms can be observed and analysed.[1]

In light of the described circumstances, the question of an "extended" Middle Ages in Serbia might become clearer, as well as the problem of the relatively late evidence of oral literature.

---

[1] See the survey of several kinds of transitional texts in LORD 1986.

Correspondences of poetical categories

The forms of oral and written literature coexisted for centuries and it is necessary to study them within the framework of a particular literary period and poetic system. Poetic systems of oral and written literature in Serbia bear more resemblance in the Middle Ages than in any other literary period. Correspondences between them may be briefly presented in the following way:

1. *The creation and transmission of oral and literary pieces.* In oral literature, work is created and transmitted orally, and in written literature through handwriting and print. However, some oral literature was written down in the late Middle Ages and in the Renaissance, and was published from the first part of the sixteenth century. In this way oral literature grew to be an established fact of written literature, but also an object of imitation and "learned redaction".

2. *The role of the individual* (author or performer) in the process of creating oral and literary works is limited and dependent on many factors. In oral literature, a piece is created by a talented person on the basis of an oral or written source, and by using traditional themes and stylistic schemas and formulas. Oral literature developed a specific formulaic style that had its own theoretic and aesthetic rules. In medieval literature, the category of authorship was respected only when the author possessed extra literary authority – spiritual or secular. On the other hand, the works of an author who did not possess authority could be changed, added to or abridged, especially if the theme was previously known. "Similarity of subjects incited borrowing of descriptions, phrases, and whole sections".[2] The same applies to oral literature: narrative patterns, units and blocks of formulas can be sequenced in chains through the principle of correlation and resemblance.

3. *The principle of collectivity* in oral literature is reflected in the creation, transmission and reception of oral work, but also in the poetic system, devices and style. In the Middle Ages, literature "tends to express the collective emotions, collective relations towards the object of presentation".[3] From the principle of collectivity result two complementary principles. In medieval literature, they are defined as the *eternal* and the *commonplace principle*:[4] The first tending to generalise and the second to concretise. In oral literature, they can be described as the creative powers of tradition that make an oral piece historical and actual, or more general and insubstantial. These principles influence poetic style. Oral literature, and to a large extent, folklore is based on repetitions of rituals and formal acts, all types of protocols and codes of behaviour. In oral literature, heroes are specific literary types, not individual characters. The medieval writer also

---

[2] Lihačov 1972, 22–23.
[3] Lihačov 1972, 68.
[4] Likhachov 1981, 20.

used literary etiquette and emblems, and depicted the hero "according to the laws regulating the category of heroes to which he belongs".[5]

Although the names and biographies oral performers are known sometimes, and although it is possible to discuss certain stylistic features and techniques of the oral poetics of one particular singer or a group of singers from a local region, every individual style is always dependent on traditional style and conventions of genre. The same applies to medieval literature: individual style was poorly expressed as authors followed the tradition already formed in the genre. Seeing in everything that is earthly the symbols of the eternal and divine, medieval writers generalised by using loan words, compilations, citations and analogies from the Bible, stereotypical phrases and constructions.

4. *The genre systems* of oral and medieval literature have a practical function. It is well known that some oral lyric genres are correlated to calendars and rituals; that incantations, charms and apocryphal prayers are part of ritual and aim to cure or harm; that laments are connected with the cult of the dead and epic poetry with the cult of ancestors. In medieval literature, genres may also have had a practical aspect in the rite and in everyday life. For example, encomia, hagiography, the divine office, comments on the books of the Bible, the Euchologion, etc., greatly influenced church life and its "liturgical rhythm". Some poetic genres even require a specific time and mode of performance: singing of various religious chants and prayers is strictly regulated in the course of liturgy, and particular conduct is sometimes needed (sitting, standing, bowing). There are genres that are strongly related to lay life, social order and commercial interests; for instance, codes, administrative and private correspondence, charters, medical and apocryphal books.

Just as the oral genres may absorb the elements of other arts, primarily music, dance and acting, the medieval genres are closely linked to painting, architecture and music. In fact, oral and written genres reflect the medieval culture and mental attitude in their complexity. If the church represented the microcosmos, then the liturgical programme in the church needed to correspond with literary and biblical stereotypes as well as with the contemporary social reality. It was common to paint decorative letters and fragments of text on the frescoes and walls, not just as the "signature" of saints on portraits, but as a part of the holy figure or the narrative scene as well. The words were represented figuratively with the help of the book: for example, the saint is holding the opened book, pointing towards it; the words are visible to the spectators and refer to the Bible. The written text could be inserted into almost any material, it

---

[5] LIKHACHOV 1981, 17.

could be a part of embroidery[6] or engraved on a ring.[7] The amalgamation of written text and picture resulted in an exceptional genre mixture called "hagiographic icons". These icons consist of several tableaux that present selected scenes from saints' lives as a sort of pictorial illustration of the text that is "outside" the manuscript (as opposed to a miniature painting that is "inside" the manuscript).

5. *The vocal component* of medieval genres (singing, reading aloud) can influence rhythm, the use of rhetorical devices, and how the audience is addressed. Even the prose intended for reading becomes rhythmical and distinctively poetic. Reading aloud could be for private purposes, individual reading (for example, prayers, psalters or chronicles), and it could also be formal, public reading in church, in liturgy, or in the dining room during meals, or in the square or market. Reception by hearing allows listeners to identify a reader or performer with the abstract figure of the author, whose traditional physiognomy is personified in the genre.[8] Medieval writers use oral knowledge as a method, equalising oral and written sources in the creative process.[9]

6. *The role of the audience* in the process of the reception and transmission of an oral piece is very important. The singer and the audience are familiar with the theme and the poetic grammar and they actively participate in the performance of the oral piece. The singer adapts not only his manner of performance (tempo, disposition, tone) to the audience, but also the content, style, idea and sometimes even language (in the case of bilingual singers). The audience may impose themes, the sequence of narrative units or the mode of singing; it can influence the course of the performance, and finally it censors (accepts or not) the work of art. In the artistic sense, this is a matter of an "aesthetic of identity".[10] In the Middle Ages, the audience that experiences the piece either by

---

[6] The best known is the piece of embroidery made by Jelena Mrnjavčević, or Nun Euphemia. The text of *The Eulogy of Prince Lazar* (1402) was embroidered with a golden thread on red cloth (67 × 49 cm) which was intended to cover the body of the Prince (today in the Serbian Orthodox Church Museum in Belgrade).

[7] For example, one of the most famous rings from the early fourteenth century, the golden ring of the Serbian Queen Theodora, mother of the Emperor Dušan (today in the National Museum in Belgrade), has the carved inscription: "May the Lord help the one who wears it".

[8] "Every genre has its own strictly developed physiognomy of author, writer, performer... In cases when genre was required to be interpreted aloud, when it was meant for reading or singing, the figure of the author becomes identical with the figure of the performer – in the same way as it is indistinguishable in folklore", Lihačov 1972, 60–61.

[9] Evangelical and hagiographical texts rely on the audience. In the beginning of *The Life of Saint Sava* (i.e. Rastko Nemanjić, 1175–1235, the first archbishop of the autocephalous Serbian church became a monk on Mount Athos by the name of Sava), Teodosije (hieromonk at the Monastery Hilandar on Mount Athos) claims that he writes on the basis of what he had *heard* about the saint as well as by using written sources.

[10] Lotman 1968 makes a distinction between the real and the anticipated structure of art work and formulates two categories for understanding artistic creation: the aesthetic of identity (*estetika tozhdestva*) and the aesthetic of contrast or difference (*estetika protivopostavlenia*). An aesthetic of identity is characteristic of folklore, the Middle Ages and Classicism (as opposed to the aesthetics of contrast in the art of the baroque, romanticism and realism).

reading or by listening participates in its creation in such a way that it "actively gains" the piece by recognising a "stylistic, aesthetic code", a unique style.[11]

Following, a few examples will be given in order to point out the complexity of the contacts between the oral and written forms.

From hagiography to historical legend: *The Synaxarion of Prince Lazar* and *The Story of the Battle of Kosovo*

The two versions of *The Synaxarion*[12] (between 1392 and 1398) of Prince Lazar, the Serbian ruler who was beheaded in the Battle of Kosovo[13] in 1389 and canonised as a martyr,[14] depict the Battle in different ways. The first version of *The Synaxarion* uses common martyrological symbols and is constructed as a consistent dramatic antithesis between Prince Lazar and the Sultan Murad I.[15] The second version of *The Synaxarion* contains various commonplaces in describing the Battle, but nonetheless presents historical details such as the Prince's speech to the lords and soldiers prior to the Battle, their confinement and the execution, and the translation of the Prince's relics from the Metropolitan church in Priština to his memorial monastery, Ravanica. These two versions of *The Synaxarion* served as the basis for the piece known as *The Story of the Battle of Kosovo*, retained in some thirty copies since the end of the seventeenth and the beginning of the eighteenth century. *The Story* is a folk adaptation of *The Synaxarion* and it includes fragments of folk epic songs and legends. In the introduction, *The Story* presents Prince Lazar's biography and closely follows *The Synaxarion*, but in the central part it incorporates the folk legend of Miloš Obilić, the Serbian feudal lord and son-in-law of Lazar who killed the Turkish Sultan Murad I in order to prove his loyalty. An unknown compiler narrates

---

[11] Lihačov 1972, 93.

[12] The synaxarion, i.e. a shortened version of a hagiography, is a genre intended for reading during a service in the church (liturgy) on the holiday of a saint. It relates the life of the saint, his virtues, deeds, suffering and miracles. The composition scheme of synaxarions is the same as in hagiography. Its main purpose is to improve continuity and maintenance of the cult of the saint and therefore it is open to folk influences.

[13] Kosovo (i.e. "The Field of Blackbirds") is a plain in south Serbia. The battle took place on the field called Gazimestan (in Turkish: "graveyard of heroes"), near Priština (Prishtina), present capital of Kosovo.

[14] Prince Lazar Hrebeljanović (1329/1371–1389) was connected with the Nemanjić dynasty through marriage (his wife Milica was a descendant of Vukan Nemanjić) and he began his service in the court of Emperor Uroš. He rose slowly by conquering lands of other district lords and by enhancing his prestige through family ties. He succeeded in uniting the traditional lands of the Nemanjićs and in partly restoring their state, but his greatest achievement was the conciliation between the Serbian church and the Patriarchate in Constantinople, after which the Serbian Patriarchate was acknowledged. After he was killed on the Kosovo plain on 15/28 June 1389, Prince Lazar was canonised as a martyr. In the first decade after the Battle of Kosovo, several texts were written in order to venerate his cult, see Mihaljčić 1989; Vucinich & Emmert 1991.

[15] The Turkish Sultan Murad I (1359–1389) was killed on the Kosovo plain in 1389 by the Serbian feudal lord whose name, Miloš Kobilić, later Obilić, appears in historical and legendary sources from the end of the fifteenth century.

the events that preceded the battle with many picturesque details, starting from the quarrel between Lazar's daughters that resulted in a duel of husbands, Miloš on one side and Vuk Branković on the other. Since Vuk was defeated and ashamed, he slandered his opponent to Prince Lazar, who in turn accused Miloš for treason. In order to prove his loyalty Miloš then commits his heroic deed. Although folk legend introduced new particulars, intrigue and another pair of positive and negative heroes, *The Story* has kept the concept of Prince Lazar as an ideal ruler who dies in the battle sacrificing himself for his nation and the country and who is proclaimed a martyr afterwards. Narrative conflict and epic types (slandered hero and traitor) taken from folk tradition are pervaded by a metaphysical historicism in the martyrological figure of Prince Lazar and are outlined in a way that is characteristic of a hagiography.

The Story of the Battle of Kosovo is a typical example of the transitional form between medieval literature and folklore. Because of the large number of copies, which are all close versions of one another, any variability in the text poses the question of whether they are cases of copying or recording of folk tradition. The fruitful synthesis of hagiographic elements with folk legend shows that it was possible to merge oral and written forms of art while still remaining in the frame of the composition of hagiography as a universal biographical model.

Dialogue as a frame for dramatic action: Danilo's *Narration about Prince Lazar* and folk poems about the Kosovo Battle

Narration about Prince Lazar (1392–1393) by Patriarch Danilo III[16] is a complex synthesis of hagiography, eulogy and homily. The author strives for this genre in order to narrate in a festive, sublime and emotional way about the origin, life, deeds and suffering of Prince Lazar. In text related solemnly and dramatically, Lazar is celebrated not only as a martyr, but as a warrior, too. Although *Narration* unites martyrological and hagiographical elements, the principle of theatrical presentation in a dialogue is dominant. Prince Lazar addresses his soldiers and nobility prior to the Battle to strengthen and encourage them, saying:

> Let us not spare ourselves,
> Knowing that we are to depart from this place
> And be mixed with earth.
> We die that forever we may live
> And offer ourselves to God, a living sacrifice,
> Not as transient creatures
> That have sinned, enjoying this world's abundance,
> But in this shedding of our blood.

[16] Danilo III (c. 1350 – c. 1396/1399) rose from the abbot of the Monastery Drenča to the Patriarch of the Serbian Orthodox Church. He wrote many offices for Serbian rulers (St Sava, St Simeon, St Milutin). Composed in the finest tradition of Orthodox hymnography, the *Narration about Prince Lazar* (also known as *Sermon*) represents Danilo III as an eye-witness to the translation of the Prince's relics and as a close friend to the royal family.

Let us not spare our life
That unto others we may be a shining example.
Let us fear not the terror that comes upon us
Nor the assault of faithless foes
Bent on our destruction.
If we should think on fear or loss,
We shall not be worthy of grace,
If we should reflect on our sins of vanity,
Our holy sacrifice shall come to naught.
We must do battle with the Mohammedans,
Though the sword smite our heads, the spear our ribs,
And death our lives.
We must do battle with the infidel.
We, and our companions in the fight,
Should be mindful of the burden set on the Roman soldiers
That did guard the crucified Christ
That we may be glorified in Him,
We are one human nature,
Assailed by the same passions,
And with one grave that awaits us
And one field for our bodies' bones
So that the bright garden of Eden shall admit us.[17]

Lazar's oration and the warriors' reply can be found in other cult writings, as well as in historical sources and the tradition of the Kosovo Battle. The essential idea of cult and epic poetry is heroic death on the battlefield that will bring freedom: "It is better to meet one's death heroically than to live shamefully, it is better to end the battle with sword than to turn our back to the enemy". Lazar's speech, like other speeches delivered by princes to their armies before battles, represents evidence of oral literary language that was formed by the traditions of oratory.[18] Danilo III brought to life the spoken word of the protagonists and gave vocal and emotional charge to a scene that has great heroic and epic potential. The dramatisation of Lazar's speech and the response of the choir of Serbian warriors can be compared to that of ancient Greek tragedies. Opposed sections of discourse correspond to the active dialogue that occurs during the reading or performing of *The Narration* between the author and the audience, or the "conscience of other" in Bakhtin's terms.[19]

The idea that honourable death in the battlefield is worth more than disgraceful life connects epic heroes and martyrs. It can be found as commonplace

[17] DANILO III, *One Human Nature*, p. 94.
[18] Examples for Old Rus literature in LIKHACHOV 1981, 59–63.
[19] Cf. BAKHTIN 1981.

in oral and written sources in different cultures and epochs.[20] In Serbian oral tradition it was verbalised in epic decasyllable and was widely transmitted as heroic formula. However, in epic poetry on the Kosovo Battle the idea was integrated in two different situations with different protagonists, but the meaning did not change and the form of dialogue was preserved. In the first example, a dialogue is held between Lazar's wife, Princess Milica, who is trying to keep at least one of her nine brothers, the Jugovići, instead of Prince Lazar and the Serbian warriors. She tries to withhold one brother after another, but they refuse her and bravely follow the Prince, bearing in mind how he had besought the soldiers. In the context of the Kosovo legend, this is the moment when the heroes prove their loyalty to the Prince and readily enter the combat. In this way folk songs preserved the fundamental concept of the soldiers' decision to die for ideals no matter what that was expressed in medieval cult writings. In the second example, in the folk song about the fall of the Serbian Empire, Prince Lazar receives a letter from the Holy Mother. All symbols are explained in the prologue of the song: the letter is in fact a swallow and it was brought from the holy city of Jerusalem by St Elias who was transformed into a falcon. The Holy Mother offers Lazar a choice between the earthly and the heavenly kingdom, and this choice enables him to gain eternal life through heroic accomplishment and a martyr's death. This is how folk tradition used Christian concepts to refine the epic poem, turning military defeat into moral and spiritual victory. On the level of structure, there is a parallelism between Lazar's choice of heavenly kingdom and his decision to confront Sultan Murad. This similarity of models shows that the idea is essential for poetic impression and that it can easily mask the structure.

Laments, funeral sermons and folk mourning songs

In Serbian oral and written literature, laments share not only a ritual function and manner of improvisation, but also the same cognitive and rhetorical patterns. Laments and the actual descriptions of the weeping of Princess Milica over Lazar's body differ in cult texts. A comparison of versions fostered the hypothesis that medieval writers, who were contemporaries (and some even participants in the translation of relics), had remembered Milica's improvised weeping and included it in their pieces while managing to keep the original motifs and tone. Authors even described how the Princess "fell as if dead over that saintly body and for a long time she was unconscious", and later, having come to herself, "as if awakened from a deep sleep, she scratched her face and pulled out her hair":

> Woe to me, o my light,
> how were you eclipsed from my sight,
> how did [you] my beauty become so darkened,

[20] See for example *The Serbian Alexandride*, *The Lay of Igor's Host*, *The Tale of Batu's Sacking of Ryazan*, the chronicles of Georgios Monachos (Hamartolos) and Konstantinos Manasses, *The Jewish War* of Josephus Flavius, but also the *Iliad* (XI, 486; 529), *Beowulf* (XXXIX: "Yea, death is better for liege-men all than a life of shame!"), *El Cid* (XCIII, 1691), etc.

how did [you] wilt, my sweet flower,
how did you go past us through your martyrdom?
Where is your sweetly-speaking tongue,
where is your honey-pouring mouth?
Oh, mountains, hills, and forest trees,
cry with me today.
Henceforth my eyes pour bloody streams of tears.[21]

Laments were also included in funeral orations. The sermon on Despot Đurađ Branković,[22] composed by an anonymous orator from Smederevo 1456/57,[23] refers to some historical facts: the appearance of Halley's Comet, the fall of Constantinople, the sufferings of Despot Đurađ and his family – the blinding of his sons Stefan and Grgur, and the forced marriage of his daughter Mara to Sultan Murad II. Appeals for help addressed to the late despot are combined with requests for lamentation, in which the orator reveals his own presence. In the final part he invites everyone to come, raise their hands and pray. Rhythm, increased emotion in the text, sincere appeal and change of grammatical persons indicate that this piece could have been performed orally at the despot's funeral.

Whether medieval laments were presented as separate narrative units or included in the narrative, they kept a specific emotional and melodic rhythm which links them with folk lyrical songs. Furthermore, folk mourning songs and lyrics intended to be sung without musical instrument were improvised exclusively on the spot (it was believed that preparation in advance would bring misery). However, weeping was also integrated into epic songs where it managed to retain the rhythm of the oral, spoken word even when formed by metrical and stylistic patterns, like in the epic song *The Death of the Mother of the Yugovichi*:

The mother took her son's hand in her own,
She dandled it: she turned it to and fro.
And then she whispered to the lifeless thing:
'How like an apple, O most precious hand,
That blossomed, came to fruit, and was cut down:
You grew up at my knee, but you were reaped
Upon the level plain of Kosovo'.[24]

Epitaph and the *bugarštica*

Epitaphs and inscriptions carved on medieval tombstones show specific orality. Their conventional form and formulaic style resemble that of epic poems. In epitaphs the hero is praised in an epic way by the mention of some particular

---

[21] Danilo III, *Milica's Lament*, p. 120
[22] Despot Đurađ Branković (George Brankovich, 1427–1456) succeeded Prince Lazar's son Stefan Lazarević.
[23] Anonymous from the fifteenth century, *Lament for Đurađ Branković*; fragments translated in Matejić & Milivojević 1978, 187–188; Dragić Kijuk 1987, 157–159.
[24] *The Death of the Mother of the Yugovichi*, p. 74.

attributes and motifs: boldness, honesty, loyalty and dedication to his lord, a proud and independent character; feast with food and wine; commitment to his company of warriors and an obligation to carry a wounded or dead friend; a metaphor of death as a wedding with earth or forest; the sacrifice of one's life as the crown of loyal service. Following are two typical epitaphs from the fifteenth century:[25]

> Here lies Vukosav voyvoda[26] Vlađević. I fought with my friends and I was killed with my lord on a restless frontier battlefield. And my company brought me to my land inherited by nobility.

And

> Here lies Bogdan Hateljević, the servant of Radič voyvoda. At a favourable moment I was born in Dabre(h) and I did right things in my company, and I died in loyal service to my lord.

A common motif in epitaphs is the burying of a faithful vassal underneath the feet of his sovereign, which symbolically assures continuance of loyal service in the other world. In reality, a lord and his vassals were often buried together, as can be seen in this inscription from the fifteenth century:

> Here lies voyvoda Miotoš with my son... beneath the feet of my lord Vlatko Vlađević, to whom I served while he was alive, and whom I buried when he had died.

This migratory motif and ritual relic from prehistoric times is poeticized in the *bugarštica*[27] about the Battle of Kosovo from the end of seventeenth and the beginning of eighteenth century. It describes how Sultan Murad honoured Miloš Obilić, the hero who inflicted him with a lethal injury. The Sultan showed his grace and respect for the heroic deed by asking Miloš to be buried under his feet, but the Serbian hero refused because he wanted to be placed under the feet of his lord, Prince Lazar. Just as on the tombstone, the parallelism is established:

> May I make this request, Oh Sultan?
> Do place me not at your right hand,
> But place me, Miloš, at your feet,
> My father-in-law, at your right hand –
> As everywhere I served him well,
> May I so do in mother earth![28]

---

[25] STOJANOVIĆ 1902–1926, III, no. 4833, 4835, 4774. See MATIĆ 1964 on the traces of oral verses on tombstones. For a selection of Serbian medieval inscriptions in German translation, see MIHALJČIĆ 1982.

[26] *Voyvoda* is the feudal title given to a commander of company, similar to that of duke.

[27] The *bugarštica* is a special kind of epic song in lines of fifteen to sixteen syllables. Many issues on the *bugarštica* have been discussed; see the bibliography in MILETICH 1990.

[28] *The Song of the Battle of Kosovo*, p. 31.

In another old *bugarštica* song, Zmaj Despot Vuk, on his deathbed, sends a message to King Matijaš that he must betray him, for he will be serving the mightier lord – the great God.

Facts from medieval reality, typical feudal relations and symbols, were absorbed into the epic generic and poetic system and conformed to the universal cultural patterns. Amalgamated, these elements created an epic world on the level of poetic genre, but also on the level of a particular epic poem, where they formed a vivid and concrete background and authentic feelings of national past. As a result, they now contribute to an understanding of the historical, cultural and social context of Serbian heroic epic as a whole.

Proskomidia, genealogies and folk genealogies

In folklore proclaiming the names of deceased ancestors in dangerous situations, when help or support is needed, is known as a special form of "crying out for ancestors".[29] The custom of asking for help from ancestors is widespread and is part of the cult of ancestors. It is deeply rooted in the mentality of Serbs, thanks mostly to *slava*, a specific Serbian family feast based on a very old, presumably pagan custom of respecting the domestic patron, who is replaced in Christianity by the saint. During the ceremony of praising the patron, a tribute is paid to the saint protector whom the host must convince to obey ethical and social norms to ensure improvement for the family. Folk poems about the celebration of the patron are a sort of exempla that set ethical, social and religious values. One depicts the Emperor Dušan as host at a dinner ceremony: while he is serving his guests and showing respect for his parents, as well as the poor and unexpected guests,[30] the angel protector stands on his right shoulder and caresses him on the cheek with his wing.

It is customary to make historical and chronological "mistakes" like merging and separating generations in folk genealogies. Despite this, however, folk genealogies are believed to be true (by narrators as well as their audience) in that they reveal the causes and consequences of historical events and explain some particular course of history. That was the case when the Serbian ruling dynasties of Nemanjić, Lazarević and Branković were joined with the Hungarian royal dynasty in the sixteenth and seventeenth centuries. The need for this emerged after the fall of the Serbian medieval state in 1459 when the struggle against the Turks was transferred to Hungary, under whose banner the descendants of ruling families and prominent Serbian feudal lords had fought. In one version of folk genealogy, a direct link was established: the "captain-general" of Hungary, Janos

---

[29] *Proskomidia* (in Serbian: *pomenik*), a list of persons to be prayed for, such as a list of names of dead and living members of royal and ruling families, church dignitaries, monks and laity in the Serbian medieval state. It begins with a liturgical formula: "Mention, o Lord, the souls of your servants in your Kingdom". Reeling off names during the service has both a ritual and sacral character. As an important source for preserving genealogical memory, *proskomidia* represents a rudimental historiographic genre and an antecedent of genealogy.

[30] Unexpected guests are specially honoured in Serbia because they are thought to be messengers from God or disguised deities.

Hunyady,[31] was proclaimed the illegitimate son of Despot Stefan Lazarević[32] and grandson of Prince Lazar, even though they were of similar age. Someone like Hunyady was needed to carry on the fight against the Turks, so he was adopted in Serbian tradition.[33] In another version of folk genealogy, Prince Lazar and Zmaj Despot Vuk[34] are connected although they are really three generations apart. The folk poem tells how Zmaj Despot Vuk fought with the Dragon of Jastrebac Mountain in order to release Princess Milica from his persistent courting (the widespread motif of a dragon lover). Vuk wins in a duel and receives a reward from Prince Lazar – an official document that legalises the province of Srem as his hereditary legacy. In the beginning of the nineteenth century, when the song was written down, Srem (which is today part of Vojvodina in north Serbia) was still under Hungarian rule although it was inhabited predominantly by a Serbian population. The song shows the actual tendency to give what is thought to be a true explanation of how Srem was legally part of Serbia from ancient times.

Folk genealogies originate from the cult of ancestors, but they are always some kind of response to concrete social and political situations, and therefore they are "true" from one perspective. The mixture of family and tribe-fraternity ties with feudal relations and the ambition to show heroes as descendants of more famous heroes or rulers does not prevent a belief in the truthfulness of genealogical legends in general and their ability to serve as credible knowledge about the past as an "oral popular chronicle".

Evidence of oral tradition and performance in medieval Serbia

From the beginnings to the end of the Serbian medieval state (4th–14th centuries)

Specific historical, social and cultural development in Serbia brought about some particular characteristics in the development of oral and written literature. The oldest testimony about the oral tradition originates from the common

[31] In Serbian tradition Janos Hunyady, governor of Hungary and father of King Matthias I Corvinus (1400–1456), is known as Ugrin Yanko Voyvoda or Sibinjanin Janko.

[32] Despot Stefan Lazarević (1402–1427) ruled after his father, Prince Lazar (1371–1389). After the Battle of Kosovo in 1389, in which Lazar was killed, Stefan accepted vassal obligations to Sultan Bayezid I Yildirim (the "Thunderbolt", 1389–1402, son of Murad I), while managing to remain partly autonomous. In 1414–1427 Janos Hunyady was in the service of Despot Stefan, possibly in the fortress Bešće.

[33] Despot Stefan died young and did not leave any children to succeed his throne. In spite of the great glory that he had won in many wars, he was linked to the motif of the uselessness of the struggle against the Turks. It is said that Stefan expelled the Turks down to the sea, and then he threw mace into the sea and said: "When this mace comes out of the sea, then Turks will return here". But the mace came to the surface straight away, confirming God's will that Turks would take over the kingdom because of Christian sins.

[34] Zmaj Despot Vuk or Zmajognjeni Vuk ('The Dragon Fire Wolf') is the epic name of Vuk Grgurević (c. 1439–1485), grandson of Despot Đurađ Branković and Serbian Despot in Hungary 1465–1485, cf. Jakobson & Ružičić 1950.

Slavic period (fourth to seventh centuries).[35] Having settled in the Balkans in the seventh century on the territory that was under Byzantine administration, Slavs became part of a rich legacy of Mediterranean Greco-Roman civilisation. The shift from oral into written forms of communication may be observed from the ninth century, which was marked by the Christianisation of Slavs (867–874), the mission of the Slavic educators Cyril and Methodios, and the creation of the first alphabets (Glagolitic and Cyrillic). Parallel to the expansion of Christianity and literacy, there are testimonies about the use of the musical instrument *gusle*[36] that speak about the condemnation of the pagan songs of the common people. In the twelfth century, an anonymous Presbyter from Dioclea wrote a pseudo-historical *Chronicle* based on oral and written sources, indirectly including folk motifs and narrative patterns.[37]

The Serbian prince Stefan Nemanja founded the independent state Rascia,[38] and his son Rastko – St Sava, the first archbishop (c. 1175–1200) – founded the Serbian Orthodox Church, as well as its literature. The Nemanjić dynasty[39] ruled until 1371 and its legitimacy and spiritual strength endured, spreading out long after the fall of the Serbian medieval state in 1459. Nemanja's second son, Stefan Prvovenčani (Stefan the First Crowned King) received the royal crown from the Pope in 1217. With these two of Nemanja's sons the original national literature actually began. The transplantation of Byzantine inheritance into medieval Serbian literature has contributed to its inclusion into the world cultural heritage. On the other hand, since medieval Serbian literature arose from an Old Slavic literary tradition, it entered *Slavia Orthodoxa*, the Russian-Bulgarian-Serbian cultural and historical area integrated with the tradition of Old Slavic language and Orthodoxy.[40]

[35] In the fourth century Wulfila in his translation of the Bible uses the Slavic loan word *plinsjan* 'to dance'. In the sixth century Procopius from Caesarea mentions that Greeks attacked the Slavs who fell asleep exhausted by singing on the feast. In the seventh century Byzantine historian Teophylactos Simokata tells about an event in 592, when Byzantines caught three men on the Propaditian Coast who had *zither* (which could be *gusle*) instead of weapons. They introduced themselves as Slavs and stated that they, as well as their compatriots, would rather sing than go to war.

[36] *Gusle* can be described as a "simple one-stringed fiddle with deeply rounded body, held upright on the knees when played upon; they were chanted by the *guslari*, the national bards", SUBOTIĆ 1932, 4. However, the *gusle* is not essential equipment for the Serbian bard because he can sing without any instrument or simply narrate the song.

[37] Dioclea is the Latin equivalent for Duklja, which was an independent kingdom in the territory of present-day Montenegro; see the extract in MATEJIĆ & MILIVOJEVIĆ 1978, 27–32.

[38] Rascia (Raška) is the name of medieval Serbia in the period of the first zhoupans. It was made after the city of Ras, the capital of Rascia (in present south-west Serbia).

[39] There were ten members of the Nemanjić dynasty on the Serbian throne: "magni iupanus" i.e. Great Zhoupan Stefan Nemanja (1168–1196), Stefan the First Crowned (1196–1228), Stefan Radoslav (1228–1234), Stefan Vladislav (1234–1243), Stefan Uroš I (1243–1265), Stefan Dragutin (1265–1282), Stefan Uroš II Milutin (1282–1321), Stefan Uroš III Decanski (1321–1331); Emperors Stefan Uroš IV Dušan (1331–1355) and Stefan Uroš V (1355–1371). In turbulent times, after the death of Emperor Dušan, other rulers emerged: King Vukašin Mrnjavcević (1365–1371), his son Marko (1371–1395), i.e. Marko Kraljević "son of the king", the national hero who rose above national borders and became the epic hero of all Balkan peoples, and Tvrtko I (1377–1391), Prince Lazar (1371–1389), Despot Stefan Lazarević (1402–1427) and Despot Đurad Branković (1429–1456).

[40] PICCHIO 1963; 1973.

Parallel to the development of medieval Serbian literature, in the early thirteenth century there are testimonies of an intense presence of orality in all social classes. In the introductory note to his translation of the Psalter from Greek into Old Serbian, St Sava requested that the monks sing the integral text of Psalms for 24 hours, five days a week. Teodosije, hagiographer of Stefan the First Crowned, mentioned that the king used to sit at the head of the table, sing during the dinner and entertain nobles and landed gentry, accompanied by drums and *gusle*. In the thirteenth century, there are records of professional singers, musicians and artists who travelled and entertained those who could afford it. In the early fourteenth century, the Byzantine historian Nikephoras Gregoras (1295–1359) observed on his journey through Serbia the sad monotony of melodies sung by soldiers in his escort, but also their singing and dancing in a special round dance, *kolo*, that is preserved up to the present day.

During the existence of the Serbian medieval state, and even when it began to collapse after the battles against the Turks on the river Marica in 1371 and on the Kosovo field in 1389, oral and written literature permeated one another constantly. Despite the invasion of the Turks, Đurađ Crnojević, ruler of Zeta (present Montenegro), established the first printing shop in the South Slavic lands at Cetinje that printed four liturgical books in the period between 1493 and 1496. In the first half of the sixteenth century there were printing shops in Venice (Božidar Vuković, 1519), at Goražde (Đurađ and Teodor Ljubavić), in the monasteries of Rujno, Gračanica and Mileševa, and in Belgrade (1552), and production was dedicated exclusively to the normal performance of the rite.[41] The influence of the printed book would intensify in the seventeenth and eighteenth centuries.

Parallel to the rise of printing technology, the earliest record of oral poetry is noted in 1497. The text of the poem and a description of its performance were presented by the Italian court poet Rogeri de Pacienza di Nardo. On June 1, 1497, the refugees from Serbia who settled in the village of Gioia del Colle near Bari on the southern Italian part of the Adriatic coast, sang and danced in *kolo* in honour of the Queen of Naples, Isabella del Balzo, and her retinue. The song was performed by some thirty Slavs, men, women and children. The names of the singers that Pacienza fortunately noted are common Serbian names. Analysis of the theme (an historical event), similar epic variants and names of the singers leaves no doubt that the song was brought over from the state of Despot Đurađ Branković. The performance was described in detail: adults and children were leaping about and jumping "like goats" and singing at the same time. Since Pacienza did not understand the language of the singers, he recorded the text he had heard or, perhaps, he was given the text after the performance. This text was incorporated in the poem *Balzino*, and reconstructed in the following way:

> An eagle flew in a circle over Smederevo city.
> No one desired to speak to it,

---

[41] Subotin-Golubović 1999, 282.

> Only Yanko voyvoda spoke from the prison:
> I pray thee, eagle, descend a little lower,
> So that I may talk to thee: I take thee as blood brother,
> Get thee to the gentry of Smederevo and ask them to beseech
> The glorious Despot to set me free from Smederevo prison;
> And if God aids me and the glorious Despot sets me free
> From Smederevo prison, I shall feed thee
> Crimson Turkish blood, white knightly flesh.[42]

The song refers to the short confinement of Janos Hunyady by the Serbian Despot Đurađ Branković that took place in the autumn of 1448. After his army was fully defeated in the so-called second Battle of Kosovo on 17–19 September, Hunyady retreated secretly from the battlefield, passing through the Serbian territory. Nevertheless, he was recognised and arrested. The Despot kept Hunyady imprisoned for less than a month in order to obtain war reparation since the united Christian troops had ridden through Serbia towards Kosovo as through a hostile country.

Artistically perfect, the ten recorded lines testify to a completely formed poetic language, motif and style register. The subject of the poem is the wide-spread motif of a hero who tries to escape from detention and seeks help. On an ideological and symbolical level, the opposition is formed between the enslaved captive and the free eagle, which is also an emblem of both the Serbian medieval state and Byzantium.[43] The short chronological distance between the actual event (1448) and the performance (1497) suggests that the principle of creating epic songs was contemporary, that is that epic songs on historical events were sung relatively soon after the occasion that inspired them.

Later evidence of the continuity of oral tradition

Since the end of the fifteenth century, the Serbs have migrated widely carrying on their tradition to the north and east towards Hungary and Romania, and

---

[42] Some changes were made in D. Bynum's original translation; in line 1: "An eagle circled over Smederevo city"; line 3: "Save only Yanko, leader of troops, who spoke to it from (where he lay in) prison"; line 5: "I have thee (as my) brother"; lines 6–7: "Get thee to the noble folk of Smederevo, let them beseech / The famous Despot to set me free from Smederevo prison"; line 10: "Crimson Turkish blood, white flesh of mounted warriors", cf. BYNUM 1986, 312.

[43] There are several possible interpretations of this song, but we draw attention to one in particular that shows the complexity of associations and forms of oral and written literature as well as medieval art. On one miniature in *Chronicle*, by Konstantinos Manasses (twelfth century) and translated into old Serbian literature in the fourteenth century, the legend of Emperor Markian is told and illustrated under the years 450–457. Being ill, the emperor fell a sleep, and in that moment the Vandal King Giserich spotted him. When he saw how the eagle provided shade for Markian, the king changed his mind and decided not to murder Markian. In the opinion of Serbian art historian S. Radojčić, this illustration could survive in art unchanged for centuries, most of all because similar scenes already existed in antiquity: Ulysses was portrayed asleep while the owl hovered over his head with open wings; Plutarch wrote that the eagle hung over the head of Alexander the Great in the battle at Gaugamela; Emperor Hadrian was depicted on coins with an eagle flying down on him. See RADOJČIĆ 1965.

down to the south towards the Adriatic coast and islands. To the north and east of the rivers of Sava and Danube, the last descendants of Branković, Jakšić and other noble families fought against the Turks. After every invasion of the frontier, many refugees were taken from the former Serbian lands to be colonised on the large estates of the Serbian gentry in exile in the south of Hungary (present Vojvodina in northern Serbia), Walachia or Moldavia. Immigrants brought their songs together with their unique way of singing known as "Serbian style" (or "measure"). This distinctive manner of singing was mentioned in 1551 in Lipa (Lipova, in present-day Romania) regarding the performance of the Serbian bard, Dimitrije Karaman, who entertained the Turkish lord, *beg*, Uluman.[44] In the description, the Serbian bard, who is sitting and holding the *gusle* between his knees, literally breaks its cords in the highly emotional artistic performance, with a sad and dedicated expression on his face. Here we can recognise the prototype of all later epic singers, up to Filip Višnjić, the celebrated blind bard of the First Serbian Uprising in the beginning of the nineteenth century.

Down to the Adriatic coast oral and written forms were intermixed, especially in urban districts. Local humanists appreciated folk literature over the masterpieces of Antiquity, pointing to the specific oral genres: proverbs, laments, love songs, wedding songs and poems sung during the work.[45] The heroic epic and the *bugarštica* were very popular in the early sixteenth century. Epic performance was collective and public: in 1547 in Split, a small town on the Adriatic coast, during distribution of bread to the poor one blind soldier initiated a song about Prince Marko and almost immediately everyone on the square accepted it. The performance must had been impressive, considering that the Italian official in charge felt the urge to record the event. Soon after this, in 1555, Petar Hektorović (1487–1572), the aristocrat and Renaissance erudite from the island of Hvar in the Adriatic Sea, recorded texts and melodies of six folk songs, among them two *bugarštica*. Two fishermen also sang in *Serbian style*, pointing out that it was an usual and widespread way of singing among their friends.[46]

From the aspect of the textology of oral literature and its contacts with written forms, the oldest records of Serbian folk literature are far from ideal. Some records were made by listening and later transcribing (as in Pacienza's case), and therefore the meaning of words, poetic meter and syntax were violated. Most recorders of folk songs were editors as well, and sometimes even the actual authors, so it is practically impossible to separate the roles of the collector,

[44] Hungarian historian Sebastian Tinody in *Transylvanian Chronicles* (1554) mentioned the Serbian singers: "There are many gusle players here in Hungary, but none is better at the Serbian style than Dimitrije Karaman".

[45] The Humanistic scholar Juraj Šižgorić (Georgius Sisgoreus) wrote the ethnographic study *De situ Illyriae et civitate Sibenici* in 1487 in Latin and it contains much evidence of oral tradition and folklore in general.

[46] In *Ribanje* Hektorović described how fishermen prepared for singing: "Having rowed a little, before becoming tired, / pouring forth his words, Nikola spoke: / Let's each of us tell off, to pass the time, / a fine song, that we may not feel our labor, / and that in Serbian measure, my dear comrade, / as in company we have always done".

copyist, redactor or editor. Another problem is the imitations of folk songs, whether they were deliberate or unconscious.

In view of the *bugarštica*, this problem is even more complex. It seems that some songs went through certain editing processes and for this reason it is difficult to distinguish between the authorial contribution and that of the singers. Texts are preserved only in later hand-written copies. The largest collection of the *bugarštica* from a Dubrovnik manuscript was altered by the erudite poet Ivan Marija Matijašević (1714–1791). While he copied songs from older manuscripts (which are not preserved) in order to create an anthology, he also consulted printed books such as the legendary history of the Slavs, *Il Regno degli Slavi* ('The Slavic Kingdom'), by Mauro Orbini (1601) and the collection of poetry written in imitation of the folk style, *Razgovor ugodni naroda slovinskoga* ('The Pleasant Conversation of Slavic People'), by Andrija Kačić Miošić (1756). He referred to these works with the intention of giving his anthology the impression of learned authority and historical accuracy, an act typical in written culture. By the time Matijašević finished his hand-written anthology, the *bugarštica* had already become extinct and could not be heard in the vicinity of Dubrovnik.

Little is known of the origin and nature of oral records in the Erlangen manuscript,[47] the collection of decasyllabic folk songs from the first half of the eighteenth century. In the course of the seventeenth and eighteenth centuries hand-written songbooks intended for private use circulated widely. They contain primarily lyric poetry, traditional and non-traditional (but were never marked as such). The selection of songs is personal and reflects the owner's taste. The collectors and copyists of these songs are often anonymous; sometimes they were both singers and editors, since the text was written down from memory. Eventually, the systematic collecting, recording and publishing of folklore "from the lips of the people" was initiated by Vuk Stefanović Karadžić (1787–1864),[48] one of the most magnificent figures of Serbian culture – a cultural reformer, lexicographer, philologist, ethnographer, and historian. His work represents the beginning of a new period in the history of Serbian literature.

Although the problem of a relatively late date for oral evidence is characteristic of all Slavic traditions, their antiquity is more or less accepted because of circumstantial evidence and the archaeological, folkloristic and linguistic analysis of layers of tradition. It is essential to study records and evidence in the framework of medieval culture, considering why and for whom they were made. An understanding of the collector's intention may offer a key to the analysis of evidence. For instance, the earliest integral oral text was written down rather accidentally and by a foreigner. Pacienza considered the song of common people as a desirable ornament in a literary poem devoted to the Queen of Naples. That act may reveal his view on oral poetry, but also the place of the oral epic in the hierarchy of genres and its social function. The other important source for oral tradition, *Memoirs of the Janissary* or *Turkish*

---

[47] Ed. GESEMANN 1925.
[48] Cf. WILSON 1970.

Chronicle by Konstantin Mihailović (1435–1501),[49] a Serbian soldier from Ostrovica in Kosovo, was written with a political ambition. Konstantin was captured by the Turks and fought on their side until he surrendered to the army of Hungarian King Matthias Corvinus. Konstantin probably wrote *Memoirs* in Poland and they are retained in many Polish and Czech copies. In his piece, which is a sort of memorandum, he addresses the European Christian kings who are able to confront the Ottoman Empire. He exposes the Byzantine idea of universal kingdom and his own practical-political views on the king's personal authority, the passive politics of the Roman pope and the necessity of achieving a Christian ideal in practice. However, apart from many unique descriptions concerning Turkish military organisation and customs, Konstantin narrates the recent Serbian past in a series of historical and legendary fragments, linking them to the broader picture of the world's history. Just like a medieval chronicler who does not really "write" history in the sense that he invents it, but includes historical data in a larger whole "in the course of history on a world scale",[50] Konstantin depicts the fall of the Serbian medieval state as a consequence of God's punishment for human sins. This explanation is not merely a rhetorical and theological metaphor, but an honest expression of the actual feelings of despair and helplessness of Christians after the fall of Constantinople. These circumstances provide a key to reading the traces of oral tradition in Konstantin's *Chronicle*.

Nevertheless, direct and circumstantial evidence for oral literature shows only a fragmentary picture of medieval orality. This picture can be enriched with specialised studies that discuss different issues, for example: research of the cliché, the recurrence of metric and syntactic patterns, repetitions and parallelisms, rhythmic prose, oral style, mixture of verse and prose in medieval texts; the assimilation of folk motifs and composition schemes in written genres; the analysis of formulas that indicate oral delivery and vocality; studies of quoting from the Bible and other written sources by memory and by heart (the latter being more often improvisation than verbatim quote). Equally important, together with the various approaches to oral evidence, is their interpretation in the frame of a wider cultural area and their comparison with related oral traditions.

Concluding remarks on orality and literacy in the Middle Ages in Serbia

Serbian oral tradition had two remarkable entrées in Europe. The first one coincided with the full bloom of Romanticism in the beginning of the nineteenth century, when the Brothers Grimm, Herder and Goethe became enchanted with folk songs from Karadžić's collections and started to learn Serbian in order to translate and study them. By the end of the nineteenth century, Serbian

---

[49] Svane 1995.
[50] Likhachov 1981, 12.

folk poetry was translated into several European languages.[51] The interest in Serbian and South Slavic oral tradition was renewed in the twentieth century when intensive field research was undertaken by Parry, Lord, Murko, Schmaus, Gesemann, along with the scholars who gathered round the journal *The Contributions to Research of Folk Poetry*.[52] Lord's study *The Singer of Tales*[53] for the second time introduced Serbian and South Slavic epic tradition to the scholars all over the world. The study was valuable for at least two reasons. Firstly, Serbian epic was linked again to the Homeric question – a connection first introduced during the Romantic period. Secondly, it was associated with performance theory, oral formulaic analysis and various ethnographical and anthropological approaches in the works of Lord's follower, J. M. Foley, and other researchers,[54] thus broadening its horizons in criticism.[55]

In view of the problem of oral and written art forms in Serbian medieval literature, one has to cope with the limitations of material, the specific circumstances of historical, social and literary development and methodological shortcomings. To summarise, it can be said that there was a balance between oral and written art forms. In medieval Serbia, literary activities in various forms, as well as manuscript tradition, were highly developed. Literacy was not reserved for the elite, but was common in everyday life. Archeographic research shows a fascinating diversity of *ductus* and handwriting styles, depending on monastic scriptoriums and local administrative offices. Illuminated manuscripts, decorated initials, miniature art and ornamented leather bookbinding demonstrate attention to detail and concern for the book in all of its aspects. Graphically and artistically, the medieval book sends a signal stating that written culture was indeed represented in the universal diversity. After the Ottoman Conquest, written culture did not die out, but accommodated itself to new circumstances. This can be illustrated by the phenomenon of professional travelling scribes – laymen, who worked in private houses or for local priests – because of the great demand for books.[56]

On the other hand, oral culture in the Middle Ages also appeared in a variety of forms. Linking orality exclusively to the illiterates is a wrong and simplified approach,[57] just as *oral* cannot simply be identified with the *folk*. It is very probable that oral genres filled in most of the gaps in the system of medieval literary genres. Oral art forms satisfied the needs of the various classes until they were written down.[58] The system of medieval literary genres was considerably conditioned by practical needs – sacral and secular – while oral

---

[51] Subotić 1932; Wilson 1970; Ivić 1995.

[52] Originally *Prilozi proučavanju narodne poezije*, ed. by R. Medenica and A. Schmaus, Belgrade, 1934–1939. The journal brought many field reports from all over the former Yugoslavia, as well as analytical studies (all texts have abstracts in German).

[53] Lord 1960.

[54] Cf. Foley 1985.

[55] Parry-Lord's theoretical views were discussed from the standpoint of literary poetics in Serbian scholarship, cf. Detelić 1996.

[56] Subotin-Golubvić 1999, 283.

[57] Cf. Matejka 1986, 511.

[58] Lihačov 1972, 76.

culture covered the genres of oral literature as well as types of oral communication. Serbian medieval literature existed in different mediums typical for the culture in general.[59] The first is the literary language of high, spiritual literature and liturgical rite,"the prestigious language of the Church, emanating from Serbian medieval ecclesiastic centers".[60] This language (or style) corresponds to the elite culture of educated social groups. The second is the language of the common and practical sphere that comprises a wide range of genres like medieval novels, apocrypha, private correspondence, administration, law codices, marginal inscriptions, etc. It corresponds to the various layers of middle class culture such as educated amateurs, laity, professionals, craftsmen and merchants. In the scope of this stratum, there is a nucleus of a specific "culture for the people". It covers simplified semiliterary works and transitional forms that can be marked by special linguistic style. The third linguistic medium that is also the least known is the native colloquial speech (vernacular). Valuable research on spoken language features in Serbian medieval manuscripts has shown that the living language penetrated on the phonetic, morphologic and lexical plane, and significantly less on the syntactic. Manifestations of the spoken language and conversational features (for instance the vocalisation of certain dialectic types) are noticed even "in a group of strictly canonical and liturgical texts",[61] which proves that layers or styles of the language can be intermixed regardless of the medium. This language corresponds to the popular, folk culture of the uneducated (but not necessarily the illiterates), that comprises specific non-literary dialects and even argot.

Layers of language and culture correspond to the system of medieval literary genres. It was noted that every medieval genre "to a great extent determined the predilection for the predominance of one or the other linguistic component":

> There are considerable linguistic and stylistic differences within a single literary form. Apart from the Byzantine literary heritage embodied in Old Church Slavonic, there is also the influence of oral folk tradition in Old Serbian. The former exists in the presentations and descriptions of war activities, diplomatic negotiations, and ceremonies in the lives of the Serbian rulers. The latter is in topical situations where the folk tradition has already provided the framework: laments, curses, as well as personal emotional situations whose informality dictated the use of an informal linguistic medium.[62]

The diachronic relation between the oral and the written tradition, conditioned by the different nature of their texts, is in a sense paradoxical. As S. Neklyudov observed, since it is not possible to restore the genuine oral situation from the past, the reconstruction of the oral text as an object of literary analysis is

---

[59] TOLSTOJ 1995.
[60] MATEJIĆ & MILIVOJEVIĆ 1978, 22.
[61] ŠTAVLJANIN ĐORĐEVIĆ 1995.
[62] MATEJIĆ & MILIVOJEVIĆ 1978, 23.

impossible. The fixation of the oral text cannot correspond to the "original", which is just one of many manifestations of tradition and should be treated as an abstract construction.[63] On the other hand, attempts have been made to overcome the methods that focus only on fixed oral text as a "final result" of communication. It has been proposed that we consider the text as a product of a direct contact in communication between representatives of tradition, while the emphasis is on the process itself, not on the fixed text. S. M. Tolstaya proposed a classification based on a level of structuration on a scale of orality to literacy. Five categories were singled out: 1) non-structured oral text (spontaneous word), 2) structured oral prose text (folk tale, *fabulata*, etc.), 3) structured oral metrical text (song or recitative), 4) literary hand-written text, and 5) literary printed text.[64] They are metaphorically described as aggregated phases in constant change. Apart from this, but in some aspects similarly, L. Honko indicated the problem of transition from orality to literacy in documentary sources on epics. He suggested that the relationship between oral and written should not be regarded as a mixture of a "pure oral" and a "pure written" discourse, but rather as a mixture of "oral and written discourses" or "performance styles, i.e. an oral style in a written text or a written style in an oral performance".[65] Challenging the concepts of "song" and "variant", he assumed a "pool of tradition" model that is more general than the genre system or calendar cycle, but still encompasses them, dealing with the basic elements of tradition and culture – "multiforms, themes and formulas reside within an internalised tradition system (of a singer, group, or region) to be activated in a particular situation of performance". Honko implied the idea of a "mental text" that constitutes a fluctuation of choices, as an "open system without final fixity".[66]

Whether a methodological approach is suitable or not depends on its applicability to a fixed text or to living tradition. Apart from the above-mentioned terms, others like "transitional" and "oral-derived text", "oral / written mentality" or "oral composition", or "quasi-folk style", "elementary-learned", "authentic", "sophisticated-learned style", etc.[67] can be helpful, too. The choice of a suitable method depends primarily on the nature of the oral and written "material" and the specific problems of every particular cultural legacy. The experience gained in field research enables us to draw some analogies between contemporary and medieval orality, but only to a certain extent. It seems that there is much dissimilarity between these categories that ought to be recognised and explained in the context of the Middle Ages, not in the framework of the poetic norms and methods of later periods. The authority of the written text, form or composition in the Middle Ages should not be underestimated, but this does not mean that medieval people were unable to recall the oral narratives of the past to incorporate them into written text, especially when they wanted to tell a

---

[63] NEKLYUDOV 1999, 290.
[64] TOLSTAYA 1989, 9–14.
[65] HONKO 1995, 1.
[66] HONKO 1996, 1.
[67] Cf. texts of Lord, Foley, Miletich, Jason and others in PETROVIĆ 1988.

true story which for some reason was considered important and thought worthy to be kept and "saved" from oblivion. Since the written text could inspire the creation of new oral texts, two-way circulation between the oral and written art forms is a phenomenon that must be taken into account for the medieval period.

Bakhtin's idea that one's own culture reveals itself more fully and deeply only in the eyes of another culture confirms the conviction that the comprehension of the specific problems and issues of one particular tradition may lead to a better understanding of the general theoretical concepts regarding orality and literacy; this paper was an attempt in that direction.

Bibliography

Primary sources

The Song of the Battle of Kosovo, transl. John S. Miletich in *The Bugarštica: A Bilingual Anthology of the Earliest Extant South Slavic Folk Narrative Song*: p. 13–32. Urbana 1990.

DANILO III, *Milica's Lament*, transl. Mateja Matejić in eds. Mateja Matejić and Dragan Milivojević *An Anthology of Medieval Serbian Literature in English*: p. 120. Columbus, Ohio 1978.

DANILO III, *One Human Nature* (= *A Fragment from Narration about Prince Lazar*, transl. Sheila Sofrenović in eds. Predrag R. Dragić Kijuk *Medieval and Renaissance Serbian Poetry*: p. 94. Beograd 1987.

The Death of the Mother of the Yugovichi, transl. Geoffrey N. W. Locke in *The Serbian Epic Ballads. An Anthology*: p. 72–74. Belgrade 2002.

PETAR HEKTOROVIĆ, *Ribanje i ribarsko prigovaranje*, transl. Edward D. Goy. Stari Grad 1997.

Secondary sources

BAKHTIN, Mikhail 1981: *The Dialogic Imagination*. Austin.

BYNUM, David E. 1986: "The collection and analysis of oral epic traditions in South Slavic: An instance." *Oral Tradition*, 1/2 302–343.

DETELIĆ, Mirjana 1996: *Urok i nevesta. Poetika epske formule*. Beograd, [The Charm and the Bride. The Poetics of Epic Formula, with English summary].

DRAGIĆ KIJUK, Predrag R. (ed.) 1987: *Medieval and Renaissance Serbian Poetry*. Serbian Literary Quarterly, Beograd.

FOLEY, John Miles 1985: *Oral-formulaic Theory and Research: An Introduction and Annotated Bibliography*. New York.

GESEMANN, Gerhard (ed.) 1925: *Erlangenski rukopis starih srpskohrvatskih narodnih pesama*. Sremski Karlovci, [The Erlangen Manuscript of Old Serbo-Croat Folk Songs].

HONKO, Lauri 1995: "Oral and semiliterary epics: A panel in Mysore." *Folklore Fellows Network*, 10 1–6.

———— 1996: "The quest for oral text: The third wave." *Folklore Fellows Network*, 12 1.

IVIĆ, Pavle (ed.) 1995: *The History of Serbian Culture*. Edgware, transl. R. A. Major.

JAKOBSON, Roman & RUŽIČIĆ, Gojko 1950: "The serbian Zmaj Ognjeni Vuk and the Russian Vseslav epos." *Annuaire de l'Institute de Philologie et d'Histoire Orientales Slaves*, 10 343–355.

LIHAČOV, Dimitrije Sergejevič 1972: *Poetika stare ruske književnosti*. Beograd, transl. D. Bogdanović. [The Poetics of Old Russian Literature, first ed. Leningrad 1971; cf. French translation: Dimitri LIKHATCHOV, *Poétique historique de la literature Russe Xe – XXe siècle*, traduction, préface et notes de la F. Lesourd, L'Age d'Homme, Lausanne, 1981].

LIKHACHOV, Dimitry 1981: *The Great Heritage. The Classical Literature of Old Rus*. Moscow, transl. D. Bradley.

LORD, Albert B. 1960: *The Singer of Tales, Harvard Studies in Comparative Literature*, vol. 24. Cambridge, Mass.

———— 1986: "The merging of two worlds: Oral and written poetry as carriers of ancient values." In John Miles Foley (ed.) *Oral Tradition in Literature: Interpretation in Context*, pp. 19–64, Columbia.

LOTMAN, Jurij M. 1968: *Lektsii po struktural'noj poetike: Vvedenie, teorija stiha*. Tartu, [Lectures on Structural Poetics].

MATEJIĆ, Mateja & MILIVOJEVIĆ, Dragan (eds.) 1978: *An Anthology of Medieval Serbian Literature in English*. Columbus, Ohio.

MATEJKA, L. 1986: "Serbo-croatian oral and written verbal art: contacts and conflicts." In *Studia slavica medievalia et humanistica. Riccardo Picchio dicata*, vol. II, Roma.

MATIĆ, Svetozar 1964: "Tragovi stiha na stećcima." In *Naš narodni ep i naš stih*, p. 249–269, [Our Folk Epic and Our Verse].

MIHALJČIĆ, Rade (ed.) 1982: *Namentragende Steininschriften in Jugoslawien vom Ende des 7. bis zur Mitte des 13. Jahrhunderts*. Weisbaden.

MIHALJČIĆ, Rade 1989: *The Battle of Kosovo in History and in Popular Tradition*. Belgrade.

MILETICH, John S. (ed.) 1990: *The Bugarštica: A Bilingual Anthology of the Earliest Extant South Slavic Folk Narrative Song, Illinois Medieval Monographs*, vol. 3. Urana.

NEKLYUDOV, S. Yu. 1999: "Tradicii ustnoi i knizhnoi kul'tury: sootnoshenie i tipologiya." In E. E. Levkievskaya (ed.) *Slavyanskie etyudy. Sbornik k yubileyu S. M. Tolstoi*, Moskva.

PETROVIĆ, Svetozar (ed.) 1988: *Usmeno i pisano/pismeno u književnosti i kulturi = Oral and Written/Literate in Literature and Culture*. Novi Sad.

PICCHIO, Ricardo 1963: "A proposito della slavia ortodossa e della comunità linguistica slava ecclesiastica." *Richerche slavistiche*, 11 105–122.

———— 1973: "Models and patterns in the literary tradition of medieval orthodox Slavdom." In Victor Terras (ed.) *American Contributions to the Seventh International Congress of Slavists*, vol. II, The Hague.

RADOJČIĆ, Svetozar 1965: "O nekim zajedničkim motivima naše narodne pesme i našeg starog slikarstva." In *Tekstovi i freske*, p. 94–115, Novi Sad.

STOJANOVIĆ, Ljub. (ed.) 1902–1926: *Stari srpski zapisi i natpisi.* Beograd, [The Old Serbian marginal and other inscriptions].

SUBOTIN-GOLUBVIĆ, Tatjana 1999: *Srpsko rukopisno nasleđe od 1557. godine do sredine XVII veka.* Beograd, [The Serbian Manuscript Tradition from 1557 until the Middle of the XVIIth Century; with English summary].

SUBOTIĆ, Dragutin 1932: *Yugoslav Popuar Ballads: Their Origin and Development.* Cambridge.

SVANE, Gunnar (ed.) 1995: *Konstantin Mihailovic fra Ostrovica: tyrkisk krønike, eller en janitschars erindringer, Arbejdspapirer, Slavisk Institut,* vol. 2. Århus.

TOLSTAYA, S. M. 1989: "Ustnyi tekst v yazyke i kul'ture." In M. Abramowicz & J. Bartmińsky (eds.) *Text ustny - Text Oral. Struktura i pragmatyka - problemy systenatyki - ustnosc w literaturze,* Wroclaw.

TOLSTOJ, Nikita Iljič 1995: "Jezik slovenske kulture." Beograd, [The Language of Slavic Culture].

VUCINICH, Wayne & EMMERT, Thomas A. (eds.) 1991: *Kosovo: Legacy of a Medieval Battle, Minnesota Mediterranean and East European Monographs,* vol. 1. Minneapolis.

WILSON, Duncan 1970: *The Life and Times of Vuk Stefanović Karadžić, 1787–1864.* Oxford.

ŠTAVLJANIN ĐORĐEVIĆ, Ljubica 1995: "Praćenje pojava govornog jezika prilikom rada na opisu srpskih srednjovekovnih rukopisa." In Ivić Pavle (ed.) *Proučavanje srednjovekovnih južnoslovenskih rukopisa: Zbornik radova sa III Međunarodne hiladarske konferencijeodržane od 28. do 30. marta 1989,* p. 447–453, Beograd, [Research on spoken language features in medieval Serbian manuscripts].

Ealdgesegena worn: What the Old English *Beowulf* Tells Us about Oral Forms

GRAHAM D. CAIE

T HE OLD ENGLISH poem *Beowulf* is full of information about the customs of early Germanic people, yet is this work of fiction to be trusted as a true record of cultural events, or is it like an historical novel in which the poet invents an imagined picture of by-gone civilisations? *Beowulf* takes us into a world we would like to think is genuinely Anglo-Saxon or Danish, where kings and thanes, tempered by peace-weaving queens, live in meadhalls, utter heroic boasts and plan blood feuds, while dragons and monsters freely roam in a world that has no trace of peasant or farmer.

If the world portrayed is fanciful, can we trust what the poem tells us about oral forms of composition and delivery? Much depends on the vexed question of the dating of *Beowulf*, as the poem we have today might be the product of oral composition with its roots in a period not long after the events narrated, or it may have been imaginatively composed almost five hundred years after these events and have as much relationship to these events as *Braveheart* has to medieval Scottish history. At least it is possible to compare references in *Beowulf* with other datable Old English poems which mention oral composition and which contain descriptions of poets or *scops* creating and reciting verse; this will help corroborate the authenticity of descriptions of poetic creation in *Beowulf*.

A brief word on some problems surrounding the dating of *Beowulf* is, however, necessary in order to highlight some issues concerning composition, even though Edward B. Irving states that if "an eighth-century date has been shown to be rather insecurely based … the late date has as yet been no more firmly established",[1] and Alain Renoir confesses: "I should be at loss to tell when, by whom, where and under what circumstances this greatest of all early Germanic epics was composed."[2]

We know that the events referred to in the poem occurred in the sixth century and we know that the poem is extant today in only one manuscript of the

---

[1] IRVING 1989, 31.
[2] RENOIR 1986, 68.

late tenth or early eleventh century.[3] Did it snowball orally over the centuries, accumulating digressions and episodes as it rolled, getting increasingly larger, from the sixth century until it was frozen in time by the poet, or scribe who captured it as in a photograph in the *Beowulf* Manuscript, London, British Library, Cotton Vitellius A XV? The 6-8-10 theory was easily remembered by undergraduates: the events were of the sixth century, the composition of the eighth and the only extant manuscript was of the tenth. Unfortunately for students the central date of composition in the eighth or ninth centuries has been questioned. Arguments for an early date included the presence of a formulaic style; the fact that the poet graphically relates events such as human cremation which ceased at the arrival of Christianity; and that no true Englishman would set his great English epic in Scandinavia after the Viking raids on England. Against such arguments were examples of poems containing many formulas which were evidently written compositions; the fact that Saxo Grammaticus and Snorri Sturluson describe human cremation graphically, although writing in post-conversion times; and that the ninth- and tenth-century English could distinguish between the marauding Danes of their time and the great heroes of the past from whom they were descended at the migration period – just as one hopes the Portuguese distinguish between English football hooligans and, say, Shakespeare.

The Old English *The Battle of Brunanburh* in four manuscripts of *The Anglo-Saxon Chronicle* provides a useful comparison. We know that a battle did indeed occur at Brunanburh in AD 937 and the events are historically accurate, according to Irish and Scottish annals. It was a battle at which two grandsons of King Alfred, Aethelstan and Eadmund, led a joint Wessex and Mercian victorious attack against the Scots, Strathclyde Britons and the Vikings from Dublin under Olaf. The victory fulfilled Alfred's dream of a united England under Wessex and is consequently a work full of patriotism and propaganda.

The large amount of metaphors, kennings and formulas in this poem makes it what Stanley Greenfield has called "a tissue of heroic formulaic cliché, themes and stylistic variation":[4] The formula applied in the battle scenes reminds one of Old Testament narrative,[5] and so it makes the victorious Anglo-Saxons seem like biblical heroes as the event is raised to cosmic heights. In addition, the poet justifies this defeat by viewing it as a continuation of the great victories which his Saxon and Anglian forebears achieved many centuries before:

> Ne wearð wæl mare
> on þis eiglande   æfre gieta
> folces gefylled   beforan þissum
> sweordes ecgum,   þæs þe us secgað bec,
> ealde uðwitan,   siþþan eastan hider

---

[3] KIERNAN 1996 suggests a date after 1016 for the making of the poem. See also CHASE 1981 and LIUZZA 1995.

[4] GREENFIELD 1986, 148.

[5] GODDEN 1991, 210 and CAIE 1994, 86–87.

Engle and Seaxe   up becoman,
ofer brad brimu   Brytena sohtan,
wlance wigsmiþas,   Wealas ofercoman,
eorlas arhwate   eard begeatan.[6]

> Nor has ever been greater slaughter of folk in this island before this, felled
> by the sword's edge, as books tell us, ancient authorities, since hither from
> the east the Angles and Saxons arrived over the wide sea to seek the land of
> Britain, the proud war-smiths, conquered the Welsh and, keen for glory,
> gained the land.

It was politically important for the West Saxons to associate with their Saxon
forefathers. John Pope calls it "a royal panegyric; but it is more than a panegyric
by reason of its strong national feeling."[7] So here we have a historically-verified
heroic poem, possibly written, if not composed, at the same time as *Beowulf*,
which looks nostalgically back at "the good old days" when "the proud war-
smiths", who lived around the same time as the historically-proven characters in
Beowulf, were victorious. S. A. J. Bradley states: "historical perspective is given
to the battle and a secular patriotism is celebrated in terms deliberately redolent
of antique themes of heroism."[8]

As in *Beowulf* there is an attempt to elevate the style and meter by making
it traditional and archaic, while the language is formulaic, as can be seen in this
translation by S. A. J. Bradley:

> The field grew wet with men's blood from when in the morning-
> tide that glorious star, the sun, glided aloft and over earth's plains,
> the bright candle of God the everlasting Lord, to whom that noble
> creation sank in rest.... They left sharing out the corpses the
> black-plumaged, horny-beaked black raven, and the dun-plum-
> aged white-tailed eagle enjoying the carrion, the greedy war-hawk
> and that grey beast, the wolf of the forest.[9]

It is a patchwork of kennings and formulas, variation and repetition, intended
to evoke the oral poetry of the heroic age. The victory is placed in cosmic and
spiritual context, as are the victories of Beowulf when fate and God are invoked.
This style and verbal echoes with both Old Testament and heroic verse raise the
battle to that of biblical narrative and Germanic epic. If we had not been able
to date and locate this poem precisely, we would undoubtedly be claiming a
much earlier date because of the style.

Anglo-Saxon scholars in the nineteenth and early twentieth centuries were
keen to highlight the remnants of heroic Old English verse as they wished
to define the quintessentially Germanic spirit of Anglo-Saxon times. In fact

[6] *The Battle of Brunanburh* 65–73.
[7] Pope 1966, 56.
[8] Bradley 1982, 516. Most of my translations are based on Bradley's translations.
[9] Bradley 1982, 516.

we have very little Old English heroic verse compared to religious poetry. We will never know if the paucity of material is because there never was such nationalistic verse earlier, or if it has been destroyed, as *Beowulf* nearly was in the Cottonian fire, or whether it was all orally delivered and later stamped out by the Church. *Quid Hinieldus cum Christo*? 'What has Ingeld to do with Christ?' asks Alcuin in 797 by way of criticising monks for listening to heroic lays: "Let the word of God be read at the meal of the clergy, not a harp-player, sermons, not songs of the laity". It is obvious that the monks at Lindisfarne were used to listening to heroic lays and that there would be no encouragement to commit them to vellum. It is curious that the best known examples of what we call secular heroic verse occur at the end of the Anglo-Saxon period, just before the Norman Conquest. It is not by chance, though, that such poetry fulfilled a political need of the Saxon rulers to create a united England with a great past and ideals of loyalty to king and country. It nourished a sense of nostalgia for a time considered to have fixed beliefs when men were heroes and heroes were immortal – a time that never was and yet will be forever at least in poetry.[10]

So after the above caveat, what *does Beowulf* tell us about oral delivery and the workings of the *scop*? The first piece of textual evidence is after the creation of a brave new civilisation in Denmark by Hrothgar who builds the magnificent hall, Heorot, described in terms of the Creation. Immediately after this description we hear of Grendel's anger which seems to have been aroused by the sound of the harp: "every day he heard the sound of joy, loud in the hall."

> þær wæs hearpan sweg,
> swutol sang scopes.   Sægde se þe cuþe
> frumsceaft fira   feorran reccan,
> cwæð þæt se ælmihtiga   eorðan worhte,
> wlitebeorhtne wang,   swa wæter bebugeð,
> gesette sigehreþig   sunnan ond monan
> leoman to leohte   landbuendum,
> ond gefrætwade   foldan sceatas
> leomum ond leafum;   lif eac gesceop
> cynna gehwylcum   þara ðe cwice hwyrfaþ.[11]

There was the sound of the harp, the clear song of the poet. He who was skilled in recounting the creation of men in distant times, declared that the Almighty made the earth, a beautiful plain, which water encircles. He, triumphing in victory, established the sun and the moon, a light to light the land-dweller; he adorned the corners of the earth with branches and leaves. He also created the life of all the species which exist.

[10] Caie 1994, 93.
[11] *Beowulf* 89–98.

We learn from this quotation that the harp and poetry are inextricably linked. The expression *swutol sang scopes* 'the clear song of the poet' is significant, as it is not recited but sung. The creation of a new order by Hrothgar, a new civilisation in social harmony, triggers off this song of the Creation, described in terms of harmony. It is that which angers Grendel who stands for all that threatens *dream*, 'joy' and 'song'. When Beowulf is about to die, the poet says that the hero laid down all *hleahtor, gamen ond gleodream* (3020) 'laughter, entertainment and convivial joy'. So song, poetry, joy, the harp – all symbolise the perfect society. The creation of poetry and song throughout the poem is connected with victory, cosmos and peace, as at the creation of the hall Heorot, while during Grendel's reign of terror we hear that the harp is silent. It is significant that in the royal burial at Sutton Hoo and the burial at Taplow there is a harp or lyre alongside the helmet, sword and other warlike treasure, as *scop* and thane must have been of equal importance. Poetry then played a vital social as well as cultural role.

Leoð 'poem' and *sang* 'song' are, therefore, synonymous in Old English;[12] Bede's verb *cantare* 'to sing or recite' is translated in his account of Caedmon by *be hearpan singan* 'to sing [accompanied] by the harp'. In poetry the verbs *singan, giddian, galan,* and *gliwian* and the nouns *sang, gidd/gied,* and *gleo* all refer to singing and reciting of poetry.[13] *Gleo* is used in compounds such as *gleo-mann* 'poet', *gleo-dream* 'the joys of poetry/song', *gleo-beam* 'harp' and are all found in *Beowulf*. Prose, however, is called *gewrit* and the act of composing in prose is *writan,* a verb which suggests the process of inscribing on vellum and is cognate with Old Norse *rita* 'to tear or scratch'.[14] Hrothgar looks at the hilt of the magic sword with which Beowulf has killed Grendel's mother and sees that *on ðæm wæs or writen / fyrngewinnes* 'on it was written the origin of the ancient strife' (1688–89) referring to the biblical story of the Flood. Such canonical, authoritative events or occurrences then are engraved and inscribed, whereas the poet's composition of vernacular oral legend is sung.

Previously, after the victory over Grendel, we hear from the *Beowulf*-poet that:

> þær wæs sang ond sweg   samod ætgædere
> fore Healfdenes   hildewisan,
> gomenwudu greted,   gid oft wrecen,
> ðonne healgamen   Hroþgares scop
> æfter medobence   mænan scolde.[15]

> There was song and music together in the presence of Healfdene's battle leader [Hrothgar], the "pleasure wood" [harp] was plucked and often a lay recited, when the time came for Hrothgar's poet to relate along the meadbench an entertainment in the hall. [The Finn episode follows]

[12] SCRAGG 1991, 58.
[13] ALEXANDER 1983, 55.
[14] FRANTZEN 1991, 327–357.
[15] *Beowulf* 1063–1067.

The song recited is the Lay of Finn and Hildeburh which concludes:

> Leoð wæs asungen,
> gleomannes gyd.   Gamen eft astah,
> beorhtode bencsweg;   byrelas sealdon
> win of wunderfatum[16]

The poem was sung, the song of the *gleomann* [poet/singer]. Revelry/en-
tertainment arose once more. The clamour from the benches glittered;
cup-bearers gave wine from wondrous vessels.

Leoð and *gyd* appear to be synonymous and refer to both song and poetry,
whereas *gamen* suggests general entertainment or games. The former commands
silence and respect and the latter is conducted with noise, clamour and wine
drinking.

The best example of a poet at work occurs after Beowulf's first victory over
Grendel. The Danes and Beowulf's men retreat to the now cleansed Heorot
and the *scop*, who is again called a thain of the king, not a minstrel or servant,
creates a new song, this time about Beowulf. He states:

> Hwilum cyninges þegn,
> guma gilphlæden,   gidda gemyndig,
> se ðe ealfela   ealdgesegena
> worn gemunde,   word oþer fand
> soðe gebunden;   secg eft ongan
> sið Beowulfes   snyttrum styrian,
> ond on sped wrecan   spel gerade,
> wordum wrixlan.   Welhwylc gecwæð
> þæt he fram Sigemunde   secgan hyrde,
> ellendædum,   uncuþes fela,[17]

At times one of the king's thanes, a man filled with eloquence, familiar
with stories and who had in memory a great multitude of traditional
tales, composed a new poem truly linked [one word would conjoin with
another, accurately linked]. This man cleverly set about reconstructing
Beowulf's exploit, and successfully recited a skilful narrative achieving
variety with his words. Almost everything he had heard about Sigemund
he told, about the deeds of courage.

This is undoubtedly an example of oral composition and delivery including a
hint in the phrase *wordum wrixlan* as to how the poetry was constructed. The
poet praises the feats of Beowulf, compares him with Sigurth, called Sigemund
in the English tradition, thereby foreshadowing Beowulf's final battle with
the dragon. He contrasts Beowulf with Heremod, who appears elsewhere in

[16] *Beowulf* 1159–1162.
[17] *Beowulf* 867-876.

Beowulf as an example of a bad king who does not distribute gifts. The poet who recites is "familiar with old stories"; he is, literally translated, "laden with high-sounding poetry, magniloquent speech".[18] The *scop*, then, is endowed with eloquence, and, equally important, his memory is stressed: this is someone who remembered the great lays 'who could call to mind a great multitude of all kinds of ancient traditions' (*ealdgesegena*). This means more than poetic works but all ancient verbal utterances such as the maxims or gnomic verse of which we have a fair amount in Old English verse. Both verbs are highly significant: *gemunde* 'remembered' and *fand* 'found' or 'invented', referring to both the remembrance of formulas and the creation of new words or recitations. Both of these then are *soðe gebunden* 'faithfully bound or linked', undoubtedly a reference to alliterative binding or linking of phrases, while adverbs and adverbial phrases such as *snyttrum* and *on sped* 'skilfully' and 'effectively' stress the poet's professionalism. *Wordum wrixlan*, meaning to interweave or create variety with words, is probably a reference to the poetic technique of variation. The same verb is used in Old English for the song of the nightingale, as it too finds variations on a theme.[19] *Wrixlan* can also mean 'wrestle with' and it adds that notion of robust and complex mental agility that is necessary for such variations. One can imagine that part of the entertainment is to see how the *scop* adapts his material and comes up with something new. Variation is an important device in alliterative poetry and certainly not just a means to fill in verses.[20] The accumulation of epithets each of which adds a new dimension to the object described is part of the art. Grendel the monster is never physically described, but each variation adds to our picture of him: he is a "death-shadow", a "denier of life", an "evil soul", of the kin of Cain, a "heathen one", "God's enemy", a "solitary one", an exile, and so on, with each adding a new detail to our understanding of Grendel. The form is expected, but there is much freedom within these patterns which create vital, original and fresh verse.

The best example of freedom within form is found in *Cædmon's Hymn*. Bede in his *Historia ecclesiastica* relates how the cowherd Caedmon of Whitby was given by God the gift of poetry and was the first to compose Christian poetry in English. Whether Caedmon ever existed is questionable, but it is clear that Bede wishes to show how Christian vernacular poetry can be fashioned out of formulaic heroic verse:

> Nu scylun hergan   hefaenricaes uard
> Metudaes maecti   end his modgidanc
> Uerc uuldurfadur,   sue he uundra gihuaes,
> Eci dryctin,   or astelidae.
> He aerist scop   aelda barnum
> Heben til hrofe,   haleg scepen;
> Tha middungeard   moncynnaes uard,

[18] Wrenn 1958, 200.
[19] Alexander 1983, 53.
[20] Greenfield 1972, 60–83.

> Eci dryctin   aefter tiadae,
> Firum foldan,   frea allmectig[21]

> Now we must praise the guardian of the heavenly kingdom, the lord's
> might, and his mind's purpose, the work of the father of glory; as he of
> all wonders, the eternal lord, established the origin. He first created for
> the children of men heaven as a roof, the holy creator, then middle earth,
> mankind's guardian, the eternal lord afterwards ordained, the earth for
> men, the almighty lord.

God is not mentioned by name, but by periphrasis eight times: he is *uard* 'a
guardian'; *Metod* 'lord or measurer of fate'; *uuldurfadur* 'father of glory'; *drihten*
'warlord'; *Frea,* a more domestic title for lord, and a term used of Beowulf; *scepen*
'creator' (a cognate form of *scop* 'poet'); *rices weard* 'guardian of the kingdom',
which is the epithet Beowulf uses for King Hrothgar. Such epithets are common
in all Christian Old English verse; Michael Alexander states that

> the traditional content of the formulaic language of Old Eng-
> lish poetry is of more significance than the terminological and
> statistical argument about whether it is "oral" or "literary". Of
> the formulaic nature of the original Old English verse vocabulary
> there can be no doubt; nor is there any doubt that in its gen-
> esis and nature it is an "oral" style ... Bede makes it clear that
> Caedmon's poems were orally composed and implies (what his
> Old English translator says) that they were then written down by
> scribes – scribes without whose presence he would not have had
> these stories to tell, just as, without the tradition of vernacular
> extempore composition, there would have been no poems to be
> written down.[22]

So Old English poetry comes from an oral tradition, according to Bede, and
when written down they retained the techniques and rhetorical devices which
were developed by this tradition. Later the trappings of oral devices gave poetry
the *gravitas* or authority that comes with age. The desire to give the illusion
of oral composition continues well beyond the Anglo-Saxon period and well
beyond the Middle Ages. *Sir Gawain and the Green Knight*, for example, written
in the West Midlands in the last quarter of the fourteenth century, contempor-
aneous with Chaucer, displays many oral features. The poet states in this highly
stylised and complex metrical form:

> If ʒe wyl lysten þis laye bot on littel quile,
> I schal telle hit as-tit, as I in toun herde,
>   with tonge,
>   As hit is stad and stoken

[21] *Cædmon's hymn* (Northumbrian version), POPE 1966, 3.
[22] ALEXANDER 1983, 51–52.

In stori stif and stronge,
With lel letteres loken,
In londe so hatz ben longe.[23]

If you will listen, this lay I shall tell in a little while as I heard it in town,
as it is laid down in stories with true interlocked letters as it has been in
this land for long.

There is no way that this poem is orally composed, but the poet gives it authority
by claiming that he heard it "with tongue" in a composition which uses *lel
letteres loken / In londe so hatz ben longe*, literally, 'loyal interlocked letters which
have been in this country for ages'. He is undoubtedly referring to alliterative
poetry, the verse form which Chaucer mocks as being parochial, but which
has its origins in oral Old English verse. This poet deliberately uses both front
and end rhyme in this highly complex versification perhaps to show that he
is capable of using the French-influenced end rhyme, but prefers the native
English form. Claims of orality are common in Middle English romances and
indeed most vernacular literature, in an age when originality is condemned and
all literary works require the *auctoritas* of an ancient, preferably Latin, source.
Chaucer, for example, borrows extensively from his contemporary Boccaccio in
Troilus and Criseyde, but attributes his work to a non-existent Latin Lollius. By
applying such formulas in vernacular, written poetry, the author gives his work
the authority of an old, oral work and avoids the accusation of originality.[24]

It is impossible, and I believe unproductive, to attempt to distinguish
between rhetorical devices which suggest oral creation and those which either
help make the poem appear archaic or are intended to aid oral *delivery* rather
than oral composition. One such device is the initial *Hwæt*, often thought to be
a call to gain silence in the hall and translated by Seamus Heaney with what he
calls an Irish "So!". Andreas Haarder gives us a Danish "Ja!" which has the sense
of "OK let's go!", but it is usually feebly translated in English as the archaic
"Lo!" or "Listen". This exclamation begins a number of other works in Old
English including saints' lives such as *Juliana*, *Andreas* and *The Fates of the
Apostles*, works which were definitely composed in written form.

Andreas begins:

Hwæt! We gefrunan   on fyrndagum
twelfe under tunglum   tireadige hæleð,
þeodnes þegnas.[25]

Listen! We have heard tell in olden days of twelve famous heroes beneath
the stars, thanes of the Lord.

---

[23] *Sir Gawain and the Green Knight* 30–36.
[24] Caie 2004, 57–71.
[25] *Andreas* 1–3.

It continues with another oral, formulaic device *we gefrunon* 'we have heard tell [in olden times]', thereby placing the poem in an ancient and so authoritative context.

Beowulf has an almost identical opening:

Hwæt! We Gardena   in geardagum,
þeodcyninga   þrym gefrunon,
hu ða æþelingas   ellen fremedon.[26]

Listen! We have heard tell in olden days of the majesty of the Spear-Danes,
of the kings of that people, how the princes performed courageous deeds.

However *Andreas* with its runic acrostic at the conclusion was definitely a written composition, as was the Old English *Judgement Day II*, a translation of Bede's *De die iudicii* – a poem which begins with a resounding *Hwæt!*

The Old English poem *Widsith* casts light on the art of the poet and composition. It is often called "a poet's poem" and begins [in translation]: "Widsith spoke out, unlocking his store of words, he who had travelled through most of the peoples, nations and tribes upon the earth", concluding:

So the minstrels of men go wandering through many lands as events direct them; they declare their need and give thanks. Always, south or north, they meet one wise in speech, generous in gifts who wishes to exalt his reputation before the tried warriors and to do what is noble, until everything passes away, light and life together. This man wins praise and a noble judgement in this world.

The *scop* was an important thane with a vital role in society, namely he had responsibility for keeping the chief's and other thanes' *lof* and *dom* 'praise and reputation or glory' alive. In *The Fortunes of Men* we hear of the poet who *mid hearpum æt his hlafordes / fotum* sitting 'with harp at his lord's feet', receives treasure, swiftly twists the strings and creates harmony. Widsith is a professional *scop* who visits tribes from Persia and India to Frisia and the land of the Picts: he lists heroes such as Alexander, Caesar, Offa and Attila the Hun, Hrothgar and Hrothulf of *Beowulf* fame and his king is Eadgils of Sweden, who also appears in *Beowulf*. All these people are now famous, he modestly says, because of his poetry.

The *Beowulf* and *Widsith* manuscripts (London, British Library, Cotton Vitellius A XV and the Exeter Book, respectively) are late Anglo-Saxon artefacts, compiled not long before the Norman Conquest. They are books to be read or at least recited from and the *Beowulf* manuscript contains scholarly works such as the prose *Letter of Alexander to Aristotle* and the prose *Marvels of the East* as well as the Old English poem *Judith*. Many Old English works translated from

---

[26] *Beowulf* 1–3.

Latin, such as *The Phoenix* and *Metres of Boethius*, contain identical formulas and stylistic features as those found in poems which are often considered orally composed. I hope to have shown how the use of formulas should not be confused with oral composition. Like variation, repetition, archaisms, circumlocution, digressions, kennings and other subtle and elaborate stylistic effects, the application of formulas was an integral part of the Old English poet's art. The *Beowulf* poet was able to synthesise style with his archaic subject matter and thereby create the greatest of English epics.

Bibliography

Primary sources

Andreas, ed. G. P. Krapp in *The Vercelli Book*. ASPR II. New York 1932.
The Battle of Brunanburh, ed. E. V. K. Dobbie in *Anglo-Saxon Minor Poems*. ASPR IV. New York 1942.
Beowulf, ed. George Jack. Oxford 1994.
Cædmon's Hymn (Northumbrian version), ed. John C. Pope in *Seven Old English Poems*. New York 1966.
Sir Gawain and the Green Knight, eds. J. R. R. Tolkien and E. V. Gordon [revised by N. Davies]. Oxford 1967.

Secondary sources

ALEXANDER, Michael 1983: *Old English Literature*. London.
BRADLEY, S. A. J. 1982: *Anglo-Saxon Poetry*. London, transl.
CAIE, Graham D. 1994: "The shorter heroic verse." In H. Aertsen & R. H. Bremmer jr. (eds.) *Companion to Old English Poetry*, pp. 79–94, Amsterdam.
———— 2004: "'New corn from old fields': The *auctor* and *compilator* in fourteenth-century English literature." *Revista Canaria de Estudois Ingleses*, 47 59–71.
CHASE, Colin 1981: *The Dating of Beowulf*. Toronto.
FRANTZEN, Allen J. 1991: "Writing the unreadable *Beowulf*: 'writan' and 'forwritan', the pen and the sword." *Exemplaria*, 3 327–357.
GODDEN, Malcolm 1991: "Biblical literature: The Old Testament." In M. Godden & Lapidge M. (eds.) *The Cambridge Companion to Old English Literature*, pp. 206–226, Cambridge.
GREENFIELD, Stanley B. 1972: *The Interpretation of Old English Poems*. London.
———— 1986: *A New Critical History of English Literature*. New York.
IRVING, E. B. 1989: *Rereading* Beowulf. Philadelphia.
KIERNAN, Kevin 1996: *Beowulf and the Beowulf Manuscript*. Michigan, revised edition.
LIUZZA, Roy Michael 1995: "On the dating of *Beowulf*." In Peter S. Baker (ed.) *Beowulf: Basic Readings*, pp. 281–302, New York.
POPE, John C. (ed.) 1966: *Seven Old English Poems*. New York.

RENOIR, Alain 1986: "Old English formulas and themes as tools for contextual interpretation." In Phyllis R. Brown, Georgia R. Crampton & Fred C. Robinson (eds.) *Modes of Interpretation in Old English Literature*, p. 65–79, Toronto.

SCRAGG, Donald G. 1991: "The nature of Old English verse." In M. Godden & Lapidge M. (eds.) *The Cambridge Companion to Old English Literature*, pp. 55–70, Cambridge.

WRENN, C. L. (ed.) 1958: *Beowulf with the Finnesburg Fragment*. London, revised edition.

The Scandinavian Medieval Ballad: From Oral Tradition to Written Texts and Back Again

Olav Solberg

S INCE THE MIDDLE of the nineteenth century, Scandinavian ballad scholarship has been preoccupied with the question of the roots of the ballad
genre. When was the ballad introduced in Scandinavia, in which country or countries – and in what way? The Danish ballad scholar Svend
Grundtvig and his contemporaries thought that the ballad came to the Nordic
countries at a very early stage, around 1100, perhaps even earlier. Since then,
ballad scholarship has changed its position and concluded that the ballad is
much younger, in any case not older than the thirteenth century. The Swedish
ballad scholar Bengt R. Jonsson has suggested that the Scandinavian ballad first
came into being at the Norwegian royal court in the 1280s or 1290s. Even
if Jonsson's theory cannot be fully documented, it is in my opinion the most
plausible theory of how and when the ballad was introduced to Scandinavia.
This is not the place to discuss Jonsson's theory in detail, but I will refer to two
of his articles on the matter.[1]

While there has been much debate concerning the origin of the ballad
genre in Scandinavia, there has never been any doubt that the ballad has always
been an oral genre. The standard ballad reference book describes the medieval
ballad in Scandinavia in the following way; it is a definition which is based on
agreement among ballad scholars past and present:

> The medieval ballad in Scandinavia is a genre of orally transmitted
> song that is defined by its form (sometimes couplets with one
> or two burdens, sometimes quatrains with one burden), by its
> narrative content, and by its objective style, the latter characterized
> not least by the frequent use of formulaic expressions and so-called
> "commonplaces". The ballad may, on the basis of these criteria, be
> effectively distinguished from other categories of folksongs which
> lack one or more of these characteristics. In fact, the ballad is one

---

[1] JONSSON 1989; 1991.

of many folksong categories, the common denominators of which are oral transmission and the fact that there is no such thing as an authorized version.[2]

Apparently, in the Middle Ages the ballad also had a dance function, as is still the case in the Faeroe Islands.

It should be pointed out, however, that the Scandinavian ballad is closely related to the romances that were translated at the court of King Hákon Hákonarson and his followers on the Norwegian throne in the thirteenth century – that is, into *written* texts. These texts were Old Norse adaptations from French (Anglo-Norman) originals, translated at the Norwegian court. It seems likely that the ballad poets were inspired by the romances when they were read aloud at the court or elsewhere, and that they chose whichever idea or topic in the romances that appealed to them to make their own *oral* ballads. When the ballad genre was firmly established, motifs and plots from other fields – both literary and nonliterary – were used, for instance from eddic lays, religious legends and folklore. It also seems highly probable that French song genres such as the *rondeau* and the *chanson de toile* inspired the Scandinavian ballad poets, even if this is hard to prove in detail. But in the French writer Jean Renart's romance, *Guillaume de Dole*, probably written in the 1220s, there are song texts that are quite similar to Scandinavian ballads, and it is tempting to assume that there is a connection of some kind.[3]

It did not, however, take long before the oral ballad made its first appearance in writing. Well before King Hákon V and Queen Eufemia married their daughter Ingebjørg to the Swedish Duke Erik in 1312, the queen had commissioned the translation of three romances into Swedish – the so-called *Eufemiavisorna* 'Eufemia's lays', *Hærra Ivan*, *Flores ok Blanzeflor* and *Hærtogher Fredrik*. *Hærra Ivan* is a version of Chrétien de Troyes' *Le chevalier au Lion*, which had already been translated from French into an Old Norse saga in the days of King Hákon Hákonarson. *Flores ok Blanzeflor* had also been translated into Old Norse before, from a French version, whereas *Hærtogher Fredrik* was translated for the first time into a Scandinavian language from German.

According to the manuscripts, *Hærra Ivan* was turned into Swedish verse in 1303, and the other two romances in 1308 and 1312, respectively. There seems to be little reason to doubt the dating of the translations.[4] This means, if Bengt Jonsson's theory about the ballad's emergence at the Norwegian court is correct, that the ballad only existed some 15 or 20 years before it was recorded. The expression recorded is exaggerated, as there is nothing like a complete ballad to be found in *Eufemiavisorna*; but on the other hand, there are many expressions and formulas that must have come from a living ballad tradition. Let me quote two passages from *Hærra Ivan*:

---

[2] JONSSON *et al.* 1978, 14.
[3] *Guillaume de Dole*, 69–71.
[4] WILLIAMS 1999, 5.

Han la þe nat til dagher var lius;
þa kom en præster for þæt hus
ok klappaþe a dyr mæþ finger sin,
baþ hærra Ivan lata sik in:
"Nu ær þær væl time til,
um I mæsso høra vil."[5]

He remained in bed until dawn. Then a priest arrived at the castle and tapped at the door with his finger and asked Sir Ivan to let him in: "Now it is high time, if you want to attend Mass".

[...] mæþ hvitæ hænder ok finger sma;
þe stolta iomfru giorþe sva.
Siþan lot hon honum klæþer fa,
þe rikasta man mæþ øghum sa,
mæþ hvit skin ok skarlakan røþ;
þe giorþo alt hvat þæn iomfru bøþ.[6]

[...] with her white hands and dainty fingers; this is what the fair maiden did. Then she had clothes brought for him, the richest ever seen, of ermine and red scarlet; they did everything the maiden commanded.

One is struck by the modernity and the simplicity of the language in *Hærra Ivan*. There is, in my opinion, a connection between the relatively straightforward language in *Eufemiavisorna* and the ballad; the ballad probably functioned as a kind of a "modernistic" poetry around 1300. Both linguistically and thematically the ballad was quite different from the eddic lays, not to mention skaldic verse, and may have influenced the translator of *Eufemiavisorna*.

There are several typical ballad formulas and ballad line endings, to be found in the two passages – for instance the expression *dagher var lius*, is related to *for þæt hus*. Indeed this is a very common way of telling a ballad story, when the point is to underline that one has to wait for dawn, *lius*, until action can take place. Then the protagonist may leave his castle, his *hus*. Furthermore, the expression *klappaþe a dyr mæþ finger sin*, related to *baþ hærra Ivan lata sik in*, is quite usual in ballads recorded at a much later time. The same goes for formulas like *mæþ hvitæ hænder ok finger sma, þe stolta iomfru* – and *mæþ hvit skin ok skarlakan røþ*. In these formulas we find important aspects of the Scandinavian ballad aesthetics verbalized, such as bright colours, rich clothes and elegant and sophisticated manners.

As demonstrated by David Colbert in his book *The Birth of the Ballad*, the ballad formulas in *Hærra Ivan* and the other two Eufemia romances do not appear in isolation.[7] On the contrary, the formulas are adapted to the motifs

---

[5] *Hærra Ivan* 3269–3274. The translations of *Hærra Ivan* are from the edition, the remaining are my own.
[6] *Hærra Ivan* 4827–4832.
[7] COLBERT 1989, 134–148.

and scenes of the romance in question. For instance, the formulas *dagher var lius* and *for þæt hus*, together with the two following lines, belong to a specific motif or scene that may be called *morning visit*, or perhaps *starting point*. Another important aspect of the ballad formulas in the Eufemia romances is that many of them are narrative or epic in nature. These formulas are not only related to the various events, but make up the central parts of the story itself, and contribute to creating a recognizable ballad style. Also, the so-called ornamental formulas, such as *mæþ hvitæ hænder ok finger sma*, are an intrinsic part of the ballad's mode of expression.[8]

It seems evident that the translator of the Eufemia romances not only must have heard ballads, but in fact must have been well familiar with the ballad genre. We do not know the translator's name. It has been suggested that it might be Peter Algotsson, a well-educated aristocrat who was the Swedish king's chancellor. If so, it would have to have been before he had to flee from Sweden to Norway, together with his brothers. One of them, Folke Algotsson, had abducted a Danish nobleman's fiancée from a nunnery in 1288, and the Swedish king became furious with the whole family. In Norway, King Håkon V gave Peter Algotsson important administrative missions, and even sent him as a diplomat to foreign countries.[9]

In any case, the oral ballad's narrative formulas, as well as the ballad rhymes, must have struck the translator as useful – even necessary – expressions when translating French written texts into written Swedish verse texts. This suggests a relatively close relationship between oral and written art forms at the beginning of the fourteenth century. It also suggests that well-educated aristocrats and ordinary people shared the same oral culture. The introduction of oral ballad formulas was probably facilitated by the knittel verse employed in the Eufemia romances; in many ways parallel to the two-lined ballad stanza, but without refrain and of course not stanzaic.

In the Eufemia romances, there are also many passages that illustrate how a medieval book was normally expected to be read – for instance the scene in *Hærra Ivan* when the protagonist enters the garden and discovers a maiden reading aloud. The nature of the passage seems to be symbolic, underlining the value of learning courtesy by listening to romances. It is a *mise-en-abyme*, telling us that, like the old knight and the fair lady, Ivan, too, should try to improve his manners:

> Þa hærra Ivan a garþin gik
> en gamal riddara han se fik
> hvar han sat ok vilde a lyþa
> hvat en iomfrua las til þyþa.
> Undir honum var bret baldakinna
> þe rikasta þær man matte finna.
> Þe iomfru las þær romanz,

8 HOLZAPFEL 1980, 21–27.
9 FERM 1997, 33–34.

> ena bok man kallar sva a franz.
> En frua þær man vænasta sa
> sat ok þær ok lydde up a
> þe iomfru moþer þær las þe bok;
> hon var baþe høvisk ok klok.[10]

> When Sir Ivan walked into the garden, he saw an old knight who sat and
> listened to a maiden who read aloud. Underneath him a gold brocade was
> spread, the most splendid fabric one could find. The maiden was reading
> a romance, a type of book so called in French. A lady, the fairest one
> could see, also sat there and listened, the mother of the maiden reading
> the book; she was both courteous and wise.

It is possible to identify ballad formulas in the Eufemia romances because the
same expressions are found in ballad recordings from the Renaissance and even
from the nineteenth century. It goes without saying that this demonstrates
a relatively conservative and stable ballad tradition. Even if certain ballads
disappeared through the centuries and were replaced by others, the singers
apparently saw no reason to change the old formulas, at least not all of them,
for new ones. That the ballad tradition was conservative is also demonstrated
by the fact that single words and expressions – not necessarily formulas - were
used by singers in the nineteenth century, even if they did not understand the
meaning of them. In some cases, we can see that formulas were modernized
– for instance the very common expression *slå ut sitt hår*, meaning 'let one's
hair fall to the shoulders'. When a lady lets her hair down, she is eager to find
someone to love, and perhaps get married. In ballad versions from the second
half of the nineteenth century or later, this meaning evidently was not clear
to the ballad singers, so they replaced the verb *slå* with 'comb' - 'combing her
hair'. Some of the singers even changed the verb *slå* for 'sun' - 'sunning her hair',
which is quite far from the original, composed at a time when the idea of sitting
in the sun to get a nice tan did not exist.

According to Milman Parry and Albert B. Lord, who analyzed Homer's
poetic language in the *Iliad* and the *Odyssey* as well as in Yugoslavian folksongs,
a formula is a group of words which is regularly employed under the same
metrical conditions to express a given essential idea. The metrical conditions
are in fact not quite the same in the Eufemia romances and in ballads, even if
they are related, but the definition seems to fit the characteristics of the ballad
genre well enough. Nevertheless, Scandinavian ballads are quite different when
it comes to the question of *how* formulas were employed. The Yugoslavian *singer*
was also a *poet* and a *composer*. The singer of tales was a composer of tales, who
did not memorize the poems, but instead – by means of formulas – recomposed
the poems at every performance. This does not seem to have been the case with
Scandinavian ballad singers, at least not in the nineteenth century. The ballad
singers must have memorized the ballads which they wanted to keep in their

---

[10] *Hærra Ivan* 4769–4780.

repertoires, although the formulas helped the singers to learn the ballads and sing them from memory. According to the ballad scholar Ådel Gjøstein Blom, who analyzed the formulas in Norwegian legendary ballads, most legendary ballads were learnt by memorizing. But it is evident that formulas made it easier to learn ballads by heart, and to hand them down to others.[11]

As far as we know, it took some two hundred years before ballads were recorded from tradition on a large scale. This happened as a result of the antiquarian search for old heroic poems during the Renaissance, especially in Denmark and Sweden – or at least the search is best documented in these countries. Furthermore, it became fashionable among the nobility to collect ballads and other song texts from oral tradition – perhaps also from flysheets – and in 1591 the Danish historian, Anders Sørensen Vedel, published *It Hundrede vduaalde Danske Viser*. In the preface, Vedel states that ballads are pleasant and useful, both to *read* and to *listen to*. They tell of dramatic events that happened long ago, and of remarkable persons; some good and some bad. Furthermore, from listening to ballads one may learn how people lived in the old days, which is very interesting in itself. Not the least, says Vedel, the rich and colourful ballad language gives the ballad poems a much higher quality than modern poetry.[12]

The first recorded Renaissance ballad text of any length however, seven stanzas in all, was recorded in Norway around 1500, by a wealthy landowner by the name of Mattis Nilsson. This ballad, of which there are later recordings in Danish, is traditionally called *The Knight in Stag's Disguise*. It is a ballad of chivalry, and tells the story of a knight who proposes to a lady, but is turned down. He then disguises himself as a stag, and the lady shows her affection for what she believes is a real deer. He removes his disguise, which comes as a shock to her – but she promises to marry him if he is able to find a treasure that her father has buried. No treasure exists, however, and while the knight is busily digging, the lady locks herself in her castle and tells the knight to go away forever. It is the seven opening stanzas of the ballad that are recorded from Norwegian oral tradition:

Drømth haffuer mik om jomfrwer i alle naath.

1. Thet wor herræ Peder,
   han taler till swene tw:
   "Kwnde i mik stolz Ose-lille
   meth fager talen fa?"
   – Drømt haffuer mik om jomfrwen alle nath.
2. Borth tha gynge the panszer-swene
   alz ther, stolz Ose-lille wor:
   "Myn herræ han holler weth sneke-bordh,
   han will alth haffue idhert taall."
3. Swaredhe ok stolz Ose-lille,
   hwn swaredhe ther-till eth ordh:

[11] BLOM 1985, 190–202.
[12] VEDEL, *It Hundrede vduaalde Danske Viser*, 13–23.

> "Thet ær ængen jomfrw-seth
> ath gange till snecke-bordh.
> 4. Theth ær ængen jomfrw-seth,
>   ath gange till snecke-bordh:
>   henne folgher hiem bode lasth oc skam,
>   swaa manthet hodigsos-ord."
> 5. Ather komme the pantzser-swene,
>   the sagde ther herræ i-fraa:
>   "Icke kwnde wij stoldz Ose-lille
>   meth fager talen faa."
> 6. "Kwnde i icke stoldz-Ose lille
>   meth fager ordhen faa:
>   tha skal jek fare i myn hiorte-ham,
>   swaa wel skal jek henne faa."
> 7. Theth een ham wor aff hwidit sølff,
>   thet annith aff rødhe gwldh:
>   thet wor herre Pedher,
>   han speller swaa frydhe-fuldh. [13]

I have dreamt of maidens the whole night through. 1. It was Sir Peter, commanding his two armoured squires: "Could you bring me proud Aase with fair words?" I have dreamt of the maiden all night. 2. The armoured squires went away to seek proud Aase at her place: "My lord is waiting at the ship's side, he wants to talk to you". 3. Proud Aase gave them her answer, she said the following words: "It is not the custom of an honourable maiden to go to the ship's side. 4. It is not the custom of an honourable maiden to go to the ship's side. Both disgrace and shame will follow her then, and many contemptful words". 5. Back came the armoured squires, and told their lord what had happened: "We were not able to bring you proud Aase with our fair words". 6. "Could you not bring me proud Aase with your fair words: then I will put on my stag's disguise, easily I will get her then". 7. The one horn was made of white silver, the other of of red gold. It was Sir Peter, he plays so full of pleasure.

Svend Grundtvig did not know that the transcription was made in Norway, and when he published the second volume of *Danmarks gamle Folkeviser*, these seven stanzas (the A-version) were printed as a Danish text. And the written text does indeed look like a Danish one, even if there are some typical Norwegian words, like the name of the female protagonist *Aase* (*Else* in later Danish versions), the expressions *fager talen* and *fager ordhen* 'fair words', and perhaps most significantly, *hodigsosordh* 'contempful words, words of shame'. In the middle of the nineteenth century, the linguist Ivar Aasen registered this word in Norwegian dialects as *haadingsord*, its equivalent in Old Norse being *háðungar-orð* or *háðingsorð*. Apparently, the word was not easily understood in Danish,

---

[13] *Ridderen i Hjorteham*, Cf. HJORTH 1976.

and was replaced by alternatives like *hedings-ordt* (the C-version) or *hadings ord* (the E-version). *The Knight in Stag's Disguise* would, of course, have been sung or recited in a Norwegian dialect, not very different from the way other Norwegian ballads were sung in the nineteenth century. At that time, however, the ballad collectors were specifically looking for texts in a Norwegian idiom, texts that could prove the connection between Old Norse literature and the nineteenth century tradition.

The main reason why this early version of *The Knight in Stag's Disguise* was transcribed in an idiom close to Danish is that around 1500, the Old Norse language was rapidly disintegrating as a *written* idiom. Danish was taking its place. The writer – probably the manuscript owner himself – might, of course, have recorded the *oral text* in the local dialect. Why did he not do this? We know that the writer was not only a wealthy landowner, but also was engaged in the administration of law – to be precise, he was what is called in Norwegian a *lagrettemann*, and consequently accustomed to writing. To the manuscript owner, written language must have had priority over a spoken or sung local dialect. When the person engaged in writing has no particular reason to bring the influence of the oral text into focus, this may seem natural enough. But in many cases, it will prove difficult to avoid the oral text altogether. I quote a stanza from a Norwegian transcription from 1612 – *Friarferdi til Gjøtland* – where the oral text clearly comes to the surface:

> Saa er hussiit indenn thiill
> som jomffruenn inde sider
> det gliemmer guld j kioriaa veg
> det er jomffruenns lydt.[14]

> This is how the house looks inside, where the maiden is sitting, gold is
> shining on each wall, such is the maiden's complexion too.

In 1612, Danish was definitely the only possible written idiom in Norway in addition to Latin, of course, and the writer of the stanza tries hard to express himself accordingly. He does not always succeed, however, which is evident in the unfortunate rhymes in lines two and four – *sider* 'is sitting', and *lydt* 'complexion'. In Old Norse as well as in the local dialect, the oral text would have been something like *sit/set* and *lit/let* – in other words a perfect rhyme. Also the pronoun *kioriaa* (from Old Norse *hverjum* 'each') looks rather peculiar in its linguistic surroundings. In fact, the writer could easily have translated the line into Danish: *det gliemmer guld i hver den veg*. It comes as a surprise, then, that the oral text is easier to detect in the transcription from 1612, than in the one from around 1500. The reason may be simply that the writer of the 1612 text was less accustomed to writing, or perhaps that he – possibly *she* – was deliberately trying to preserve some oral expressions that sounded right.

In Iceland, the collection of ballads started around the middle of the seventeenth century. The first collector, Gissur Sveinsson, was probably influenced

---

[14] *Friarferdi til Gjøtland* st. 3.

by the example of Anders Sørensen Vedel. According to Vésteinn Ólason, most ballads were brought to Iceland either from western Scandinavia, that is Norway or the Faeroe Islands, or from Denmark. Because the old Icelandic written language did not deteriorate as the old language in Norway did, the imported – and oral – ballads were translated into Icelandic, but not in quite the same way as written literature. Many of the words and sentences were allowed to stand unchanged. As Vésteinn Ólason writes, people evidently "did not bother to give [the imported ballads] a completely Icelandic appearance; this language was fully comprehensible, and probably even took on a slightly poetic air because of its connection with exotic subjects".[15]

Therefore it comes as no surprise that when ballads were collected in the sixteenth and seventeenth centuries, the existing written language in the area in question functioned as a model for the transcription. In Norway the written language was Danish, and consequently ballads handed down from tradition were recorded in Danish – while ballads in Iceland were recorded in Icelandic. One of the interesting things is that many of the peculiarities of the oral ballad language – such as loan words and other linguistic features – were accepted in writing. This suggests that the collectors looked upon the ballad as a distinct literary genre, with qualities of its own.

One of the most influential ballad books in Denmark and Norway was probably that of the linguist Peder Syv, whose edition was published in 1695. This book, which contained the one hundred ballads published by Vedel in 1591 with the addition of another hundred, became very popular. It was reprinted at least three times during the eighteenth century, and many of the ballad singers in Norway not only knew the book, but owned it themselves. Peder Syv's book of two hundred ballads made a solid impact on the Norwegian ballad tradition – to the extent that collectors in the early 1840s suspected that no real Norwegian ballad tradition existed at all. Jørgen Moe, one of the early collectors, says that when he was told of the ballad tradition in Telemark, he took it for granted that these ballads were no more than translations, or at best variations and improvisations in the local idiom of the songs in Syv's collection. Moe then adds that he later found his suspicions to be wrong. There certainly was a considerable number of ballads borrowed from Syv in the Norwegian tradition, but also a great number of original Norwegian ballads:

> Jeg formodede, at dette Viseforraad ei bestod i Andet end Over-
> sættelser eller høist Afændringer og Omdigtninger i Folkesproget
> af Viserne i Syvs Samling, som jeg vidste var alminnelig kjendt
> i hine Dalfører. Jeg overbeviste mig imidlertid efterhaanden om,
> hvormeget jeg heri havde feilet. Vistnok synges i Thelemarken en
> heel Deel Viser af "Kjæmpeboka", stykkeviis overførte i Folkets
> Mundart, men ved Siden af disse har man et meget stort Antal ori-

[15] Vésteinn Ólason 1982, 97–98.

ginale Viser, til hvilke man oftere finder Pendanter hos Svenskerne end hos de Danske.[16]

In the summer of 1847, Jørgen Moe collected ballads from an elderly man, whose name was Bendik Ånundsson Felland. According to Moe, this singer knew most of Peder Syv's book by heart. In fact, he knew it so well that he could tell immediately whether a certain song was to be found there or not. A brief look at Bendik Felland's repertoire shows that he was indeed familiar with Syv's edition. As an example, I quote the first stanza from Felland's version of *Liti Kjersti*, a ballad which tells the story of a woman forced to return to her mountain husband, recorded by Sophus Bugge in 1857. This stanza is quite similar to the opening stanza in Syv's version:
Felland:

> Liti Kjersti og hendes modir.
> – Hvem bryder løvet af lindegren –
> dei leika gulltavl uppå bori.
> – Sjell træder hun duggen af jorden –[17]

Little Kjersti and her mother. Who breaks the leaf of the linden branch – they played at golden chess on the table. She herself treads the dew from the ground.

Syv:

> Liden Kirsten og hendes moder
> Hvo bryder løven af de træer,
> De syde de silke-huer.
> Saa træder hun duggen af jorden.[18]

Little Kirsten and her mother. Who breaks the leaves of the trees – they were sewing silken hoods. She then treads the dew from the ground.

There can be little doubt that Bendik Felland borrowed this stanza from Syv, along with the refrain; but on the other hand, his version does not contain other borrowed stanzas. However, in Felland's version there are quite a few formulas and expressions in Danish, which clearly show the impact that writing had on this singer's repertoire. If we are to believe Jørgen Moe's statement about Felland, we should expect even more likeness between his version and Syv, but it may well be that Moe and other collectors did not take down ballads that were more or less copies from Syv.

It is clear that writing influenced the ballad tradition, and the nineteenth century collectors were, of course, aware of this. What most of them – at least the Norwegian collectors – seem to have preferred, was a tradition without

---

[16] Moe 1964, 52–53.
[17] *Liti Kjersti* st. 1.
[18] *Liden Kirsten* st. 1.

traces of booklore, or at least with as few traces of written culture as possible. They seem to have had an idea of a primary, oral text still within reach, in the sense that it could be recreated, and of singers who handed down their versions without tampering with them. For that reason, nineteenth century collectors did not like singers who improvised, but preferred the type of singers who performed their ballads with no, or only few, variations. For instance, the philologist and ballad collector Sophus Bugge writes that some of the singers were unreliable and not be trusted.[19] In a way, the collectors thought of oral texts as something not very different from texts in writing. There can be no doubt that the attitude of the collectors was felt by the singers, even if this is difficult to prove. However, I think the reason that surprisingly few jocular and bawdy ballads were recorded has more to do with the collectors' prudery, as many of the singers probably felt too embarrassed to perform them.[20]

It is, of course, impossible to say how a ballad recorded in the nineteenth century would have sounded three or five hundred years before. As already mentioned, the formulas definitely seem to have been a stable element in the tradition, but the ballad stories themselves may have changed. Some stories simply disintegrated and disappeared, others were shortened or embroidered upon. If a ballad was composed to depict a certain historical event, this depiction would tend to become more general and less specific, as the ballad was handed down from generation to generation. A political conflict would, for instance, develop into a love story, or a story of revenge. This is why the so-called historical ballads are not really historical after all. As a rule, the only historical information in them are the names of the protagonists.

From the beginning of the ballad genre's existence, there were probably ballads of different kinds: jocular ballads as well as ballads of chivalry, religious ballads as well as ballads of the supernatural. Some ballads were more closely related to written sources than others, and therefore more complicated structurally, for instance the ballads derived from the Old Norse *Þiðriks saga*, and from the romances in vogue at the Norwegian court. The ballad's success was due to its linguistic and thematic modernity; it was a new and popular kind of poetry, expressing romantic and fashionable feelings in a straightforward way. From the 1280s until the nineteenth century the ballad genre has been remarkably stable and long-lived. It is important, however, to distinguish between the ballad's *creative period*, which is not so long, and the much longer period of tradition.

[19] BLOM 1982, 127.
[20] SOLBERG 1993, 16–17.

Bibliography

Primary sources

Friarferdi til Gjøtland, ed. Ådel Gjøstein Blom & Olav Bø in *Norske balladar*: 257–261. Oslo 1981.

Guillaume de Dole, ed. Félix Lecoy. Paris 1979.

Hærra Ivan, ed. Marianne E. Kalinke, *Norse Romance III: Hærra Ivan, Arthurian archives* vol. 5. Cambridge 1999.

Liti Kjersti, ed. Ådel Gjøstein Blom & Olav Bø in *Norske balladar*: 54–56. Oslo 1981.

Liden Kirsten, ed. Peder Syv in *200 Viser om Konger, Kemper oc Andre*: 524–525. Copenhagen 1787.

Ridderen i hjorteham, ed. Svend Grundtvig in *Danmarks gamle Folkeviser* II: 220. København 1854–1856.

VEDEL, *It hundrede vduaalde Danske Viser*, ed. Paul V. Rubow: *Anders Sørensen Vedels Folkevisebog*. København 1926–1927.

Secondary sources

BLOM, Ådel Gjøstein (ed.) 1982: *Norske mellomalderballadar*. Oslo.

BLOM, Ådel Gjøstein 1985: *Norsk legendevisemateriale. En muntlig overlevert diktning*. Oslo.

COLBERT, David 1989: *The Birth of the Ballad: The Scandinavian Medieval Genre*. Stockholm.

FERM, Olle 1997: "Introduction." In Olle Ferm & Bridget Morris (eds.) *Master Golyas: The Transformation of a Clerical Satire*, p. 11–41, Stockholm.

HJORTH, Poul Lindegård 1976: "Linköping-håndskriftet og 'Ridderen i hjorteham'." *Danske studier*, pp. 5–35.

HOLZAPFEL, Otto 1980: *Det balladeske: Fortællemåden i den ældre episke folkevise*. Odense.

JONSSON, Bengt R. 1989: "Bråvalla och Lena: Kring balladen SMB 56." *Sumlen: Årsbok för vis- och folkmusikforskning*, pp. 49–166.

———— 1991: "Oral literature, written literature: The ballad and Old Norse genres." In *The Ballad and Oral Literature, Harvard English Studies*, vol. 17, pp. 139–170, London.

JONSSON, Bengt R., SOLHEIM, Svale & JERSILD, Margareta (eds.) 1978: *The Types of the Scandinavian Medieval Ballad: A Descriptive Catalogue*. Oslo.

MOE, Jørgen 1964: "Indberetning fra Cand. theol. Jørgen Moe om en af ham i Maanederne Juli og August 1847 med offentligt Stipendium foretagen Reise gjennem Thelemarken og Sætersdalen, for at samle Folkedigtninger." In *Tradisjonsinnsamling på 1800-tallet*, Norsk Folkeminnelags skrifter, pp. 47–88, Oslo.

SOLBERG, Olav 1993: *Den omsnudde verda: Ein studie i dei norske skjemteballadane*. Oslo.

VÉSTEINN ÓLASON 1982: *The Traditional Ballads of Iceland*. Reykjavík.

WILLIAMS, Henrik 1999: "Introduction." In Marianne E. Kalinke (ed.) *Norse Romance III: Hærra Ivan, Arthurian archives*, vol. V, p. 3–9, Cambridge.

Apocalypse Now? The *Draumkvæde* and Visionary Literature

JONAS WELLENDORF

A FAIRLY RECENT mammoth article on the dating of *Draumkvæde* (*TSB* B 31, *NMB* 54) by Bengt R. Jonsson, a prominent scholar of balladry, sets off by stating the fact that *Draumkvæde* has been studied, analysed, and commented upon more intensively than any other Scandinavian ballad, and that many of the contributors to this discussion lack a more general familiarity with the ballad genre and its specific problems and methods.[1] I will begin by admitting that this description fits the present contribution only too well. It is therefore not without doubts and hesitation that I have decided to venture out into the weird and wonderful world of *Draumkvæde* scholarship.

But first a few words for the uninitiated about the nature and content of *Draumkvæde*. The ballad was discovered in Telemark in the early 1840s. A sexton of Vinje wrote the earliest preserved version (I).[2] This version is not recorded directly from oral tradition, but compiled from a range of informants and is a conflation of several ballads.[3] The ballad is, however, thought to be much older than the 1840s, although its exact age is unknown. Attempts at dating the ballad are numerous; but suggestions that have not only been proposed by individual scholars, but also accepted by other scholars are significantly fewer. Datings that have met some approval are ca. 1300, the late Middle Ages, and the period of the Counter Reformation.

Other recordings followed the first; most notably one dictated by Maren Ramskeid (II) and two dictated by Anne Lillegaard (V & VI). The versions of these two informants are generally regarded as the best versions and together they form the nucleus of the most successful of the subsequent reconstructions. These reconstructions were felt to be necessary because one saw in the preserved recordings of *Draumkvæde* the ruins of something far greater than the scattered fragments preserved. A number of reconstructions exist, but the most famous is the fifty-two-stanza-long reconstruction of Moltke Moe from around the turn

---

[1] JONSSON 1996.
[2] Roman numerals refer to the number attributed to the individual recordings in *NMB*.
[3] E.g. *NF* 4, 10 and 89.

of the twentieth century;[4] the latest is that of Magne Myhren from 2002.[5] The differences between these two reconstructions are considerable as are the differences between them and the original recordings, even though the reconstruction of Myhren sticks closer to what is commonly regarded as the core version of the ballad, the thirty-stanza-long version of Ramskeid. The original recordings vary in length: the longest covers seventy-four stanzas, those from Lillegaard twenty-four and twenty-two stanzas, while the greater part of the remaining recordings is much shorter. The total number of written records of *Draumkvæde* directly from oral tradition surpasses one hundred, but only fourteen of these contain more than nine stanzas.

Because of these differences it is virtually impossible to give a summary of the ballad, but according to common opinion it begins with the following framework: a young man, Olav, falls asleep on Christmas Eve and sleeps until Epiphany, i.e. thirteen days. He rides to church to tell what he has dreamt during his long sleep.[6] The exact content of his dream and the order in which he experiences the various parts is a matter of dispute because of the divergences between the main versions and the rest of the versions in general.

Even though the story-line of the ballad is not altogether coherent it was soon realised that these orally transmitted accounts of Olav's dream had some connection to the widespread and immensely popular medieval genre of visionary literature.[7] The next thing that happened, to make a long story short, was that Molkte Moe read the most important visions, and 'reconstructed' *Draumkvæde* in accordance with the knowledge he had gained from his readings of how texts belonging to this genre were constructed. The result was the *Draumkvæde* most Norwegians nowadays are familiar with, but the choices made by Moe were highly subjective, and any other scholar would no doubt have made a significantly different reconstruction. Moe's revision of the poem was quite extensive, and in fact only a single stanza of the fifty-two of which his reconstruction consists is verbatim identical with a stanza that can be found in the original manuscripts.[8] The recent reconstruction of Myhren is more sober than that of Moe in that it sticks relatively close to a single text, but he, too, cuts and pastes from the two other core versions. Myhren makes the following postulate regarding the three versions he builds upon:

---

[4] Reprinted in MOE 1927, 199–208.

[5] Bø & MYHREN 2002, 7–12.

[6] This framework is largely held in the third person, but from hereon the viewpoint shifts from a narrator to Olav himself, and the rest of the ballad is held more or less in the first person. This shift of viewpoint is quite common in the genre of visions even though there are visions held largely in the third person. See Tableau VII in CAROZZI 1994, 521 for a survey of the Latin material. *Visio Godeschalci* is supposedly recorded twice from oral tradition and extant as a first person narrative (the B-text) and as a third person narrative (the A-text).

[7] The bibliography by GARDINER 1993 lists 64 visions from medieval Western Europe, but this number is far from complete. In the terminology of DINZELBACHER 1981 this kind of vision belongs to 'Type I'.

[8] BARNES 1974, 13.

He who wishes to examine these recordings need [...] not go beyond the tradition itself; i.e. there is no reason to use Old English
or Old Norse writings or Old Norse medieval literature translated
from Latin as the main foundation of an analysis. These three
sources [i.e. the three core recordings] can be understood in light
of domestic tradition and Norwegian language [*my translation*].[9]

I do not agree. The remaining part of this paper will, I hope, show that it
is crucial for an understanding of the ballad to see it in light of the genre of
visionary literature. The position I have adopted is the traditional one, and
the question that has been posed most frequently is: 'How does *Draumkvæde*
correspond with the genre of visionary literature?' In order not to tread too
closely in the footsteps of others I have chosen not to answer this question,
but to turn it upside-down, and ask how it differs from visionary literature as
we know it from the medieval tradition.[10] I have chosen to elaborate on two
characteristic disagreements only. My general ideological point of departure is
that the visions were more or less based on real experiences, and that they were
believed to be so by their audience as well, even though most visions surely had
their sceptics.

The guide

Aeneas is led through the underworld by the sibyl and his father, Dante through
Hell by Vergil, and Garborg's Veslemøy through Helheimen by a volve. So, too,
in the authentic visionary literature is the guide indispensable. The visionary
never walks alone but always has a guide to show him the way.[11] The guide
interprets the meaning of the various sights in the beyond, and thus ensures
that the audience makes the intended interpretation. This interpretation is most
often given in the form of an informative dialogue between the visionary and
his guide and follows the basic pattern of question and answer. The guide is
also of importance because the visionary would not stand a chance against the
servants of Hell alone. One of the returning topoi of the genre is indeed that
the angelic guide abandons the soul of the visionary for a short moment in the
Otherworld;[12] and left to its own devices without protection the soul almost

---

[9] "Den som vil granska desse oppskriftene, tarv [...] ikkje gå utom sjølve tradisjonen; dvs at det er
ingen grunn til bruka gamalengelsk og norrøn dikting og norrøn mellomalderlitteratur omsett frå
latin til hovud-grunnlag for ein analyse. Desse tri kjeldene kan ein forstå i ljos av heimleg fråsegn
og norsk språk". Bø & MYHREN 2002, 60–61.

[10] MORTENSSON-EGNUND 1927, 12–13 presents a list of divergences from the genre as well: "1.
Skildring av overgangen, døri, frå det medvitelege til visjonen og kjenslune som kjem over ein
då (såleis som der er i „Solarljod"). 2. Skildring av millomverdi fyrr ein når brui, jordhimmelen
eller Jotunheimen. 3. Skildring av langsynet langt burte mot det målet som gjev motvekt mot det
nærmaste stygge og leide. 4. Rikare skildring av Helvete og Paradis, og attvending til fødesheimen.
5. Når der skal vera ein bolk til kvar av dei 13 dagane, so er det sume som vanta. 6. Fleire umkvede.
Hev det vori eit serskilt umkvede til kvar bolk?"

[11] Exceptions to this rule are few, but one is *Visio Bernoldi*. Bernoldus only has a guide for a smaller
part of his journey.

[12] For example in *Visio Baronti*, *Visio Drycthelmi*, *Visio Karoli Crassi* and *Visio Tnugdali*.

falls prey to the ever-eager emissaries of the King of Darkness. An example of this is found in *Drycthelms leizla*:

> og þa hvarf mier minn leidtoge enn eg stod eftter å backanum eirnsamann, þa vard eg ögurlega hræddur, og vissa eg ei huad eg skylldi til giøra, edur huọrt eg skylldi vykja minne gøngu, edur huorn enda þetta skylldi hafa, og ei huxadi eg annad enn eg mundi þar ofann J fara, heyrda eg nærre mier họrmulegt kall andanna edur salnanna, huorjar þar voru so họrmulega dregnar af Diøflunum enn fiøndunnar spottandi hrundu þeim ofann J Viti, Enn þeir ohrejnu andar køfudu vpp af vnderdiupenu vtblasandi af nọsum og munne brennanda elldi ódaun og lóga og ætludu ad samre svipan mig ad taka med elldlegum tøngum, og J þeirre minne hrædslu kom leidtogi minn, enn þeir hrucku aller nidur J pittenn undann, med grimmre røddu, og þegar tok af mier allann ótta[13]

> Then my guide disappeared, and I was left alone. I became terribly frightened and did not know what to do or where to go or how this would end, and I could not think of anything else than that I would fall down [in the mouth of Hell]. Nearby I heard the distressed calls of the souls that were dragged away by devils and hurled down in the punishments by the mocking enemies. The unclean spirits emerged from the lower Hell blowing fire, stench, and flames out of their nostrils and mouths. They planned to grab hold of me in this very instant with their glowing tongs. And as I stood there struck by terror my guide returned and they withdrew to the pit with foul shouts. At the same time my horror vanished...

The Old Norse term for a vision of this kind, *leizla*, also underlines the importance of the guide. *Leizla* seems to be an Old Norse neologism. It is made up of the same verbal root as *leiða* 'to lead'. Thus the angelic guide literally leads, in some visions even drags, the soul through the Otherworld. Now what about the guide in *Draumkvæde*?[14] In fact there is no guide. Olav walks all by himself through the Otherworld, even though he meets the Mother of God in some of the versions. But her function is not that of a guide: she gives him a new pair of shoes (V, VI, VII) or asks him to proceed to where the judgement will take place (II).[15] On his journey Olav never appears to be threatened by unclean spirits, and Olav himself spells out the proper interpretation of the

---

[13] *Drycthelms leizla* p. 149–150.

[14] Moe 1927, 259 writes in his commentary to *Draumkvæde* that some variants utilise a *dei*, 'they', who leads the visionary, which seems to indicate that some versions have not one but two or more guides, but none of the published variants contain this word in the right context. The nearest one comes to a guide in the published variants is in XV 4–5: "De fyste va me i utext/ me gjek ivi dynne-tra/ sode va mi skarlagenskappe/ å neglanne af kvor mi tå.// De fyste me va i utext/ eg gjek ivi dynne ring/ sonde va mi skarllagenskåpe/ å naglan af kvor min fing". But this text, number K5 in the edition of Barnes, seems, according to Barnes 1974, 79, to rely on the printed edition of *NF*.

[15] Other versions where he sees her or she recognises him are: XV 17, XVIII 10.

various torments for the audience. The basic structure of such stanzas is two
verses with description and two with explanation:[16]

> Der såg æg dei ormane tvei
> dei hoggje kvorare i kjæfte
> å dæ va syskjenboni i denni heimen
> dei mone kvorare ægte.[17]

> Next I came on serpents twain, each other's tails they chewed: cousins
> they who in this life were joined in marriage lewd.[18]

Sometimes the description occupies all four verses of a stanza and no interpretation is provided, such as in the following:[19]

> Kiæm eg mæg at manno dei
> de blei mæg då fyste ve
> lite bån i fanie bar
> giek i jori alt unde kne.[20]

> I saw a young man trudge around, — the first that I did see — he bore a
> boy-child in his arms and sank in earth to's knee.[21]

Here no interpretation of the stanza is provided, and the audience must assign
the proper meaning to the scene themselves. How can they know what the
intended interpretation is? They cannot, and neither can we, except that we
can surmise that the original sin involved children in one way or another. An
informative angelic guide would have come in handy here. There is, however,
another resort: the visionary can engage in dialogue with the souls in the other
world. This device is used to great effect by Dante in his *Commedia*, but it also
occurs in some 'real' visions (examples are *Visio monachi de Eynsham* composed
in 1197 and *Visio Bernoldi* from the ninth century).[22] In such a dialogue the
visionary, instead of asking the guide as usual, asks the tormented souls why
they suffer as they do or, alternatively, the tormented souls declare their sins on
their own initiative. One recording of *Draumkvæde* follows this last principle;
the stanza following the stanza which mentions the men sunk in earth to their
knees is in direct speech:

---

[16] A variation on this pattern is found in XIII 8–11, where a description occupying a whole stanza is
followed by an interpretation that also occupies a whole stanza. This pattern is repeated once.

[17] *NMB* 54 II st. 10.

[18] Trans. LIESTØL 1946, 14 st. 43.

[19] This stanza is found in five versions, but the wording changes considerably: III 3+4, V 8, VI 10, XI
26, XII 4.

[20] *NMB* 54 V st. 8.

[21] LIESTØL 1946, 13 st. 38.

[22] When conversation does occur it is often a soul that begs the visionary to deliver a message to those
left behind or asks for prayers for his soul to relieve his torment. As in *Visio Godeschalci* A 52, B 23.

Eg ha' meg eigong eitt lite bån
eg ville 'kje mæ dæ kanne
derfor må eg i denne heimen
lie den store vande.[23]

I once had a little child; I would not acknowledge it as mine, because of
this I suffer the great torment in this (i.e. the other) world.

Because the soul told us, we now know that this punishment is intended for
those who would not acknowledge their paternity to a child. But this is the
only stanza I have found in the entire *Draumkvæde* corpus that contains an
example of interaction between Olav and other souls. This single stanza makes
us wonder whether the almost absolute absence of personal contact between
the visionary and the other souls is due to the fortuitousness of transmission,
or whether this was once a typical feature of *Draumkvæde* which has been
muddled up by the singer of this otherwise very forgettable seven-stanza-long
variant with the number XII. No definite answers can be given in this parlour
game, but the conventions of the genre demand an explanation of the torments,
and to let the tormented soul speak for itself is a way to compensate for the
missing guide. Another compensational strategy is followed by Mortensson-
Egnund who introduces a guide in his own reconstruction of the poem. In his
commentary he underlines the importance of the guide and praises the way in
which the guide is introduced in the text, but he does not inform his readers
that the guide is in fact his own invention.[24]

The Notion of Time

In our worldly universe time passes incessantly, and it will continue to do so
until the end of time. Beyond the grave lies eternity, but nonetheless time passes
there as well, and the souls of the eternally damned are, according to the fourth
redaction of *Visio Pauli* (p. 79), granted a respite once a week lasting from
Saturday afternoon until Monday morning. So even in eternity time passes, but
not without an end. All the souls in the Otherworld, except those in the lower
Hell, look forward to the end of time and the second coming of Christ when
they will be rejoined with their bodies and enter Heaven. In visionary literature
it is, however, the Otherworld at its present stage that is in focus, i.e. the now
in the hereafter.

In the Middle Ages the concept of two judgements was current: one minor,
the individual or particular which took place right after death, and one major,
the universal at the end of time. The visionary might experience individual
judgements, and the souls he encounters in the Otherworld have all gone
through some kind of judgement before the visionary meets them, but the
visionary never experiences the final judgement. The end of time is the subject

---

[23] *NMB* 54 XII st. 5.
[24] Mortensson-Egnund 1927, 5.

of other genres such as the apocalyptic revelations, mystical visions, homilies, theological treatises and scriptural commentaries. The visions of Heaven and hell concern themselves with a 'now' in the Otherworld, which corresponds to the historical 'now' in the present world where the body of the visionary lies.[25]

Is this also the case with *Draumkvæde*? Well, this has been a matter of dispute. Scholars well-versed in visionary literature argue that *Draumkvæde* deals with the contemporary Otherworld and see the judgement scene depicted at the end of Maren Ramskeid's version as a description of the individual judgement,[26] whereas others readily accept that the ballad describes the final judgement.[27] The prelude to the judgement scene, the lining up of the two hosts, is described near the end of *Draumkvæde* in Ramskeid's version but somewhere in the middle in the variants of Lillegaard. The angelic host is led by the archangel Michael who is followed by Christ, whereas a certain Grutte Gråskjæggje (as it is spelled in II st. 23), often interpreted as the devil, leads the hellish host. Ramskeid continues:

> Dæ va St Saale Mechael
> han blæs i Luren den lange
> aa no sko alle Synde-Sjæline
> fram fe Domen stande.
>
> Men daa skolv alle Synde Sjæline
> som Aaspelauv for Vinde
> aa kvor den, kvor den Sjæl der va
> dei gret for Syndine sine.
> I Broksvalin—
>
> Og det var St. sále Mikkjel
> han vóg med skálevigt
> sá vóg han alle syndesjælene
> hen til Jesum Krist.[28]

> It was St. Michael, lord of souls, he blew his trumpet clear: «And now must every living soul to judgment forth appear!» Then every sinful soul did shake like aspens in the wind, and every single soul there was wept sore for every sin. It was St. Michael, lord of souls, he weighed them fair and even, — he weighed in scales the sinful souls away to Christ in Heaven.[29]

---

[25] GUREVICH 1992, 83 argues that "the vision [of Bernoldus] takes place in its own time where the present and the future do not form a linear chronological plane but are united in one mythological continuum" (see also DUTTON 1994, 190 on this point), but this is the exception, not the rule.

[26] Examples are MOE 1927, 282 ff. and DINZELBACHER 1980, 93.

[27] BLOM 1971, 267–268; JONSSON 1996, 81 ff.; BØ & MYHREN 2002, 40–46. The middle course is chosen by LIESTØL 1946, 37–38, who, like me, considers the judgement scene a depiction of the final judgement, and supposes that it replaced a depiction of an individual judgement during the oral transmission of the ballad.

[28] *K1* 26–28

[29] Trans. LIESTØL 1946, 13 st. 35–37.

I tend to agree with those who think that this is indeed intended as a description of the final judgement.[30] One of my reasons for this is the size of the hosts; in the visions where we witness an individual judgement, as in *Visio Thurkilli* and *Visio Fursei*, the two sides never roll out their heaviest guns, but the matter is dealt with by Michael or, at a lower administrative level, by some angels and a few emissaries from Hell. Furthermore, the focus of the ballad is not on the individual souls, but on all the souls, even though the poem only mentions the souls of the sinners. One problem, however, is that the three stanzas describing the judgement of the souls are *only* found in the version by Ramskeid, and the last of them is even added in the manuscript at a later stage than the remaining text (we can also notice that the orthography is different).[31] Lillegaard only describes the hosts riding from north and south and there is no indication that she saw this as a prelude to a judgement, be it a particular or the universal.

I have pointed out two ways in which the visionary ballad *Draumkvæde* differs from visionary literature in general: 1) The lack of a guide, and 2) The enlarged perspective of time. Now, what to make of these deviances? We can say that the *Draumkvæde* does not belong to the genre of visionary journeys through Heaven and Hell in a strict sense, but that would simply be to follow the line of least resistance. A more rewarding path is to accept that *Draumkvæde* does in fact belong to this genre even though it contains features we usually do not find in such texts, and then try to account for these deviances to the best of our ability.

The following argument requires us to endorse one of the datings that have been proposed for the ballad, but the choice is not an easy one. Any dating of *Draumkvæde* must take the genre of visionary literature as well as the genre of balladry into consideration, but for chronological reasons it is impossible to satisfy the demands of both groups of texts at the same time. The visionary genre seems to have been fully developed before the eighth century and its grande finale is 1206. From this point in time the genre more or less stops being productive.[32] A dating between 800 and 1200 is, however, far too early for the genre of balladry to come into consideration. Even so, we have to consider the possibility that the content of the ballad (i.e. the vision it narrates) can be significantly older than the form in which it is narrated. The age of the genre of visions as well as its *floruit* tempts me to follow Jonsson who dates the genre of balladry to the end of the thirteenth century.[33] A vital part of Jonsson's theory is that the genre of balladry had a short creative period in Norway, lasting only a few decades. Accordingly, he dates the *Draumkvæde* to around 1300.[34] This

---

[30] However, I do not follow JONSSON 1996, 82 when he reasons as follows: "Liestøls försök att försvara åsikten i fråga genom påståendet att visionens innehållsliga tidsram skulle vara begränsad till »the thirteen days when Olav slept full fast» måste bero på ett tankefel och kan icke tas på allvar".

[31] See *NMB*: 177n and BARNES 1974, 179n.

[32] Even though the creativity comes to a halt, the genre lives on and the most popular visions are copied extensively during the later Middle Ages (cf. e.g. WELLENDORF 2006).

[33] JONSSON 1996.

[34] Around the same time most of the visions preserved in Old Norse were translated, see WELLENDORF 2007, 93–245.

theory about the origin of the ballad genre at the Norwegian court in the late thirteenth century is not uncontroversial,[35] but if we accept this dating we have to account for a period of more than five centuries of presumably exclusive oral transmission. The language of the ballad is not Norwegian as it was spoken or written in the year 1300, and this, in combination with the many variant recordings, excludes the theoretically possible scenario of a transmission in which the ballad was memorised word-for-word and stanza-for-stanza by the singers and eventually committed to writing in exactly the same form as it was once composed.[36] Verbal changes led to changes in content, but is it possible to pin down some of the changes the ballad must have undergone during its oral transmission before it was committed to writing? I think it is; and likely candidates for such innovations are the generic deviances from the genre of visionary literature, such as those pointed out above.

We can take for granted that a thorough knowledge, at least on an unconscious level, of the rules according to which narratives of different types should be constructed existed. The visions were mostly written down by a cleric who had spoken directly with the visionary or from a second-hand source.[37] This literalisation usually implied a translation from the vulgar tongue of the visionary to the Latin of the recorder of the vision (exceptions are the visions from Ireland and Iceland). With the transformation to the new medium of the Latin language the content of the vision was compared and, subsequently, harmonised, unwittingly, and often wittingly, by the recorder with the existing body of visions. Simultaneously the visionary lost control over the content of his narrative.

The underlying thought and the guarantee of the veracity of a vision was: we know this is true because it has happened to others.[38] Pushing it a little, we

---

[35] No one has, as far as I know, attempted a full-scale discussion or refutation of Jonsson's theories. The latest overview of the discussion I am familiar with is the chapter "Dateringen af folkeviserne" in LUNDGREEN-NIELSEN 2002. He makes no mention of supporters of Jonsson's theories, but one is SOLBERG 2003, 7.

[36] The singers were well aware that the language changed. Bugge writes regarding Hæge Aarmote, who had learned many ballads from her father, that her language was particularly archaic, "dog pleiede hun ikke nu at kvæde disse i den samme gamle Sprogform, i hvilken hun havde modtaget dem af Faderen, og med Sikkerhed vidste hun ofte at angive, hvor Faderen havde brugt andre Ordformer og Udtryk eller udtalt Ordene anderledes, end hun nu pleiede. Saaledes brugte Hæge nu ikke gjerne Dativ [...] Heller ikke pleiede hun nu at bruge egne Former for Verbernes Flertal". Cited after SOLBERG 2003, 219.

[37] See CAROZZI 1994, 519–522. There is a few instances where a vision is recorded by the person who actually experienced it. Examples are the *Visio cuiusdam monachi in Vaucellis claustro* and the *Visio Ulrici*.

[38] Compare with the following authorial statement from *Visio Godeschalci* p. 198: *Nec tamen diffidendum est vera esse, eciam si ratio difficile reperitur, cum similia quibusdam accidisse legamus*, or with *Visio Bernoldi* coll. 1118: *Ego per quosdam divulgari haec audiens, quia ille redivivus ad me venire non potuit, praefatum presbyterum bonae intelligentiae ac bonae vitae, cui haec retulit, ad me accersitum quae scripta sunt mihi ex ordine feci nararre, vera illa esse credens, quia hujusmodi, et in libro Dialogorum sancti Gregorii, et in historia Anglorum, et in scriptis sancti Bonifacii episcopi et martyris, sed et tempore domni Ludovici imperatoris aetate nostra cuidam Witino viro religioso revelata relegi.*

can say that no written vision can contain elements that are not already found within the tradition.[39] Ehlen writes:

> Paradoxerweise ist eine verschriftlichte Einzelvision nicht dann wahr, wenn sie der Erzählung des Visionärs, der sich genau erinnert, genau folgt, sondern dann, wenn sie das eliminiert, was der Tradition widerspricht, und das einfügt, was dieser unabdingbar zugehört. Der verschriftlichte Visionstext hat im Regelfall mit den Erlebnissen des Schauenden wohl weniger zu tun als mit der Erwartungen der Rezipienten.[40]

Ehlen might be pushing it too far here because it was not only the recorders who had the "power of harmonisation".[41] The visionary was not a clean sheet either, but well acquainted with other visions which he could have heard used as exempla in sermons or elsewhere. This knowledge would have guided his experience as much as the redactors' knowledge of the genre guided their writing down of the text.[42] If a particular vision did not conform with what was expected of a vision it would soon be adjusted to fit with the conventions. The overwhelming mass of visionary literature shows that the individual visions were cut more or less from the same cloth. A vision did not come out of nowhere, and the experience of a vision was to a high degree culturally and socially determined. But even if the vision was quite unconventional at first it would not attain a wider circulation and enter the tradition of visions as such unless it was adapted to the generic constraints that governed this genre. But there is, of course, a caveat: *Draumkvæde* is the only visionary ballad we posses, so we do not have any comparative material that allows us to see how a vision usually fared when transformed into a ballad. Furthermore, *Draumkvæde* is not a vision written in Latin and preserved up to our time through the medium of parchment, but an oral ballad written down in the middle of the nineteenth century. But still, it is unlikely that the composer of the initial *Draumkvæde* was unfamiliar with the genre and its requirements. Whether he based his work on a written account of an *Óláfs leizla* in Old Norse or, perhaps, a *Visio Olavi* written in Latin[43] is unknown, but even though the argument presented above takes its starting point in written literature, it holds true for oral literature as well where the drift towards the stereotype is equally dominant. But how did the text fare during oral transmission?

One of the salient features postulated as typical of oral transmission is its homoeostatic qualities; i.e. the content of orally transmitted texts is never

---

[39] On the writing down of visions see EHLEN 1998 and GUREVICH 1984.

[40] EHLEN 1998, 282.

[41] EHLEN 1998, 296 sharpens his point further when he writes: "Es ist offenbar nicht entscheidend, was der Visionär in seiner Ekstase gesehen hat, sondern daß er gesehen hat".

[42] See DINZELBACHER 1999, 44 for an entirely different view. He writes inter alia: "Diese parallelen [between the works belonging to the genre of visions] erklären sich nicht so sehr dadurch, weil die Verfasser der Texte ältere Vorlagen nachschrieben (was vorkommt) sondern v. a., weil gleiche seelische Erfahrungen zu gleichen Beschreibungen führen".

[43] As DINZELBACHER 1980 has suggested.

entirely redundant.[44] What is no longer important disappears from the tradition or changes after some time through this 'structural amnesia'[45] to something that is relevant. These innovations introduced consciously or unconsciously by the individual tradition carriers may enter tradition or be forgotten. As Goody formulates it: "Each performance of a long poem [...] reshapes the work and (since performance is transmission) provides a new model for future versions".[46] As the individual preserved recording is only one possible recension of a multiform,[47] so the preserved *Draumkvæde* is not the individual recordings but the total sum of all recordings. This sum is but a tiny fragment of the total sum of *Draumkvæde* performances through the centuries.[48] On the other hand, the two recordings from Anne Lillegaard show us that the ballad could be rather stable in two different recitations by the same singer.[49] It is important not to overstate the instability of the text as well.[50]

With the *Draumkvæde* we are more fortunate than with the Homeric or the Eddic poems in that we posses many recordings directly from oral tradition. The entire corpus of variants consists, according to Barnes's calculations, of one hundred and sixty-nine stanzas;[51] i.e. enough stanzas to compile no less than five and one-half ballads of the same length as that of Ramskeid without repeating as much as a single stanza. The reason for this large corpus is to be found in the eagerness of the collectors to find stanzas belonging to the *Draumkvæde* in combination with the lack of a strict story-line where event follows logically upon event. This lack might have loosened up the narrative in such a way that the ballad was more open to changes. I will therefore suggest that the visionary innovations in *Draumkvæde* are brought about by a disappearance of the need to live up to the generic demands when the genre of vision literature stopped being an active and integral part of the tradition carriers' everyday reality. When the knowledge of the genre faded, it was e.g. no longer seen as a matter of course that such a text should deal exclusively with the otherworldly present.

Is it then possible to find material that was known in Norway in the later Middle Ages and the Post-Reformation Era, a material that will substantiate our claim that an unguided vision of the final judgement could have made its way into the poem in this period? Blom has, I think, shown the way in the concluding pages of her book *Ballader og legender fra norsk middelalderdiktning*,

---

[44] See e.g. ONG 1982, 46–49; GREEN 1994, 22. This theory is, of course, very hard to prove in an historical context such as Old Norse, as the consequences of this 'structural amnesia' are that everything that was somehow unimportant or irrelevant is now lost, and therefore unavailable to scholars seeking to prove the theory. When used in an historical context, it rests therefore entirely on analogy.

[45] The inventor of this term is J. A. Barnes, but I have taken it from GOODY & WATT 1968, 33.

[46] GOODY 2000, 44.

[47] FOLEY 1984, 81.

[48] JANSSON 1991, 168 writes regarding ballads in general: "den tekstdokumentation vi har representerar endast en försvinnande liten del av många seklers framföranden".

[49] Up to five years may have passed between the two recordings.

[50] An interestingly different approach to the study of the stability of ballad texts from the perspective of psychology is found in WALLACE & RUBIN 1998.

[51] For his criteria see BARNES 1974, 80–85.

where she utilises two late-medieval religious texts written in Swedish, one of which is among the so-called 'Birgittiner-norske' texts as an indicator of beliefs current in the late-medieval milieu where the *Draumkvæde* might have circulated.[52] On the other hand, the quotations she gives from these works are not unusual or specific enough to be convincing. I am, however, certain that a more thorough search of this material will shed light on the later history of *Draumkvæde*, even though a perfunctory examination of two medieval books of sermons known to have been present in the area where the ballad was later found has not yielded any convincing results.[53]

In summation: deliberations such as these on the changeability of orally transmitted texts in combination with the strict generic regulation of the genre of visions allow us to suggest that the initial *Draumkvæde* would have kept itself largely within the confines of the accepted visionary framework. But as time passed the genre of visions went out of fashion, resulting in the disappearance of the need to live up to the generic regulations and, consequently, the ballad was open for a structural and thematic refashioning to fit a new and different context. Elements in the ballad that do not fit into the narrative morphology of visions, are in other words, likely to belong to a later period of the transmission. Elements that do fit into this morphology, will on the other hand, possibly, and I stress possibly date back to an earlier layer in the textual transmission. Such elements can be found in the entire corpus of stanzas and I see no reason to confine the hunt for such stanzas to the 'best' recordings as is done in the latest reconstruction.[54] Given the extreme fluctuation of the tradition, it seems less reasonable to reconstruct a version from two select tradition carriers as Myhren does, than to do as Moe did. I will therefore suggest that future reconstructors fire on all cylinders and pick and choose stanzas as they see fit from the entire published *Draumkvæde* corpus, and even compose new stanzas, as Moe and Mortensson-Egnund did. I will also suggest that the more adventurous attempt to translate the ballad back into Old Norse, as Bugge did with the *Hildina* ballad from Shetland.[55] In this way reconstructors will become creators and partake actively in the tradition. It is in the nature of this kind of literature that the oldest version is no less genuine than the youngest, and maybe we will end up with a new masterpiece akin to that of Moe. The alternative is of course to present, appreciate, elucidate, and carry out research on all the texts as they are

---

[52] BLOM 1971, 273–278.

[53] The manuscripts are Cod Linc T 180 (edited by EJDER 1974), which is famous because it contains the oldest written ballad fragment of some length, and Cod Holm A 111 (edited by RIETZ 1850). A survey of these manuscripts, and the manuscript group they belong to, is found in ANDERSSON 1993.

[54] Examples of such material are stanzas containing the worried neighbour-motif in the version of Anne Skålen (XI, 2) and the *smådrengje* stanzas in the same version (XI, 44–47), e.g.: "Så kjæm dei fram smådrengjinne/ å mine finganne feslar/ eg sleit sunde mi skarlakskåpa/ i tynnyrringjen meg refsa (XI 46)". The other stanzas also mention *smådrenggjinne*. MOE 1908 has discussed these stanzas, but whereas he regards *smådrengjinne* as the lost souls of exposed unbaptised children, I am more inclined to see them as devils or evil spirits, as 'smådreng' is a common word for 'servant' in the ballads (e.g. *DgF* 145 A 5), and could in this connection be a servant of the devil.

[55] Bugge's attempt at a translation is published by GRÜNER-NIELSEN 1939.

recorded from oral tradition and use their social *and* literary contexts for what they are worth.

Bibliography

Primary sources

DgF – Danmarks gamle Folkeviser, ed. S. Grundtvig, A. Olrik *et al.*. København 1953–1976.

Drycthelms leizla, ed. Einar G. Pétursson in *Einn atburðr og leiðsla um Óðáinsakur: Leiðsla Drycthelms eða CI ævintýri í safni Gerings. Gripla* 4, 138–165.

K1, ed. M. Barnes in *Draumkvæde: An Edition and a Study*: 174–178. Oslo 1974.

NF – Norske folkeviser, ed. M.B. Landsted. Kristania 1853.

NMB – Norske mellomalderballadar, ed. Å.G. Blom. Oslo 1982.

TSB – The Types of the Scandinavian Medieval Ballad: A Descriptive Catalogue, ed. B.R. Jonsson *et al.*. Oslo 1978.

Visio Baronti, ed. W. Levison, *Visio Baronti monachi longoretensis, Monumenta Germaniae historica: Scriptores rerum merovingicarum* 5: 368–394. Hannover 1910

Visio Bernoldi, ed. J.-P. Migne, *Patrologia Latina* 125 coll. 1115–1120. Paris 1844–1865.

Visio cuiusdam monachi in Vaucellis claustro, ed. Paul Gerhard Schmidt, *Die Vision von Vaucelles (1195/1196)*, *Mittellateinisches Jarhbuch* 20 155–163. 1985.

Visio Drycthelmi, ed. Bertram Colgrave and R. A. B. Mynors, *Beda Venerabilis: Ecclesiastical History of the English People*: 488–499. Oxford 1969

Visio Edmundi monachi de Eynsham, ed. Robert Easting, *The Revelation of the monk of Eynsham*. The Early English Text Society 318. Oxford: 2002.

Visio Fursei, ed. Maria Pia Ciccarese,
Le visioni de S. Fursa: 279–303. *Romanobarbarica* 1: 231–303. 1984.

Visio Godeschalci, ed. Erwin Assmann, *Godeschalcus und Visio Godeschalci: mit deutscher Übersetzung*. Neumünster 1979.

Visio Karoli Crassi, ed. R. A. B. Mynors, R. M. Thomson and M. Winterbottom, *William of Malmesbury: Gesta regum anglorum*: 162–170. Oxford 1998.

Visio Pauli, ed. Herman Brandes, *Ein Beitrag zur Visionslitteratur mit einem deutschen und zwei lateinischen Texten*: 75–80. Halle 1885

Visio Thurkilli, ed. P. G. Schmidt. Leipzig 1978.

Visio Tnugdali, ed. Albrecht Wagner, *Visio Tnugdali: Lateinisch und Altdeutsch*: 1–56. Erlangen 1882.

Visio Ulrici, ed. Johannes Grabmayer, *Visio quam Ulricus sacerdos vidit. Die Vision des Propstes Ulrich von Völkermarkt im Jahre 1240*: 210–215. *Mediaevistik* 9: 189–221. 1996.

Secondary sources

ANDERSSON, Roger 1993: *Postillor oc predikan: En medeltida texttradition i filologisk och funktionell belysning*. Stockholm.

BARNES, Michael 1974: *Draumkvæde: An Edition and a Study*. Oslo.

BLOM, Ådel Gjøstein 1971: *Ballader og legender fra norsk middelalderdiktning*. Oslo.

BØ, Gudleiv & MYHREN, Magne 2002: *Draumkvædet: Diktverket og teksthistoria*. Oslo.

CAROZZI, Claude 1994: *La voyage de l'âme dans l'au-delà d'après la littérature latine (Ve–XIIIe siècle)*. Palais Farnèse.

DINZELBACHER, Peter 1980: "Zur Entstehung von Draumkvæde." *Skandinavistik*, 10 89–96.

——— 1981: *Vision und Visionsliteratur im Mittelalter*. Stuttgart.

——— 1999: *Die letzten Dinge: Himmel, Hölle, Fegefeuer im Mittelalter*. Freiburg.

DUTTON, Paul Edward 1994: *The Politics of Dreaming in the Carolingian Empire*. Lincoln.

EHLEN, Thomas 1998: "Vision und Schrift — Interessen, Prozeß und Typik der Verschriftlichung hochmittelalterlicher Jenseitsreisen in lateinischer Sprache am Beispiel der 'Visio Edmundi monache de Eynsham'." In Thomas Ehlen, Johannes Mangei & Elisabeth Stein (eds.) *Visio Edmundi monachi de Eynsham: Interdisziplinäre Studien zur mittelalterlichen Visionslitteratur*, pp. 251–300, Tübingen.

EJDER, Bertil (ed.) 1974: *Svenska medeltidspostillor: Delarna 6 och 7*. Stockholm.

FOLEY, John Miles 1984: "Editing oral epic texts: Theory and practice." *Text: Transactions of the Society for Textual Scholarship*, 1 75–94.

GARDINER, Eileen 1993: *Medieval Visions of Heaven and Hell: A Sourcebook*. New York.

GOODY, Jack 2000: *The Power of the Written Tradition*. Washington.

GOODY, Jack & WATT, Ian 1968: "The consequences of literacy." In Jack Goody (ed.) *Literacy in Traditional Societies*, pp. 27–68, Cambridge.

GREEN, Dennis H. 1994: *Medieval Listening and Reading: The Primary Reception of German Literature 800–1300*. Cambridge.

GRÜNER-NIELSEN, Hakon 1939: "Den shetlandske Hildina-vise og Sophus Bugges tolkning." In *Heidersskrift til Gustav Indrebø på femtiårsdagen 17. november 1939*, pp. 139–165, Bergen.

GUREVICH, Aaron J. 1984: "Oral and written culture of the Middle Ages: Two "peasant visions" of the late twelfth–early thirteenth centuries." *New Literary History*, 16 51–66.

——— 1992: "Perceptions of the individual and the hereafter in the middle ages." In Jana Howlett (ed.) *Historical Anthropology of the Middle Ages*, pp. 65–89, Cambridge.

JANSSON, Sven-Bertil 1991: "Textkritiken och den muntliga traditionen: Om utgivning av äldre visor." In Barbro Ståhle Sjönell (ed.) *Textkritik: Teori och praktik vid edering av litterära texter: Föredrag vid Svenska Vitterhetssamfundets symposium 10–11 september 1990*, pp. 168–179, Stockholm.

JONSSON, Bengt R. 1996: "Om Draumkvædet och dess datering." *Sumlen: Årsbok för vis- och folkmusikforskning*, 1994-1995 9–153.

LIESTØL, Knut 1946: "Draumkvæde: A norwegian visionary poem from the Middle Ages." *Studia Norvegica: Ethnologica & folkloristica*, 3.

LUNDGREEN-NIELSEN, Flemming 2002: "Anders Sørensen Vedel og Peder Syv: To lærde folkeviseudgivere." In Flemming Lundgreen-Nielsen & Hanne Ruus (eds.) *Lærdom og Overtro*, pp. 135–374, København.

MOE, Molkte 1908: "Limbus puerorum: Et par vers av Draumkvædet." In Magnus Olsen (ed.) *Sproglige og historiske Afhandlinger viede Sophus Bugges Minde*, pp. 247–257, Kristania.

———— 1927: "Draumkvædet." In Knut Liestøl (ed.) *Molkte Moes samlede skrifter*, vol. III, pp. 197–345.

MORTENSSON-EGNUND, Ivar 1927: *Grunnsteinen i norsk bokheim: Utgreidingar um Draumkvedet og storskalden Olav Åsteson (med Draumkvedet i ny uppsetjing)*. Oslo.

ONG, Walter 1982: *Orality and Literacy: The Technologizing of the Word*. London.

RIETZ, Ernst (ed.) 1850: *Svensk Jærteckens Postilla: Efter en gammal handskrift från Norrige*.

SOLBERG, Olav 2003: *Norske folkeviser: Våre beste ballader*. Oslo.

WALLACE, Wanda T. & RUBIN, David 1998: ""The Wreck of the Old 97": A real event remembered in song." In Ulric Niesser & Eugene Winograd (eds.) *Remembering Reconsidered: Ecological and Traditional Approaches to the Study of Memory*, pp. 289–310, Cambridge.

WELLENDORF, Jonas 2006: "Homogeneity and heterogeneity in Old Norse cosmology." In Anders Andrén, Kristina Jennbert & Catharina Raudvere (eds.) *Old Norse religion in long-term perspectives: Origins, changes, and interactions*, p. 50–53, Lund.

———— 2007: *Kristelig visionslitteratur i norrøn tradition*. Bergen, unpublished PhD thesis.

The Eddic Form and Its Contexts: An Oral Art Form Performed in Writing

Bernt Øyvind Thorvaldsen

'PERFORMANCE' IS A term that is frequently used within studies of oral art forms in living cultures, where it refers to different contextual aspects of the actual events of performance. Thus it is related to the speech act theory because it focuses on verbal language in its context, "how things are done with words" – but also what things, namely non-linguistic phenomena, do to words.

However, research on oral art forms from old written sources is fundament-ally different from the study of live performance. Richard Bauman writes about his own rendering of live performance in the introduction to *Story, Performance, Event: Contextual Studies of Oral Narrative*, a book on oral narratives among dog traders and hunters in Texas:

> What makes the task so problematic is that orally performed narrative, for example, will be organized by a complex and inter-penetrating range of discourse and performance structures. One is thus confronted by the prospect of loading down the printed text with so much formal furniture that it is inaccessible to the reader, or alternatively of making motivated choices among presentational formats to emphasize specific patterning principles.[1]

Bauman describes different contextual aspects of communication in his render-ing of performance, for example that participants interrupt, are angry or are speaking loudly.[2] However, these ways of expressing non-linguistic phenomena are not enough to make the stories understandable to readers unfamiliar with the milieu he describes. Bauman analyzes and explains the social interaction and the norms at work in narrative performance, and by establishing this framework he makes it possible for the reader to understand how contextual phenomena affects and even constitutes meaning.

If we leave the hunters and dog traders and turn to Old Norse, the problem of context and performance is quite different. The events of oral performance

---

[1] BAUMAN 1986, ix.
[2] See for example BAUMAN 1986, 16–17.

are, of course, not accessible to direct observation. The sources are all written texts, and the motivation behind them and the context in which they were produced, read and heard are also only accessible by reconstruction.

In this paper I will focus on the text/context relationship in written texts that make use of one specific form, the eddic. I define the 'eddic form' simply as poetic diction characterized by two features: first, it applies two basic metrical patterns, *fornyrðislag* and *ljóðaháttr*, and variants of those patterns; secondly, the poetical language is simple. Its syntax is close to everyday speech, and metaphors appear infrequently. In three different examples I will discuss the context, or rather contexts, in which this form is applied. The origin of the eddic form is considered to be oral: it is a form that has been used in oral performance. It is, as far as I know, also the oldest known form of oral poetry in the Nordic area. The reason why I call the form 'eddic' is because the most well-known poems in this form are those of the *Older Edda*, even though they were so named due to a mistake made by the seventeenth century Icelander, Brynjólfur Sveinsson, who thought the manuscript *Codex Regius* (GKS 2365 4°) was some sort of predecessor for Snorri Sturluson's *Edda*, and that it was composed by Sæmundr fróði.[3]

When an oral art form such as the eddic appears in written contexts, the sources can be considered to represent some kind of performance, a written performance of an oral form. There are many different perspectives when oral forms are studied from a performance-oriented angle. In *Oral Traditions and the Verbal Arts* Ruth Finnegan mentions some main focal points in performance studies: both verbal and non-verbal techniques and elements of performance, interaction between participants (audience, performers, researcher), the organisation of the event, but also the relationship between the individual performance and cultural conventions.[4] In the following examples I will discuss the relationship between the oral form and the written performance, paying special attention to the following three aspects of performance: non-verbal aspects, the interaction of participants and the social aspect of art forms (norms, conventions, genres). My intention is to raise some questions about how an oral form and its contexts can be understood, and I shall also suggest how these examples are expressions of 'orality' and 'literacy'.

The first example is within the group of runic inscriptions where the eddic form is applied. Most of them are memorial inscriptions which deal with the death of kinsmen.[5] It seems likely that some sort of oral performance was associated with the erection of these stones,[6] but it is, of course, impossible to study the performance of lost events. So, what can be said of these inscriptions as documents of performance needs to be related to their written performance.

---

[3] Jónas Kristjánsson 1997, 25–26.
[4] Finnegan 1992, 93–94.
[5] Hübler 1996.
[6] Jesch 1998, 471.

I will use the stone that now stands in the church in Turinge in Söderman-
land (Sweden) as an example:

Kætill ok Biorn þæiʀ ræistu stæin þenna at Þorstæin, faður sinn,
Anundr at broður sinn ok huskarlaʀ æf[t]iʀ(?) iafna, Kætiløy at
boanda sinn.

> Brøðr vaʀu þæiʀ
> bæstra manna,
> a landi
> ok i liði uti,
> h[eld]u sin[a]
> huskarla ve[l].
> Hann fioll i orrostu
> austr i Garðum,
> liðs forungi,
> landmanna bæstr.[7]

Kättel and Björn they raised this stone in memory of Torsten, their father,
Anund in memory of his brother, and *huskarla* (the 'housecarls') after
iafna ('the just one'?), Kättilö in memory of her husband: [In eddic form:]
The brothers were / among the best men / in the land, / and out in the
host (*liþi*) / treated their retainers well./ He fell in battle / east in Russia /
the host's captain (*liþs forungi*) / of 'landmen' the best.[8]

First some words on the the participants: the stone is raised in memory of a
man named Torsten, and by his sons (Kætill and Biorn, his brother Anundr, his
huskarlar 'housecarls' and his wife Kætiløy. The poetic part of the inscription
mentions brothers who were among the best men in the land, but the identity
of them is not certain.

Regarding the material or non-verbal side of the text, the artefact is ornamented, which is a way of raising the message of the inscription above ordinary
everyday communication, and of expressing status; secondly, the writing of text
has the function of fixating and preserving the message, which of course is a
general function of writing. However, carving on *stone* (although sandstone)
emphasizes that function. In fact, many memorial inscriptions express a wish
that the stone might stand on a certain location,[9] and for an almost eternal
period of time, as in the following example from Gotland: *Æi meðan verald
vakir, liggr merki hiar yfir manni.*[10] 'As long as the world is awake (i.e. stands)
lies the landmark here in memory of that man'.

The oral art form, the eddic, appears together with metrically unbound
text, in prosimetrum. As in many other of the memorial runic inscriptions,

---

[7] *Sö* 338.
[8] Translation from SAWYER 2000, 132.
[9] HÜBLER 1996, 139–147.
[10] HÜBLER 1996, 145.

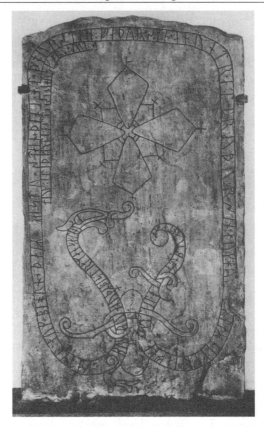

Figure 1: The Turinge stone. Note that the last part of the inscription is located on the right side of the stone, and not visible on the photo. Photo by H. Faith-Ell (*Sö*, II, image 173).

there seems to be a certain congruence between the contents and the poetically marked and unmarked text. The prose is in this case referring, in a quite "objective" style, to the kinship relations to the dead, while the poetic part focuses on the location of his death and praises him. In this manner, the eddic form could be said to have the most fundamental function of poetry, which is to "raise" the text above ordinary language.

There are two perspectives regarding cultural conventions and genre. First, this stone is a part of a large group of runic memorial inscriptions, customary to eleventh century Sweden, and the motifs on the stone, the snake-motif and the cross (see Figure 1), are frequently carved on runestones. However, it is hard to say what the symbols represent except, obviously, being elements in the craft of decorating runestones.[11] The stones themselves form a genre in one sense

---

[11] On the tradition of ornamented runestones, see HORN FUGLESANG 1986; 1998.

of the word, because they share a function (they are memorial) and are quite similar in form (both non-verbal and verbal). Secondly, the eddic part of the inscription is related to some 150–200 other memorial inscriptions in which the eddic meter also appears, although in many cases it is disputed whether it really is the eddic metre, as there is disagreement on the metrical criteria.[12]

In addition to the immediate "musical" effect of metre, the poetic form also gives associations to other texts applying the same form. The eddic form is also used in two Old Norse memorial poems, *erfikvæði*, that usually are considered to have originated in the tenth century: the anonymous *Eiríksmál* and *Hákonarmál*, composed by Eyvindr skáldaspillir. The possibility that an oral genre of eddic memorial poems has existed and also has been used and known in Sweden, can neither be confirmed nor excluded. To praise the dead person as the most outstanding among men (*landmanna bæstr*), as the inscription does, has close variants in the *erfikvæði*, for example in the twentieth stanza of the already mentioned *Hákonarmál*:

> Mun óbundinn
> á ýta sjǫt
> fenrisulfr fara,
> áðr jafngóðr
> á auða trǫð
> konungmaðr komi.

The unbound Fenriswolf shall attack the abodes of men (meaning the end of the world will come), until such a good king comes on the empty road (i.e. fills the empty place).

Another possibility is that the form might not have associations to a genre of memorial poems, but to other kinds of poems in eddic form, for example heroic or mythic, if such eddic poetry existed in Sweden at that time.

There might be several communicative functions underlying the whole memorial stone as a "text", making it appeal to the general audience capable of reading runes. If we are to believe Birgit Sawyer, memorial stones could have functioned as verification of the participants' rights to inheritance.[13] If that is the case, kinship played the central role; the stone can also be considered as a way of expressing the status of the living, both from the material point of view (the techniques applied) and from its information on kinship. I think the Turinge stone, to some extent, as with other memorial inscriptions, has to be considered an expression of emotions – a close relative is dead and those who erect the stone praise his memory.

What then can the Turinge stone tell us of the interaction between orality and literacy? The non-verbal elements are very important communicative aspects. The ornaments and other visual elements have almost the same function as the application of eddic metre: to raise the text and the message of the text

---

[12] See for example WULF 1998 on HÜBLER 1996.
[13] SAWYER 2000.

above ordinary speech and everyday activities. Both these aspects are connected to social expressions: the practice of raising memorial stones, a written tradition, and the application of an oral art form, namely the eddic. Basically, the eddic form raises the text, but it also brings associations to other poems in the same form. Of course the closest group is eddic poetry used within other runic memorial inscriptions, but it could also refer to an eddic *erfikvæði* tradition or other known or unknown groups of eddic poetry.

The Turinge stone, raised by the relatives of Torsten in his memory, and maybe to confirm the status and rights to heritage for themselves, is a kind of performance integrating visual and textual means. On the textual level the material aspect of writing and the oral form appear as integrated parts of this performance.

The next two examples belong to another category, as they are sources written in Latin script on parchment or paper, and I will discuss the performance of eddic poetry in examples from two very different prose genres: the contemporary sagas and the legendary sagas. The contemporary sagas are written close to the events they describe and they are dominated by what Margaret Clunies Ross calls a 'realistic/historical' mode. They seem to present their narratives as retelling of what actually happened. The legendary sagas, however, most often describe events of a distant past and it is probably more correct to call the mode that dominates most of them 'fantastic/supernatural'.[14] Whether this mode was considered fiction is difficult to say. Did those who read and heard the sagas believe they presented events as something that had actually happened, and that it happened in the way the texts presented it? Torfi Tulinius argues in *The Matter of the North* that the audience seems to have considered them fiction, as expressed by the term *lygisǫgur* in *Þorgils saga ok Hafliða*.[15]

The Jóreiðr cycle in *Íslendinga saga*

Poetry in eddic form appears in contemporary sagas, and particularly in *Íslendinga saga*. This saga was composed by Sturla Þórðarson. It appears within the framework of the larger compilation, *Sturlunga saga*, probably made by Þórðr Narfason. The eddic poetry in *Sturlunga saga* typically appears, as Judy Quinn writes, "within dreams and visions by supernatural figures, such as valkyries, large imposing men, ravens and other figures who indicate in their speech that they have recently passed from the land of the living".[16] Quinn also writes that the "dreams and visions are presented as authentic and significant to the telling of contemporary events".[17]

The perspective on the interactions of the participants is quite complicated when the oral form appears within a written narrative, especially when the

[14] CLUNIES ROSS 1998, 50–51.
[15] TULINIUS 2002, 63–65.
[16] QUINN 1987, 54.
[17] QUINN 1987, 54.

Reality	Compiler
	Saga-writer
Narrative reality	Dreamer
Dreams	Dream figures

Figure 2

original performance of the poems is said to be within a dream. In this case there are at least four levels in which different performers participate (See Figure 2).

I will, in the following, use the Jóreiðr cycle of dreams[18] as an example. This is a story about a girl who lives with a priest called Páll. Jóreiðr has four dreams in which she meets and communicates with a woman who reveals that she is Guðrún Gjúkadóttir, known from the heroic tales. It should be mentioned that the chapter in which these dreams appear has a disputed authorship. The fact that the author, who may be Sturla Þórðarson, mentions that Jóreiðr lived with Páll and also names the exact place where they lived, seems to be a signal to the readers or listeners that they should *regard* the story as true.[19]

Jóreiðr's dreams form another level in which she meets Guðrún, who claims to come from Násheimr 'The land of the dead'. The two participants in the dream level of the text are Jóreiðr and Guðrún Gjúkadóttir. A tension exists between Jóreiðr and Guðrún that has little to do with them as persons. Jóreiðr asks what Guðrún, as a pagan, is doing there, and Guðrún simply says that Jóreiðr should not mind because she is a friend. As Quinn states, the focus is thus moved from the pagan/Christian dimension, to the ethical one: Guðrún appears as an ethical authority on the contemporary events which are the subject of the dialogue – and her judgement reflects a contemporary ethic mentality. For example, the "pagan" Guðrún considers it bad that Eyjólfr Þorsteinsson, responsible for the burning on Flúgumýrr intended, in her view, to spread paganism. Quinn writes: "the dream speaker [Guðrún] contextualises the forces of good and evil in an ahistorical framework".[20]

The author thus places the story in which the eddic form appears in the periphery of the narrated events; Jóreiðr appears nowhere else in *Sturlunga saga*. Furthermore, the story takes place within the dreams of this girl. The events that Guðrún passes ethical judgements on are thus not commented upon by the author, but by a figure from a distant past. Both the dream framework and the identity of the speaker might signal that the message in the words of Guðrún represents some kind of higher ethical judgement.

The Jóreiðr cycle is within the typical use of the eddic form in contemporary sagas: inside dreams and visions where the speaking voices are supernatural beings, and associated in different ways with the pagan and distant past. This is

[18] *Sturlunga saga*, 673–677.
[19] Quinn 1987, 54 and 71.
[20] Quinn 1987, 60.

an interesting tendency because it seems that the eddic form is still alive in a "pluralistic dream tradition, in which figures of traditional authority could be accommodated within a Christian framework".[21]

Genre generally plays an important role in the use of eddic poetry in the contemporary sagas in which there seems to be a link to the poems of the *Older Edda*. Some of the points Judy Quinn mentions are that the characters speaking in eddic metre are or resemble heroic, mythological or supernatural beings, or people who are passed off, and that the speakers have knowledge of the past and the future, a motif that appears in many of the poems in the *Older Edda*. There are also verbal associations between the *Older Edda* and the stanzas in the sagas, as seen for example in the expression *Villtu enn lengra* which is present in *Vǫluspá* and *Hyndluljóð*, and also in a stanza in *Íslendinga saga*.[22] In the Jóreiðr cycle there is an expression which also appears in the mythological eddic poem *Hávamál*. Guðrún says that *vinur em eg vinar míns* 'I am the friend of my friend', and she also plays with the same expression in one of the stanzas.[23] In *Hávamál* the lines *Vin sínom / skal maþr vinr vera* 'One shall be the friend of one's friend' are repeated in stanzas 42 and 43.

A work like *Sturlunga saga*, in which *Íslendinga saga* is integrated, is obviously a work that relies heavily on the technology of writing. The presentation of information in these texts is probably also related to the intended audience: if the author wants his text to be understood as a truthful account of what has happened, then his presentation probably reflects what people considered to be likely. The use of the eddic form in *Íslendinga saga* is then very interesting. In the Jóreiðr cycle the textual function in the written context is quite clear: Guðrún, who visits Jóreiðr in her dreams, expresses an ethical evaluation of certain historical events. Why the eddic form is chosen in the Jóreiðr cycle and in other similar stories probably has something to do with the horizon of the narrated events: dreams in which the past, or supernatural beings or phenomena associated with the past, appear. As Quinn notes, it seems that the dream stories containing eddic verse is associated with socially peripheral persons and women, while those presented as more important are attributed skaldic stanzas. Since it is the same peripheral group that typically have dreams containing motifs from mythology and heroic tales,[24] it is possible to argue that this specific way of merging elements from the past into the present might have been a phenomenon belonging to the social periphery.

An example from *Hrólfs saga kraka*

I will treat this last example very briefly. It is from a legendary saga, namely *Hrólfs saga kraka*. The eddic form is used in similar ways as in the contemporary sagas; it is integrated with prose in prosimetrum. The significant differences

---

[21] QUINN 1987, 60.
[22] *Sturlunga saga*, 306.
[23] *Sturlunga saga*, 675.
[24] QUINN 1987, 63–64.

that might illustrate the problems of context are the relationship between the narrative, the eddic form and the modes of the narrative.

In *Hrólfs saga* the eddic form is applied within the main thread of the narrated events and it seems impossible to say that those who speak in eddic form are different from the other figures in the saga. Generally many human figures within the legendary sagas have some features which are in accordance with the fantastic/supernatural narrative mode. Two of them, who both speak in the eddic form, are Þórir hundsfótr, a human with the legs of a dog, and Elg-Fróði, who is a moose from the navel down – the latter a kind of Old Norse version of the centaur. However, one of the speakers in *Hrólfs saga* is described as a *seiðkona* 'sorceress' and a *vǫlva* 'seeress', which seems to reflect a relationship to mythological eddic poetry and poems such as *Vǫluspá*, *Hyndluljóð* and *Baldrs draumar*. She also predicts by whom king Fróði will be killed:

> Hróarr ok Helgi,
> heilir báðir,
> þeir munu Fróða
> fjǫrvi ræna.[25]

Hróarr and Helgi, both in good health, shall steal the life of Fróði.

Thus, the function is equal to that of some dreams in the contemporary sagas, where the death of a person is predicted in eddic form.

If we compare the use of the eddic form in *Íslendinga saga* with that of this legendary saga there is one dimension that is very interesting. In the contemporary sagas the eddic form appears within dreams of peripheral persons, and these dreams are characterized by an ahistoric combination of phenomena from the past and contemporary events. The performers of the eddic form are, as in the Jóreiðr cycle, some kind of supernatural beings associated with the past or with dead people. In *Hrólfs saga*, however, the events described are located in the past, and the eddic form is performed by persons in the middle of the narrated events.

Richard Bauman underlines the difference between the "narrated event" and the "narrative event" in performance, terms that originate from Roman Jakobson.[26] They denote the relationship between the events which are told, on one hand, and the event of telling or being told, on the other hand. If we apply these terms to the two examples from the two saga types, we can describe the difference in the two narrative contexts according to Figure 3. In these cases it looks as though the contexts in which the eddic form appears have some similarities. When the horizon within the narratives is associated with the past, the eddic form is applied. Within the fantastic/supernatural

---

[25] *Hrólfs saga kraka*, 13.
[26] BAUMAN 1986, 2.

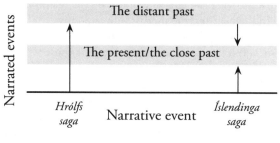

Figure 3

mode where the events are temporally located in the distant and different past, the eddic form is typically spoken by all characters. In the realistic/historical mode of *Íslendinga saga* it appears within dreams in which past and present meet.

While Bauman described the challenge of transforming performance events into written texts, as quoted in my introduction, the challenge which I have pointed out is to understand how the Old Norse, or rather Old Nordic, texts represent performance. The three examples I have used to illustrate the perspectives of participants, the cultural conventions/genre and non-verbal elements show that the study of the written performance of oral art forms means a study of the *interaction* of oral form, written text and non-verbal phenomena. The Turinge stone is a kind of performance in which the oral art form is integrated with orna-mental and textual elements, and the relationship between the participants and the performed expression is close. The saga examples are far more complicated, as the oral form appears in a well-developed storytelling tradition. In *Íslendinga saga* and *Hrólfs saga* the perspective of participants must be understood as a multilevelled phenomenon: the saga compilers, authors and the textual figures are all participants at different levels of the performance of the eddic form. It appears within different literary modes connected to mental horizons that, as we have seen, share some properties (as references to the past). Both the verbal and non-verbal elements are partly products of socially defined norms and tradition: the ornaments of the Turinge stone, the oral art form, the prose text. In the case of the sagas, the saga genres and literary modes determine the use of the oral form. All in all, I think these three examples illustrate that the performance perspective, when applied to oral art forms, indicates that "orality" and "literacy" must be viewed as integrated aspects of the expressions and in no way as a dichotomy between two basically different communicative cultures.

Robert Kellogg states in his article *Literacy and Orality in the Poetic Edda* that one should understand texts like the *Older Edda* as results of a "collaboration between two contemporary cultures, one essentially oral and the other essentially literate".[27] I think both the Turinge stone and the sagas clearly show that one cannot speak of two cultures, but one culture in which oral, written and non-

---

[27] KELLOGG 1991, 90.

verbal modes of communication live side by side and interact. Kellogg also comments on the prosimetrum of the *Codex Regius* of the *Older Edda* and the function of the prose text, but he does not take into account the use of the eddic form in runic inscriptions and prose narratives. Such a perspective is needed, because, as we have seen, runic inscriptions are unique in that they mirror real life, and the sagas are valuable sources to conceptions of the past in which the eddic form is integrated.

A performance perspective which takes into account the interaction between different verbal and non-verbal elements is interesting because earlier scholarship has had a tendency to focus on the oral prehistory of the eddic poetry. Although an important field to investigate, it is an extremely difficult task, because oral art forms are in many cases very hard to understand outside of live performance. Some of the dialogues of the Texas dog traders in Bauman's book are, at least for me, quite meaningless without the particular aids to understanding used by Bauman in his analysis. In that respect the written performance of old art forms, might be a key to an understanding of the text themselves, and to avoiding a strong dichotomy between the written and the oral when studying sources where orality and literacy merge.

Bibliography

Primary sources

Hákonarmál, ed. Finnur Jónsson in *Den norsk-islandske skjaldedigtning* I B: 57–60. København 1912–1915.

Hávamál, ed. Sophus Bugge in *Norrœn fornkvæði, Islandsk Samling af folkelige Oldtidsdigte om Nordens Guder og Heroer almindelig kaldet Sæmundar Edda hins fróða*: 43–64. Christania 1867.

Hrólfs saga kraka, ed. Finnur Jónsson, STUAGNL 32. København 1904.

Sturlunga saga, ed. Örnulfur Thorsson. Reykjavík 1988.

Sö – Södermanlands runinskrifter, ed. Erik Brate & Elias Wessén. Stockholm 1924–1936.

Secondary sources

BAUMAN, Richard 1986: *Story, Performance, Event: Contextual Studies of Oral Narrative, Cambridge Studies in Oral and Literate Culture*, vol. 10. Cambridge.

CLUNIES ROSS, Margaret 1998: *Prolonged Echoes II: The Reception of Norse Myths in Medieval Northern Society, The Viking Collection*, vol. 7. Odense.

FINNEGAN, Ruth 1992: *Oral Traditions and the Verbal Arts: A Guide to Research Practices*. London.

HORN FUGLESANG, Signe 1986: "Ikonographie der skandinavischen Runensteine der jüngeren Wikingerzeit." In Helmut Roth (ed.) *Zum Problem der Deutung frühmittelalterlicher Bildinhalte*, pp. 183–210, Sigmaringen.

———— 1998: "Swedish runestones of the eleventh century: Ornament and dating." In Klaus Düwel (ed.) *Runeninschriften als Quellen interdisziplinärer Forschung, Ergänzungsbände zum Reallexicon der Germanischen Altertumskunde*, vol. 15, pp. 197–218, Berlin.

Hübler, Frank 1996: *Schwedische Runendichtung der Wikingerzeit*, Runrön, vol. 10. Uppsala.

Jesch, Judith 1998: "Still standing in Ågersta: Textuality and literacy in late Viking-Age rune stone inscriptions." In Klaus Düwel (ed.) *Runeninschriften als Quellen interdisziplinärer Forschung, Ergänzungsbände zum Reallexicon der Germanischen Altertumskunde*, vol. 15, pp. 462–475, Berlin.

Jónas Kristjánsson 1997: *Eddas and Sagas: Iceland's Medieval Literature*. Reykjavík, transl. Peter Foote.

Kellogg, Robert 1991: "Literacy and orality in the Poetic Edda." In A. N. Doane & Carol Braun Pasternack (eds.) *Vox Intexta: Orality and Textuality in the Middle Ages*, pp. 89–101, Madison, Wisconsin.

Quinn, Judy 1987: "The use of Eddic poetry in contemporary sagas." *Frá suðlægri strönd*, 3 54–72.

Sawyer, Birgit 2000: *The Viking-Age Rune-Stones: Custom and Commemoration in Early Medieval Scandinavia*. Oxford.

Tulinius, Torfi 2002: *The Matter of the North: The Rise of Literary Fiction in Thirteenth-Century Iceland*, The Viking Collection, vol. 13. Odense.

Wulf, Frank 1998: "Recension of Hübler 1996." *Alvíssmál*, 8 93–98.

What Have We Lost by Writing?
Cognitive Archaisms in Skaldic Poetry

BERGSVEINN BIRGISSON

T HE TITLE OF this paper may seem strange to some. We are used to hearing about languages, poems and chronicles that are lost, either because they were not written down or because the parchments that held them have faded away. We thus associate writing with preserving, and that which is not written down to the lost.

In addition to the obvious fact that living memory is not as reliable as letters on vellum, one could also link these associations to a positivistic way of understanding cultural development. The new way of thinking and living, praying and writing, always inherits the bygone, while adding a little bit to it. The positivistic way of understanding the development from oral to written could, in these terms, be understood as a development that subsumes the oral culture, its artistic and functional characteristics, while adding some new features to it. In this paper, I would like to look at this from the opposite perspective. Is there something in the poetic expression of the oldest skalds in the North that the converted and learned skalds did not adapt to or bring forth in their poetic endeavour?

The idea of the discontinuity of human cultural progress is well known. We might refer to Gaston Bachelard, or his successor Michel Foucault who, in *The Order of Things*, presented the discontinuity in the way of thinking in the transition from medieval times to the classical epistemology.[1] Both stress that when a new *episteme* (way of thinking) marches on to the field of human cognition, the old way of thinking is by no means taken over by the new one. Bachelard likened the cultural development with the fate of words in an etymological perspective; one meaning is chosen while others fade away.[2]

We are used to the term "cultural continuity" in relation to the Christianisation of the North. In this paper I would like to shed some light on this continuity, or development, in poetic expression as it appears in the genre of skaldic poetry. I would like to ask if something more could exist in the deeper layers of the poems of old, saved on the vellum by the writing copyists, that can

---

[1] FOUCAULT 1996.
[2] GAUDIN 1987, xxxiv.

be distinguished from their own way of thinking and expressing themselves. Is there a continuity or discontinuity, and if there is a discontinuity – what does that involve?

The aim of this study is to search for cognitive characteristics in the oldest corpus of skaldic poetry (which medieval skaldic scholars have dated to the oral milieu in the North in the ninth and tenth century AD) and compare their characteristics to those of skaldic poetry from later centuries. What has happened to the genre in the transition from heathen to Christian times, from the oral to the written?

In order to address the topic in some depth, this kind of comparison study has to be delimited, and here I have chosen to focus on the metaphorical way of thinking. One could say that this choice is in harmony with the *Poetics* (4.5.5) of Aristotle, where metaphor is expressed as the heart of poetry as it "... (a) cannot be acquired from someone else, and (b) is an indication of genius".[3] According to contemporary theory, metaphor is not to be understood as an innocent figure or a trope delimited to decorative language, but rather as the heart of human cognition. Cognitive metaphor theory also maintains that a metaphor is an important factor in the construction of meaning in language. Through a metaphor one can unravel both direct and indirect thoughts and feelings, as, according to the cognitive theory, metaphors are mirrors of mentality.

My methodological point of departure is cognitive metaphor theory. Special attention will be given to so-called novel metaphors, and in addition to cognitive psychology, more specifically the studies addressing the topics of memory and mental imagery.

Some classical questions immediately arise: Can we be sure that the so-called "oldest skaldic poetry", as dated by the medieval writers, is authentic? Have not the oldest poems been "re-written", that is, adapted to the new Christian way of thinking through centuries of oral preservation and later on changed by the shortcomings of those who copied the manuscripts?

Such questions have been the subject of debate for centuries. Some ana-chronistic falsifications have been revealed, although the main conclusions point to the fact that the earliest skaldic poetry is so different from later poetry that to some degree it must be authentic. Some scholars have argued that the strict poetical form of skaldic poetry allowed it to enjoy a relatively stable life in oral circumstances, in contrast to the more unstable, epic genre of eddic poetry.[4] Every scholar engaged in skaldic poetry should be clear of one thing: skaldic poetry is so different, both in form and concept, from the thousand-line epic tradition in the Balkans, that adopting the conclusions from Milman Parry and Albert Lord[5] (namely that whatever is oral must be fleeting and constantly changing) into the study of skaldic poetry of the North, would only lead to fallacy. Whatever the answers may be, they must be sought after in the texts themselves, and each text must be studied on its own terms. A solid method of

---

3 ARISTOTLE, *Poetics*, 4.5.5.
4 MEULENGRACHT SØRENSEN 1993, 76–77; STEBLIN-KAMENSKIJ 1979.
5 LORD 1960.

analysis should, in my opinion, be able to confirm authenticity as well as reveal anachronisms and falsifications.

I have made use of the term 'cognitive archaism' (see Appendix: Table 1). Some of the archaisms such as 1, 2ab and 4, never occurred in examples from Christian times, and others such as 2aa and 5, occurred once or twice. I will explain the criteria as we consider the examples in the following.

Before we turn to analysis, I would like to draw attention to the potential mnemonic functions of the Old Norse metaphors, mostly found in the figures called *kennings*.

Much has been written on oral verbal culture and the technical and structural aspects that might aid memorization within such a culture. As my point of departure for this study is the metaphor, it is only appropriate to focus on the mnemonics of mental imagery, since the novel, or should I say, the original, metaphor is a way of evoking a picture or an image for our inner eye.

Studies of Greek and Roman literature on the "Art of memory", as Frances Yates termed it, reveal a salient rule for memorization: the rule of visualizing that which one wants to remember. We should make mental images (Latin *imago*) of the essential things in a text, and then place them against a well-known background. This is often termed as *loci-mnemonics*. However, there is yet another rule which also appears in the oldest Roman texts. From the anonymous rhetorical work *Ad Herennium*, from around 80 BC, and from Cicero's *De oratore*, composed a few decades later, we learn that the images we are advised to use should be bizarre and distinctive in character, in order to imprint themselves on the mind and help us remember with greater ease: "...images that are effective (*agentibus*) and sharply outlined and distinctive, with the capacity of encountering and speedily penetrating the mind."[6]

It is interesting to notice that among later Roman scholars like Quintilian, who wrote in the second part of the first century AD, a dramatic change occurred regarding the use of imagery for the improvement of memory. Quintilian simply does not advise imagery at all as an aid to memory. This led scholars such as Frances Yates to make the following remark: "Has Roman society moved into greater sophistication in which some intense, archaic, almost magical, immediate association of memory with images has been lost?" [7]

I would like to raise the question of whether this development can be understood in terms of the oral and the written – that the older works still convey archaic rules from the oral past, while the learned Quintilian can be understood as representing the mentality of the writing scholar who relies more on the repetition of the written word for memorization than the archaic rule of bizarre imagery.

I believe some obvious parallels to the art of memory in Rome can be traced among the Scandinavians, although an attempt to establish direct links between Rome and the pre-Christian North will not be made here. Regarding the old rule of visualizing for the improvement of memory, we can mention the

---

[6] II 87.358, transl. from CARRUTHERS 1993, 73.
[7] YATES 1966, 41.

etymological connections between the Old Norse words *muna* 'remember' and *mynd* 'image', which is assumed to refer to a "visual or a sensual mental image".

Keeping in mind the archaic rule of the bizarre image, I wish to emphasize some salient features of the Old Norse system of kennings which the skalds made use of to produce their metaphors. In later times scholars have drawn more attention to the visual aspects of the kenning-metaphors, and in a recent paper, Else Mundal points out the possible mnemonic aid of the images:

> The images that the skaldic language produces are often so penetrating that the verses could possibly be reconstructed with the help of those images and a few rhyming words [my translation].[8]

In the kennings we find an aesthetic tendency which I have termed the *aesthetics of contrast tension*. That is to say, in the two elements of the kenning – e.g. the basic word (fish) and the determinant (valley) – we often have two domains that stem from the basic contrast elements of nature: sea versus land, air versus earth, sea versus air, and so forth. This is also expressed in the clash of elements representing contrasting categories, or "semantic frames" as Margaret Clunies Ross has termed them in her discussion on skaldic poetics.[9] Thus we have categories such as wild versus tame, peasant versus aristocratic, life versus death, weak versus strong, erotic terms versus brutality, and so forth. I favour the example from *Ynglingatal*,[10] where the wife of Agni conspires and hangs her husband, while the kenning applied alludes to the hanging of Hagbarðr, a history of a complete faithfulness since Hagbarðr's wife, Signý, followed her beloved into the realm of death,[11] thus creating tension between the contrasting categories of conspiracy and faithfulness.[12]

If we visualize the images of these contrasting elements, we either elaborate the two clashing images into one, or allow them to interact side by side. In any case, the outcome can be understood as a bizarre, or a distinctive image as it is termed in modern cognitive psychology. A bizarre image is also a distinctive image, because it shares fewer features with the schematic images in memory than the so-called common images.[13] The skalds produce images that we cannot find in nature. The bear that struggles with a plough, the seaweed on the mountain, fish in the valley or reindeer in the sea, are all examples of what Hallvard Lie has termed as a-naturalistic.[14] Prior to Lie's insights into heathen aesthetics, these figures were often called barbaric or understood as immature attempts to make good metaphors by the classical educated philologists of the early twentieth century.[15]

---

[8] MUNDAL 2002, 155.
[9] CLUNIES ROSS 1989, 279–281.
[10] Stanza 10, *Skj.* B I, 9.
[11] SAXO GRAMMATICUS, *Gesta Danorum* 7.7.
[12] For further analysis see BERGSVEINN BIRGISSON 2003, 58–62.
[13] WOLLEN & MARGRES 1987, 118.
[14] LIE 1957.
[15] See KRAUSE 1930, 10; FINNUR JÓNSSON 1920, 383–384.

In my view, this aesthetic tendency of the skalds of old indicates that the Greek credo of art as a presentation of the nature/world as it is perceived had not yet made a breakthrough in the North. Instead of the cultural model of *mimesis* and the aesthetics of clarity and natural harmony, the Old Norse skald is much more interested in making something new, unseen or unexpected with his metaphors. And nature is the raw-material with which to create something new. Thus, the Old Norse pre-Christian poetry seems to be far more able to appreciate originality in visual metaphorical expression than Christian poetry.

But it would be wrong to limit this "bizarreness endeavour" to pure aesthetics.

I believe that the creation of the distinctive images we encounter in the Old Norse kennings is a Scandinavian expression of the same rule we find in the ancient Roman texts, that bizarre images are easier to remember than common ones. In other words, one of the original functions of the images of the contrasting kennings, and indeed the system of kennings in general, must have been a mnemonic one since these figures originate in oral contexts. It is also worth noting that originality in metaphorical expression requires visualization to a much greater degree than is the case with imitated metaphors. Cognitive psychology maintains that imagery is used to retrieve information from memory primarily "... when the property has not been explicitly considered previously".[16] Thus, one could maintain that metaphorical originality calls for the use of imagery which, in an oral context, is known to improve memorization.

Interestingly, these old rules of memory have been put to the test in a number of prominent studies in psychological research on human memory. There are, of course, some methodological problems that arise when scientists have tried to test out the mnemonic aid of bizarre images in contrast to common images, though it seems that in almost all cases the bizarre image has proved better for long-term memory.[17]

What I have done in my study is to adopt the standard criteria from the psychology of memory, such as the observations that the mind remembers best what draws its attention, and that images which make sense and give spontaneous meaning, and images which are distinctive and interactive are the easiest to retrieve from memory. The fact is that the bizarre image seems to fulfil these criteria better than other images. Thus, one could maintain that modern cognitive psychology has provided empirical support for the ancient claim that imagery mnemonics are useful in memorization. In addition, I would like to draw attention to an insight from studies of imagery, that it is perhaps not only the distinction of images and the fact that they interact, but the so-called *distinctive, specific relationships* of the images involved that have the greatest potential for improving memory.[18] Looking at the context of many of the old poems, one invariably finds such unusual and distinctive relationships between the visual figures. Here it must suffice to point to *Ynglingatal*, assumed to be

[16] Kosslyn 1995, 268.
[17] Wollen & Margres 1987; Einstein & McDaniel 1987.
[18] Buggie 1974; Hintzman 1993; Rubin 1995.

from around 900 AD, where the visual blending image of the death figure Hel is depicted as having sexual intercourse with the dead kings,[19] or where "the house-thief in the fire-stockings" (the fire) is stepping through the living king (see fig. 8 and 2). We could also allude to the *Lausavísa* of Egill Skallagrímsson where we find the blending image of the *hail-chisel*, where the storm is depicted as a wolf pressing the swan (of the sea-king = the ship) on the file (*þél*) of the ocean (here the teeth of the file are to be mapped on the waves of the sea). Such constructions could be termed as a mastery of unusual distinctive relationships in imagery. Scholars like David C. Rubin have presented the hypotheses that this is a criterion for understanding the effect of imagery in oral traditions.[20] I have not, however, included this criterion in this particular study.

The archaisms I will present have the cognitive characteristics of stimulating the listener to visualize mentally, some even demanding image inspection in order to understand the grounds of the metaphor. It could therefore be claimed that they promote memorization. I am not arguing, of course, that the poetic mind of old can be delimited to pure mnemonic endeavour. Nevertheless, one criterion for good poetry seems to have been the originality of the imagery, which one can assume has had a multifunctional value, of which key-value has been its mnemonic power.

The first archaism in the appendix falls under the category of distinctive images (see Table 1 in Appendix). I have termed this cognitive archaism as *the visual blending image*. The first example derives from the skald Þjóðólfr ór Hvini's *Ynglingatal*.[21]

In the last decade or so, cognitive theory has rendered some important insights into metaphorical language. One of those insights is the *blending theory*, whose main protagonists are Gilles Fauconnier and Mark Turner. Blending theory presents a new model of understanding metaphors in which the older two-dimensional model of topic and vehicle is given an additional third dimension that emerges in-between the topic and the vehicle. This is called the blending space, which is informally said to consist "in integrating partial structures from two separate domains into a single structure".[22] Blending theory is a language-theory, some would say a model that is focused on the dimension of meaning construction in language. Accordingly, it is a vast field of research and in the following I wish to draw this theory into the field of metaphor and mental imagery. In the last decade or so, more attention has been drawn to the role of non-verbal processes like imagery in the understanding of metaphors. It has been maintained that the use of imagery can explain why metaphors can be more effective, that is, more easily processed and understood, than the literal language.[23] The claim has been made that there are both people who are active, or so-called "vivid-imagers", and people who claim they never visualize. As I

---

[19] Stanza 7 and 32, *Skj.* B I, 8 and 13.
[20] RUBIN 1995, 54–55.
[21] Stanza 4, *Skj.* B I, 7.
[22] FAUCONNIER 1997, 22.
[23] PAIVIO & CLARK 1986; PAIVIO & WALSH 1993; ENDESTAD & HELSTRUP 2002.

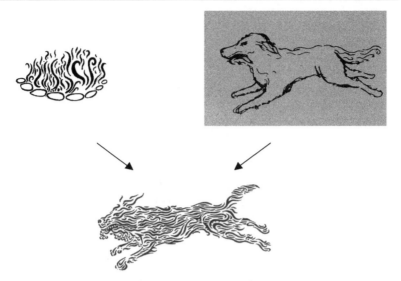

Figure 1: The fire-wolf

said, however, it is common knowledge that freshness and originality in meta-phorical expressions is more conducive to visual stimulation than the standard, classical expressions we find, for example, in idioms or imitated metaphors.

The Old Norse kenning system has the ability to counteract the tendency to make the imitated metaphors fossil, or "dead" in terms of visualization. The countless variations, or the so-called kenning variants of the standard kenning model, allow the skald to breathe new and personal metaphors into the stagnated phrases. The famous kenning model for ship, ANIMAL OF THE SEA, could perhaps coincide with what is termed as "skeletal file" among scholars of mental imagery, while the kenning variant and its adjectives reminds one of the more detailed image files, such as when the black sea-horse is depicted galloping on the waves of the ocean.[24]

The premise for the construction of a visual blending image is that both parts of the metaphor, the topic and vehicle, are fairly concrete objects, or what is termed as "high in imagery" (see fig. 1). In the example of the fire-wolf, *glóða garmr* in Old Norse, there are structures from two concrete elements, a fire and a wolf, which partially blend together to form a single image of the fire-wolf. Notice that we do not hear that the fire is like a wolf, as we would put it according to the two-dimensional model for metaphors. Rather, we receive an independent visual image of a fire-wolf that attacks King Vísburr in *Ynglingatal*.

It is important to note that the blending-image not only appears in archaic thought; these kinds of constructions are encountered every day in cartoons or comic literature. When we see a banana roller-skating, a car that cries or a

[24] On skeletal and image files see KOSSLYN 1995. One can find such a sea-horse in *Lausavísa* 13 of Eyvindr Finnsson (*Skj.* B I, 65).

Figure 2: House-thief in fire-stockings

tree that walks we have structures from the human body and structures from inanimate things projected into a blended space where a new visual image is elaborated. On the other hand, I would maintain that there is a clear tendency to make blending images in the oldest corpus, but I have not found this to be the case among the converted skalds. Concrete blending images can also be spotted on the Oseberg carpet from around 800, where the image of a tree and horses are blended into a single structure.[25] A point can also be made of the terms *nykrat* or *finngálknat,* the Old Norse medieval translations of the Latin *barbarismus.* The *nykur,* or the *finngálkn,* are creatures whose heads are not in harmony with their bodies, and thus make ideal images for the blending concept. But, as Snorri teaches in his poetics, we are advised not to make use of such figures in poetry, and thus he brings forth the new aesthetics of natural harmony and clarity.[26]

My point is that we cannot make use of the two-dimensional metaphor model if we are to appreciate the oldest skaldic poetry. Without the blending concept, or the aesthetic feeling of *nykrat,* the beauty and the construction of meaning in this poetry will remain hidden. Fortunately, the metaphorical expressions of fire and wolf can be found in the works of a distinguished thirteenth-century skald and scholar. The many differences in the metaphorical expressions of the two skalds could suggest the metaphorical development between the two periods. The Christian skald is Sturla Þórðarson, who praises King Hákon in the poem *Hákonarkviða* (1263). There is evidence that suggests Sturla knew *Ynglingatal* and Bjarne Fidjestøl has wondered why Sturla makes so much use of metaphors that clearly allude to heathen mythology in a poem which aims to praise a Christian king.[27] One explanation could be that the allusions to the heathen myths are no longer threatening or blasphemous, as

---

[25] MYHRE *et al.* 1992, 242.
[26] SNORRI STURLUSON, *Snorra-Edda, Háttatal*, 6.
[27] FIDJESTØL 1999, 289.

they had been among the skalds of the early eleventh century who excluded kennings referring to heathen mythology from their poems.

In *Hákonarkviða* the visual blending image of the fire-wolf has been replaced by using the abstract kenning model for fire THE WOLF OF THE TREE, without adding much visual details to the model. In Old Norse the kennings *elris gramr, viðar hundr* and *selju rakki* are other variants of this model.[28] In other words, the kenning model is so abstract that it does not bring forth an image with the same visual power as before. The fire-wolf is no longer to be seen. The two domains of the metaphor, topic and vehicle, are separated by the kenning model; the fire is like a wolf. It is also interesting to note that the Christian skalds, such as Þjóðólfr Arnórsson in the eleventh century and Markús Skeggjason in the twelfth century,[29] do not apply imagery when they praise the manner in which their Christian kings burn down the houses of the heathens.

Some other examples of the visual blending image in heathen poetry could be the 'house-thief in fire-stockings', *húspjófr á hyrjar leistum* (fig. 2),[30] the 'herring-tern', *sporðfjǫðruð spáperna nóta* (fig. 3),[31] 'hail-chisel', *éla-meitill* (fig. 4,[32] or Hel – the erotic death (fig. 8).[33]

It is of great theoretical interest to ask why such visual blending constructions seem to disappear with the Christian skalds. Could it be because the Christian skald was more eager to make clear and harmonically grounded metaphors which were influenced by the aesthetic criteria of *claritas*, as opposed to constructions that did not have any parallels in the natural world? Or does it have something to do with their skills in writing, since the prerequisite for their poems was no longer the living memory? Was there, at this point in time, no longer a need to make such bizarre and distinctive images mnemonic in function? Was it, perhaps, because of the popularity of allegorical metaphors, where the topic often was an abstract dimension like mercy, sin, justice, and God, and only the vehicle was concrete? Or does it have something to do with a new and more formulaic attitude towards the kennings?

I would now like to draw attention to cognitive archaism Number 4 in the appendix, which involves the effect of allusion. Here I will apply the same examples of the fire descriptions by Þjóðólfr and Sturla. Firstly, I would like to point out that this criterion has a long history. As early as 1933 Wolfgang Mohr introduced the term "treffenden Kenning", meaning a kenning that had semantic value for the topic, instead of the substitution theory of the kennings, i.e. that the kenning was a mere substitution for a noun. Later on, scholars like Ladislaus Mittner and Hallvard Lie,[34] maintained that at the heart of the art

---

[28] *Skj.* B II, 120. It is worth pointing out the fact that the blending construction *glóða garmr* is not a "correct kenning" according to the standard definition, and the same could be said about the hail-chisel of Egill Skallagrímsson. This could suggest a more liberalistic and imagery-based view on kennings among the older skalds.

[29] Stanza 2, *Skj.* B I, 347, see Table 2 in Appendix. Stanza 22, *Skj.* B I, 417.

[30] *Ynglingatal* 27, *Skj.* B I, 12.

[31] Eyvindr skáldaspillir, *Lausavísa* 13, *Skj.* B I, 65.

[32] Egill Skallagrímsson, *Lausavísa* 23, *Skj.* B I, 47.

[33] *Ynglingatal* stanzas 7 and 32, *Skj.* B I, 8 and 13.

[34] MITTNER 1955; LIE 1957, 1982.

Figure 3: The herring-tern

of kennings was the potential of the kenning to create a bridge between the concrete world of the skald and his mythological universe. According to Edith Marold, the kenning can be capable of subliming the king to the realm of the gods as well as justifying the killing of enemies.[35] I have termed this perspective on the kennings as functionalistic, in contrast to the linguistic view of kennings inherited from Snorri in which the substitution theory is essential.[36]

The fire-wolf in the poem *Ynglingatal* can easily be seen as carrying the effect of allusion. The stanza tells of two sons who burn their father in his house in order to take over his kingdom. It is said that they excite and release the fire-wolf on their father, who is bitten to death by the fatal beast. This reminds us of the myth of Ragnarǫk where Fenrir attacks and kills the god Óðinn (see fig. 5). The allusion could have had more than one function, and a key-function could be recalling to the Viking-mind which members of the mythological universe attack the gods. According to *Vǫluspá* (stanza 48 in *Codex Regius*) the wolf Fenrir was accompanied by Loki and the giants to the battle in Ragnarǫk. Dómaldi and his brother in *Ynglingatal*, who broke the ethical code, could therefore be associated with the giants. This could both explain and justify the sacrifice of the cruel son Dómaldi in the next stanza of *Ynglingatal*. It was perfectly logical to sacrifice him, because that is what usually happens to giants, as we know from the story of the giant Ymir and the creation of earth.[37] Another source on King Dómaldi, *Historia Norvegie*, also describes his death as a sacrificial offering to: "... ensure the fruitfulness of the crops",[38] as demonstrated in *Ynglingatal* with the Old Norse *árgjǫrn Svía kind*.[39] The case of cruel Dómaldi could thus agree with the hypotheses of sacrifice as a popular type of punishment for the worst criminals in the pre-Christian Scandinavia.[40] In the case of Sturla (1263), it is clear that such an allusion is impossible in the context of the poem. In this poem King Hákon himself releases the WOLF OF THE WOOD in order to punish the Swedes for their bad manners. If one

---

[35] MAROLD 1988.
[36] For further discussion on kenning-theory, see BERGSVEINN BIRGISSON 2001, 23–52.
[37] SNORRI STURLUSON, *Snorra-Edda, Gylfaginning*, 8.
[38] *Historia Norvegie*, IX.
[39] Stanza 5, *Skj.* B I, 8.
[40] See JÓN HNEFILL AÐALSTEINSSON 2001.

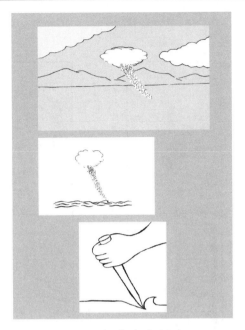

Figure 4: The hail-chisel

associates the wolf with Fenrir, then it would be logical to associate the king with either Loki or the giants – an association with which he would not be content.

Thus, in relation to the fire-wolf of *Ynglingatal* we can speak of a *non-verbal allusion*, and furthermore, a religious function of a visual image. It is the imagery itself that alludes to the myth, and informs us about the skald's ethical judgement on the act of the brothers. To kill one's father for gain is to break the ethical code of society – they prove themselves to be outcasts like the wolf and the giant.[41] The history of Vísburr and Dómaldi can thus be seen as parabolic rather than historical in nature because it conveys the ethics of the skald's society. Thus, in the case of Sturla, the metaphorical expression has become a mere poetical decoration. Perhaps the allusion to heathen mythology in *Ynglingatal* could also explain why skalds in the eleventh and twelfth century did not use the metaphor of the fire-wolf. Possibly they did not want to evoke the allusion-effect associated with the fire-wolf. In any case, this could give one answer to the interesting theoretical question of how the new credo-based way of thinking among the converted altered the attitude towards mental imagery. As a matter of fact, I have not found such imagery-based allusions anywhere in the Christian skaldic-corpus.

---

[41] That this is killing in the name of gain is implied by the kenning used on the brothers: *setrs verjendr*, "they who will take over the kingdom", and in *Historia Norvegie* it says that they burnt their father: "...so that they might attain their inheritance more swiftly" (chapter IX).

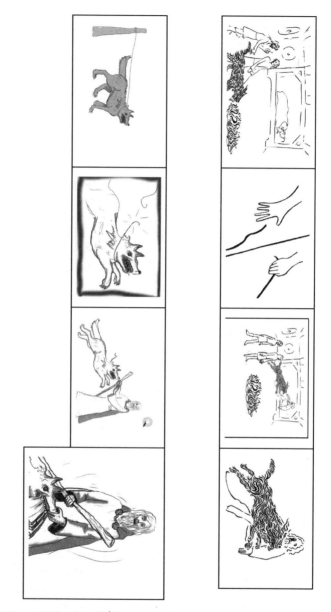

Figure 5: The fate of Óðinn and Vísburr. Upper: Scene in Ynglingatal.
Lower: Scene in the myth of Fenrir and Óðinn

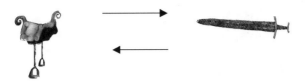

Figure 6: Saddle of the whetstone

The next cognitive archaism I wish to examine is movement-based mapping (2a in Table 1). This is also a rare feature to find among the converted skalds. In fact, I have only found one example of this in the corpus. It appears in Sturla Þórðarson's *Hákonarkviða* where he describes the eagerness to fight, or the war itself, as the 'tremble-disease of the sword', or *riðusótt bauga bliks*. Here the mapping is between the symptoms of a sick animal who trembles and the frequent movement of a soldier's sword.[42]

But the example I will focus on here derives from Egill Skallagrímsson in his poem to Eiríkr blóðøx: *Hǫfuðlausn*.[43] The kenning has a sword as its topic: *heinsǫðull* in Old Norse, or the "saddle of the whetstone" (fig. 6). As we can see in the figure, there are no formal grounds for the metaphor; a sword has nothing in common with a saddle. How then is the metaphor to be understood?

In my view, there is no way of understanding the grounds for the metaphor without a close inspection of the images involved, as well as the associative factors attached to a saddle, i.e. a horse and rider (see fig. 7). Only then can we see that the movement of the whetstone sharpening the sword is identical to the movement of the rider in the saddle. There is a clear interaction between the images and, as we noted this is one of the criteria for images easiest retrieved from memory. This represents an example of cognitive archaism 2ab, in which the grounds of the metaphor are only found in the movement of the associative factors of the images involved. I suspect the modern reader would have considerable difficulty in constructing a metaphor of this kind. The metaphors "we live by" are to be understood effectively and quickly (popular words in the capitalistic society!) or else they are doomed metaphors. The question remains as to whether we can unravel the mentality of the skald in this complex metaphorical structure. Poetry, as Egill understood it, was craftsmanship of the mind, in Old Norse *íþrótt*. It was meant to be pondered on long and dark winter-evenings; it made demands on its listeners who were also rewarded. In this context, it is of great interest to take a look at modern cognitive metaphor theory, especially the "Invariance Principle" of George Lakoff and Mark Turner.[44] The principle of invariance maintains that image-metaphors always preserve structural harmony between the topic and vehicle, that is "each metaphorical mapping preserves

---

[42] *Skj.* B II, 123.

[43] Stanza 8, *Skj.* A I, 37/B I, 32.

[44] Lakoff & Turner 1989.

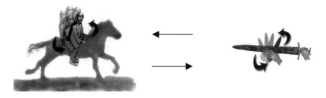

Figure 7: Movement based mapping between rider and whetstone

image-schema structure".[45] In Egill's example there is complete disharmony between the domains, the sword could be characterised as a *part* while the saddle is a kind of a *container*. Structural harmony is only found by inspecting some of the associative factors of the vehicle, the rider in the saddle, and mapping his movement to the movement of the whetstone on the sword: This leads us to some questions of a theoretical nature. The hypothesis of invariance in all metaphorical mappings, which I understand to signify a universal value, undeniably reminds us of the classical aesthetics of harmony and clarity from the Greek-Roman inheritance. Metaphorical thinking of this kind could, for example, be traced to Aristotle's writings. In his third book of *Rhetorics* he claims that "metaphor most of all has clarity"[46], and in *Poetics* he also demonstrates the aesthetics of harmony: "For to make metaphors well is to observe what is like [something else]".[47]

If these criteria were applied to the metaphors of the oldest skaldic poetry we would come to exactly the same results as did the scholars of the early twentieth century: that their metaphors are both barbaric and immature. The metaphor of the saddle and the sword would have no clarity of this kind. Accordingly, it cannot be seen as a well-made metaphor in terms of classical aesthetics, nor can we appreciate it on the grounds of our modern "fast and effective-mentality" which I assume also applies to metaphorical thinking. If, on the other hand, the Old Norse metaphors are valued on the basis of the aesthetics of contrast tension – of likening things that are not alike, and of making a-naturalistic images and metaphors that we are forced to delve into with an inner eye in order to understand the mapping – we would not hesitate to judge them as the offspring of genius minds.

It is my contention that the kind of aesthetic criteria we find in the oldest corpus of skaldic poetry must, to some extent, have been based on social conditions in which it was seen as an aid to the memorization of poetry if it contained some bizarre and penetrating imagery. These cognitive features could, perhaps, be termed as "mnemonic aesthetics". One must assume that the mnemonic rule of the bizarre image was of great value in oral culture. The unwillingness of the Christian skalds to use such imagery was clearly based on

---

[45] Lakoff 1993, 231.
[46] Aristotle, *Rhetorics*, III 2.1405a4.
[47] Aristotle, *Poetics* 4.5.5.

aesthetic and religious grounds, but in addition we might ask whether the need to penetrate human memory with bizarre imagery was less important for them because they didn't have to rely totally on living memory.

It is also worth noting that the skalds of old were by no means unfamiliar with the aesthetics of harmony and clarity. In the oldest poetry we find metaphors governed by the criterion of harmony in the form and nature of the images involved "... *með líkindum ferr ok eðli*",[48] as Snorri terms this style in his *Edda*. But this was by no means the overall aesthetic aim of the early skalds – as it would later become.

Finally, I would like to briefly examine cognitive archaism 3 in the appendix, the images of contrast tension aesthetics. As you may note, I have put the word *original* in front of the images. This is important in order to distinguish the originality we often find in the heathen corpus from the mere imitation of the same kenning variations in Christian times. The criterion is based on an analysis of the metaphorical mappings involved. If I find a new kind of mapping in the skaldic language – a new image-based mapping on top of the basic expressions – then it is termed "original image". Thus, when Snorri Sturluson obviously imitates the grotesque image from Haraldr harðráði on axe killing (1029), where the "soldier kisses the mouth of the axe", the image is not original. On the other hand, when Snorri calls the warrior "the one who satisfies the wolf of the sea" *elfar ulfseðjandi*,[49] it is an original mapping between the belly of the wolf who, in the old models, constantly feeds on dead warriors, and the "belly" of the ship, where the seafarer goes onboard. This novel mapping I have not found anywhere else, and while pondering, one can easily see the play of images intended for our inner eye.[50] The old and often used phrase for war, like "the warrior satisfied the wolf", does not call for visualization to the same extent. Thus, it is an original image of a grotesque nature which might be described as visually stimulating.

It would perhaps be better to speak about levels of originality or levels of grotesque. If, for example, we again turn to *Ynglingatal*, we find images that are far more grotesque than anything in later poetry. Here I refer especially to the female personification of Death in Old Norse mythology, Hel. In Þjóðólfr's poem, Hel is depicted in terms of erotic splendour (fig. 8). This can easily be understood as an original grotesque image from the hand of the skald, because all other examples of Hel in the oldest poetry picture this Death-figure as black, terrifying and merciless. If, on the other hand, we choose to refrain from all other empirical data on Hel, we can end up with the idea that the erotic Hel in *Ynglingatal* is based on an old religious belief, i.e. that pre-Christian Scandinavians experienced death as sexual pleasure with the figure of Hel.[51]

I would prefer to understand this in terms of the contrast-tension aesthetics which I discussed earlier. The skald can offer us the clash of many contrasts with

---

[48] Snorri Sturluson, *Snorra-Edda, Skáldskaparmál*, 121.
[49] Stanza 6, *Skj*. B II, 91.
[50] When I speak of images, I am referring to visual images, that is, what one sees in his inner eye.
[51] See e.g. this hypothesis in Steinsland 1992.

Figure 8: The grotesque Death in *Ynglingatal* (?)

his imagery: the erotic and the brutal, life and death, beauty versus ugliness, and so forth. Indeed, through the blending of the erotic and the ugly, Hel reminds us of the figures called "Kerch terracotta" with which Mikhail Bakhtin used to demonstrate the grotesque concept of the body. Those figures were old and crippled women who were also pregnant; they were *pregnant deaths* we might say.[52] But what does the Old Norse construction of grotesque imagery signify?

I would like to read the grotesque images within the context of the skald's social circumstances. Þjóðólfr was a skald at King Haraldr hárfagri's court, if we are to believe the medieval scholars, where constant wars made death visible and omnipresent, and, of course, the fear of death as well.[53] According to Bakhtin and Aron Gurevich,[54] the grotesque in medieval times, with its roots in the heathen past, is not to be understood as mere wordplay. The grotesque is instead a means of laughing at that which is serious and depressing, thus

[52] BAKHTIN 1968, 25.
[53] For a deeper grounding in this hypothesis see BERGSVEINN BIRGISSON 2003.
[54] GUREVICH 1988.

producing reconciliation with some of the hard facts of human existence.[55] Interestingly enough, the German artist Otto Dix (1891–1969) presents us with the same motifs of the erotic woman versus the dark/old woman in his war paintings.[56] This could point to the fact that such images should be understood in the context of their psychological circumstances of brutality and death. The trickster-nature of the Viking skald and the German artist is perhaps to be understood as Carl Gustav Jung proposed, as an essential archetype or dimension in the human psyche, rather than as a relative cultural model.

I would argue that the archaisms I have presented here can be used for dating and judging the authenticity of skaldic poetry in conjunction, of course, with other methods. The analysis manifests both a clear *discontinuity* in terms of metaphorical structures and expressions, as well as an obvious reduction in the function of visual imagery between the two periods mentioned. It is, of course, hard to tell how much this can be explained by the influence of writing, how much by the new credo-based way of thinking. Indeed it could be regarded as a Sisyphean toil to try to separate these two factors.

The question of whether the development of skaldic poetry in the North can be seen as a model for poetry in other cultures exposed to the same cultural fate remains for further research.[57]

Bibliography

Primary sources

ARISTOTLE, *Potics – with the Tractatus Coislianus, reconstruction of Poetics II, and the fragments of the On Poets*, transl. Richard Janko. Cambridge 1987.

Historia Norvegie, ed. Inger Ekrem & Lars Boje Mortensen, English transl. P. Fisher. Copenhagen 2003.

LexPoet see FINNUR JÓNSSON 1931.

SAXO GRAMMATICUS, *Gesta Danorum (Saxos Danmarkshistorie)*, transl. Peter Zeeberg. Copenhagen 2000.

Skj. – Den Norsk-Islandske Skjaldedigtning, vol IA/IB & IIA/IIB, ed. Finnur Jónsson. Copenhagen 1912–1915.

SNORRI STURLUSON, *Edda Snorra Sturlusonar*, ed. Finnur Jónsson. Copenhagen 1931.

Secondary sources

BAKHTIN, Mikhail 1968: *Rabelais and His World*. Cambridge, transl. Helene Iswolsky.

---

[55] GUREVICH 1988, 193.

[56] KARCHER 1992, 174, see also p. 125 for similar motifs to those we find in *Ynglingatal* (stanza 7, 32).

[57] I would like to thank Haki Antonsson who read the manuscript in its entirety for helpful advice and comments.

BERGSVEINN BIRGISSON 2001: *Hel – Heimildargildi dróttkvæðra kenninga um fornt hugarfar.* Unpublished cand.philol. dissertation, Bergen.

——— 2003: "Å elska med øyrelaus hund og skummel død – om Gro Steinslands hypotese om døden som erotisk lystreise i norrøn tid." *Nordica Bergensia*, 29 47–80.

BUGGIE, S. E. 1974: *Imagery and Relational Variety in Associative Learning.* Unpublished doctoral dissertation, Eugene.

CARRUTHERS, Mary 1993: *The Book of Memory: A Study of Memory in Medieval Culture.* Cambridge.

CLUNIES ROSS, Margaret 1989: "The cognitive approach to Skaldic poetics, from Snorri to Vigfússon and beyond." In Rory McTurk & Andrew Wawn (eds.) *Úr Dölum til Dala – Guðbrandur Vigfússon Centenary Essays*, pp. 267–286, Leeds.

EINSTEIN, Gilles O. & McDANIEL, Mark A. 1987: "Distinctiveness and the mnemonic benefits of bizarre imagery." In Mark A. McDaniel & Michael Pressley (eds.) *Imagery and Related Mnemonic Processes: Theories, Individual Differences, and Applications*, pp. 78–102, New York.

ENDESTAD, T. & HELSTRUP, T. 2002: *Imagery and Verbal Processes in Metaphor Comprehension.* Paper II in Endestad, T.: Cognitive Mechanisms in the Comprehension of Metaphors. Unpublished doctoral dissertation, Oslo.

FAUCONNIER, Gilles 1997: *Mappings in Thought and Language.* Cambridge.

FIDJESTØL, Bjarne 1999: *The Dating of Eddic Poetry, Bibliotheca Arnamagnæana*, vol. 41. Copenhagen.

FINNUR JÓNSSON 1920: *Den oldnorske og oldislandske Litteraturs Historie.* Copenhagen, 2 ed.

FINNUR JÓNSSON (ed.) 1931: *Lexicon poeticum antiquæ linguæ septentrionalis. Ordbog over det norsk-islandske skjaldesprog.* Copenhagen.

FOUCAULT, Michel 1996: *Tingenes orden - En arkeologisk undersøkelse av vitenskapene om mennesket.* Oslo, transl. Knut Ove Eliassen.

GAUDIN, Colette 1987: *On Poetic Imagination and Reverie: Selections from Gaston Bachelard.* Dallas, Texas.

GUREVICH, Aaron J. 1988: *Medieval Popular Culture: Problems of Belief and Perception.* Cambridge, transl. János M. Bak & Paul A. Hollingsworth.

HINTZMAN, D. L. 1993: "Twenty-five years of learning and memory: Was the cognitive revolution a mistake?" In D. E. Meyer & S. Kornblum (eds.) *Attention and Performance XIV: Synergies in Experimental Psychology, Artificial Intelligence, and Cognitive Neuroscience*, pp. 359–391, Cambridge.

JÓN HNEFILL AÐALSTEINSSON 2001: "Mannblót í norrænum sið." In Michael Stausberg (ed.) *Kontinuitäten und Brüche in der Religionsgeschichte*, pp. 1–11, Berlin.

KARCHER, Eva 1992: *Otto Dix 1891–1969.* Köln.

KOSSLYN, Stephen M. 1995: "Mental imagery." In Stephen M. Kosslyn & Daniel N. Osherson (eds.) *An Invitation to Cognitive Science*, vol. 2, pp. 267–296, Cambridge, 2 ed.

KRAUSE, Wolfgang 1930: *Die Kenning als typischer Stilfigur der germanischen und keltischen Dichtersprache, Schriften der Königsberger Gelehrten Gesellschaft 7. Jahr*, vol. 1.

LAKOFF, George 1993: "The contemporary theory of metaphor." In A. Ortony (ed.) *Metaphor and Thought*, pp. 202–251, Cambridge, 2. edition.

LAKOFF, George & TURNER, Mark 1989: *More than Cool Reason: A Field Guide to Poetic Metaphor*. Chicago.

LIE, Hallvard 1957: *Natur og unatur i skaldekunsten*. Oslo.

———— 1982: *Om sagakunst og skaldskap – Utvalgte avhandlinger*. Oslo.

LORD, Albert B. 1960: *The Singer of Tales, Harvard Studies in Comparative Literature*, vol. 24. Cambridge, Mass.

MAROLD, Edith 1988: "Skaldendichtung und Mythologie." In *The Seventh International Saga Conference, Spoleto 4–10 sept 1988. Poetry in the Scandinavian Middle Ages*, pp. 201–213, Spoleto.

MEULENGRACHT SØRENSEN, Preben 1993: *Saga and Society: An Introduction to Old Norse Literature*. Studia borealia, Copenhagen.

MITTNER, Ladislaus 1955: *Wurd: Das Sakrale in der Altgermanischen Epik*. Bern.

MOHR, Wolfgang 1933: *Kenningstudien: Beiträge zur Stilgeschichte der Altgermanischen Dichtung*. Stuttgart.

MUNDAL, Else 2002: "Skaldekunsten – det biletskapande ordet." In Else Mundal & Anne Ågotnes (eds.) *Ting og tekst*, pp. 145–157, Bergen.

MYHRE, Bjørn, INGSTAD, Anne Stine & CHRISTENSEN, Arne Emil 1992: *Osebergdronningens grav – Vår arkeologiske nasjonalskatt i nytt lys*. Oslo.

PAIVIO, A. & CLARK, J. M. 1986: "The role of topic and vehicle imagery in metaphor comprehension." *Communication & Cognition*, 19 367–388.

PAIVIO, A. & WALSH, M. 1993: "Psychological processes in metaphor comprehension." In A. Ortony (ed.) *Metaphor and Thought*, pp. 307–328, Cambridge, 2 ed.

RUBIN, David C. 1995: *Memory in Oral Traditions – The Cognitive Psychology of Epic, Ballads, and Counting-Out Rhymes*. New York.

STEBLIN-KAMENSKIJ, Mikhail I. 1979: "Skaldicheskaya poeziya." In S. V. Perov (ed.) *Poeziya skaldov*, pp. 77–130, Leningrad, transl. in FIDJESTØL, BJARNE 1999 pp. 187–188.

STEINSLAND, Gro 1992: "Døden som erotisk lystreise." In Finn Hødnebø (ed.) *Eyvindarbók: Festskrift til Eyvind Fjeld Halvorsen*, pp. 319–332, Oslo.

WOLLEN, Keith A. & MARGRES, Matthew G. 1987: "Bizarreness and the imagery multiprocess model." In Mark A. McDaniel & Michael Pressley (eds.) *Imagery and Related Mnemonic Processes: Theories, Individual Differences, and Applications*, pp. 103–127, New York.

YATES, Frances 1966: *The Art of Memory*. London.

Appendix

Table 1. Types of cognitive archaisms in metaphors of Skaldic poetry

1 The visual blending-image

2 Demand of Image Inspection for understanding grounds of metaphor:

    2a Movement-based mapping (projection from topic to vehicle)

        2aa Movement of topic and vehicle Movement of topic and vehicle
        2ab Movement of associative factors

    2b Image Inspection demanded in form-based mapping

3 "Contrast tension Aesthetics" expressed in visual imagery:

    3a Original images of contrast categories/frames (Wolf/holy site)
    3b Original a-naturalistic images(seaweed of the mountain)
    3c Original grotesque images (erotic terms/war and death)

4 Allusion effect (allusion to heathen mythology with meaning-construction in context of a poem)

5 Animism of nature

Table 2. Conclusions from the analyses

Period*	Skald**	Corpus	Cogn. arch.	Cogn. arch. per stanza
c900	Þjóð	Ynglingatal 1–37	28	0.70
925–38	Eg	Lausav. 11–30	24	1.10
961–70	Eyv	Lausav. 1–14	12	0.78
1019	Sigv	Austrfararvísur 1–21	5	0.14
1046	Arn	Hrynhenda 1–20	3	0.10
1033–66	ÞjóðA	Lausav. 1–27	4	0.15
1104	Mark	Eiríksdrápa 1–32	2	0.03
1153	ESk	Geisli 1–15	0	0.00
c1160(?)	ESk	Øxarflokkr 1–11	3	0.18
c1136–52	Rv	Lausav. 1–17	5	0.23
12. cent.†	HVal	Íslendingadr. 1–26	1	0.04
12. cent.	Gmlkan	Harmsól 1–20	0	0.00
1190	Anon	Nóregs kon.-tal 1–83	1	0.01
12. cent.	Anon	Óláfsdr. Trg. 1–28‡	2	0.01
1197–1208	Kolb	Lausav.1–9	1	0.11
1221–39	SnSt	Lausav. 1–7	2	0.28
1240	Ólhv	Hrynhenda 1–12	2	0.16
1263–4	Sturl	Hákonarkviða 1–42	2	0.05
13. cent.	Anon	Líknarbraut 1–26	0	0.00
14. cent.	Eyst	Lilja 1–20	0	0.00
14. cent.	Anon	Maríugrátr 31–40	0	0.00
14. cent.	Anon	Gyðingsvísur 1–8	0	0.00

* Based on classical dating.

** The names of the skalds have been abbreviated as in *LexPoet*.

† The three poems dated to twelfth century, and the three poems dated to fourteenth century, have been aligned to 1149, 1150 and 1151, and 1349, 1350 and 1351 in order to use them in fig. 9. Other poems who have a time span in regards of dating, have been aligned to the middle of the span, thus the *Lausavísur* of Eyvindr skáldaspillir assumed from 961–970, have the year 966 on fig. 9.

‡ Not authentic.

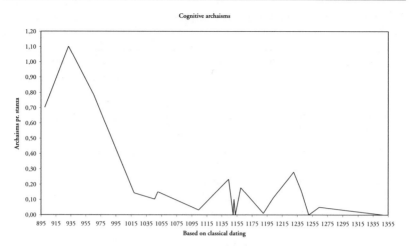

Table 3: Frequency of cognitive archaisms in Skaldic poetry 900–1350

The Dialogue between Audience and Text: The Variants in Verse Citations in *Njáls saga*'s Manuscripts

GUÐRÚN NORDAL

N JÁLS SAGA IS thought to have been written in Iceland in the 1280s.[1] The oldest extant manuscript of the saga, *Reykjabók* (the Book from Reykjar, AM 468 4to), was written in 1300–25, or only two decades or so later. Two manuscript fragments of the saga may antedate *Reykjabók*, bringing the first written evidence within twenty years of the original composition of the saga. *Reykjabók*, six manuscript fragments of *Njáls saga* from the period c. 1300–50, and *Kálfalækjarbók* (AM 133 fol., c. 1350) belong to the so-called *X* group of *Njáls saga*'s manuscripts, which is partly characterized by its citation of more verse than the other two manuscripts groups, *Y* and *Z*, represented also by two early manuscripts *Möðruvallabók* (AM 132 fol.) and the *Gráskinna* (GKS 2870 4to) fragments respectively (see Table 1).[2] The variance among the earliest manuscripts in their citation of skaldic verse shows that the earliest text of *Njáls saga* elicited a response from its readers and users, and indeed an appreciation of the early reception of *Njáls saga*, in the guise of the additional stanzas, can sharpen our understanding of saga composition in the late thirteenth and fourteenth centuries.[3] In this paper I will analyse six passages in *Njáls saga* where the audience in the early fourteenth century put its stamp on the narrative by enriching the prose with new verse creations.[4]

[1] On the dating of *Njáls saga*, see EINAR ÓL. SVEINSSON 1954, lxxv–lxxxiv.

[2] On the manuscripts of *Njáls saga*, see EINAR ÓL. SVEINSSON 1953, 5–14, and JÓN KARL HELGASON 1999, 13–43 on the transmission of the saga in the manuscripts and in later traditions.

[3] This verse is printed as an appendix to the most widely-used edition of *Njáls saga* by EINAR ÓL. SVEINSSON 1954, and in this article the verses will be called 'additional verses or stanzas' in order to distinguish them from verses common to all manuscripts of the saga and cited in the main text of his edition.

[4] The paper given at the conference in Bergen in June 2004 was partly based on an article which appeared in 2005. I refer to this article for a further discussion on many issues pertaining to the use of verse in the sagas of Icelanders. As my study of *Njáls saga* is in progress, and in order to avoid repetition, I have chosen to omit some parts of the original paper, and to add instead some new material in this printed version. Some repetition, however, can not be avoided.

The thirteenth- and fourteenth-century manuscripts of *Njáls saga* are unusually numerous in comparison with the preservation of other sagas of Icelanders, revealing the popularity of the saga among those who had books made for them. It is immediately clear that *Reykjabók* stands out. The codex is a unique testimony to the text of *Njáls saga* at the beginning of the fourteenth century, and the only manuscript to reflect a tangible development in how skaldic verse was incorporated in a saga. The first ten stanzas are cited in the narrative, seventeen are written as marginalia with a clear reference to their place in the prose, and three are written at the end of the saga. The marginal stanzas and the end verses are written in a different hand from that of the prose text, but date from about the same time.[5] The additional stanzas belong, therefore, to the first stage in the history of the text, and they may hold a key to the saga's reception in that early period.

Because of the fragmentary condition of some of the other manuscripts of *Njáls saga* it is not possible to reconstruct their 'original' text, but now five cite the additional verse: *Reykjabók*, *Kálfalækjarbók*, *Skafinskinna* (GSK 2868 4to; aligning itself with both *X* and *Z* according to Einar Ól. Sveinsson) and the fragments AM 162 B δ fol., and AM 162 B ε fol. The other fragments belonging to the *X* group are defective in those places where the verse would be preserved. Moreover, the additional verse of the *X* group is solely found in the first part of *Njáls saga*, in the so-called *Gunnars saga, that is in that part of the saga covering the life, and death, of Gunnarr Hámundarson. The distribution of the verse in the early manuscripts is shown in Table 1.

Einar Ól. Sveinsson tried to make sense of the distribution of the stanzas in the manuscripts of *Njáls saga* and came to no definite conclusion.[6] The poor quality of the early manuscripts causes obvious problems. *Kálfalækjarbók* is mostly defective in the first part of *Gunnars saga, only preserving Unnr's verse (1–3), but is the only manuscript to cite stanzas 11–12 by Skarpheðinn and Þormóðr's stanza. The δ and ε fragments contain only some of the passages where we find additional verses. The δ fragment is defective up to the point of Sigmundr Lambason's entrance to the saga, preserving two of his stanzas (13–14). The stanzas by Sigmundr are not added in the margins of *Reykjabók*, as are all the other stanzas in the second part of *Gunnars saga, but at the end of the saga by yet another scribe. The writer of δ omits verse in the second part, except for two stanzas by Skarpheðinn cited after the death of Gunnarr Hámundarson, one describing Hallgerðr (27) and the other Hrappr (28). The ε fragment preserves only Skarpheðinn's offensive commentary on Hallgerðr in stanza 27. All of Skarpheðinn's late stanzas (26–9) are in *Skafinskinna*, whose writer otherwise does not include the additional verses.

How did the verse find its way into an early manuscript of *Njáls saga*? We can think of at least four possibilities:

---

[5] See JÓN HELGASON 1962, xi.
[6] EINAR ÓL. SVEINSSON 1953, 21.

Table 1: Additional verse in *Njáls saga*

	R*	Rm	δ	K	ε	S	M	G
Unnr 1	x		def	x	def	-	def	-
Unnr 2	x		def	x	def	-	def	-
Unnr 3	x		def	x	def	-	def	-
Gunnarr 4	x		def	def	def	-	def	-
Gunnarr 5	x		def	def	def	-	def	-
Gunnarr 6	x		def	def	def	-	def	-
Gunnarr 7	x		def	def	def	-	-	-
Gunnarr 8	x		def	def	def	-	-	-
Gunnarr 9	x		def	def	def	-	-	-
Gunnarr 10	x		def	def	def	-	-	-
Skarpheðinn 11	-		-	x	def	-	-	-
Skarpheðinn 12	-		def	x	def	-	-	-
Sigmundr 13		x	x	x	def	-	-	-
Sigmundr 14		x	x	x	def	-	-	-
Sigmundr 15		x	-	x	def	-	-	-
Skarpheðinn 16		x	-	x	def	-	-	-
Skarpheðinn 17		x	-	x	def	-	-	-
Gunnarr 18		x	def	x	def	-	-	-
Skarpheðinn 19		x	-	x	def	-	-	-
Gunnarr 20		x	-	x	def	def	-	-
Gunnarr 21		x	-	x	def	def	-	-
Gunnarr 22		x	-	x	def	-	-	-
Gunnarr 23		x	-	x	def	-	-	-
Gunnarr 24		x	def	x	def	def	-	-
Þormóðr 25	-		def	x	def	def	-	-
Skarpheðinn 26		x	def	x	def	x	-	-
Skarpheðinn 27		x	x	x	x	x	-	-
Skarpheðinn 28		x	x	x	def	x	-	-
Skarpheðinn 29		x	-	x	def	-	-	-
Skarpheðinn 30		x	def	-	def	-	-	-

* See EINAR ÓL. SVEINSSON 1953, 22–23. The manuscripts are abbreviated as follows: R = *Reykjabók*; Rm = marginal verses, and those written at the end of *Njáls saga* in *Reykjabók*; δ = delta-fragment; K = *Kálfalækjarbók*; ε = epsilon-fragment; S = *Skafinskinna*; M = *Möðruvallabók*; G = *Gráskinna*. Other abbreviations in the table: x = verse cited; - = not cited; def = manuscript is defective.

1. Authentic verse transmitted orally from the tenth and eleventh centuries, and written down in the thirteenth century. This could apply to the stanzas in the conversion section,[7] which are also found in *Kristni saga*, as well as the poem *Darraðarljóð*, considered by Russell Poole to be a tenth-

---

[7] *ÍF* 12, ch. 102.

century composition.[8] These stanzas are preserved in all manuscripts of the saga.

2. Skaldic verse composed, and associated, with oral tales of Gunnarr Hámundarson, Skarpheðinn Njálsson and Kári Sǫlmundarson in the centuries after the events took place, and then written down in the thirteenth century. All of Kári's stanzas, but only two attributed to Skarpheðinn and Gunnarr are preserved in all manuscripts of the saga.

3. Skaldic verse composed at the time of writing the saga and incorporated into some manuscripts of the saga.

4. Skaldic verse composed after the writing of the saga, and then inserted into some manuscripts of the saga.

All four options seem to be at play in the first century after the writing of *Njáls saga*. A clearer understanding of the making and reshaping of the saga, and of other sagas in this early period, not least their use of skaldic verse composed at the same time, can shed a light on the active reception of the sagas of Icelanders in the fourteenth century.[9] Some of the additional verses may have existed when the first version of *Njáls saga* was written in the late thirteenth century, but others were evidently composed in appreciation of, or indeed reaction against, the written story. It is important to note that most of the additional verse (except stanzas 11–12 by Skarpheðinn, and stanza 25 by Þormóðr Óláfsson which are only in *Kálfalækjarbók*) is preserved in more than one manuscript from the fourteenth century, and therefore the inclusion of the so-called additional stanzas is not an idiosyncrasy by one editor or writer at the time, but suggests, rather, a strong interest in the use of verse within the sagas and a preference for endowing certain characters with poetic talents.

Einar Ól. Sveinsson divided *Njáls saga* into three parts: the first part, from the beginning of the saga to the death of Gunnarr Hámundarson, the second part, relating events up to the burning of Bergþórshváll and the third part depicting Kári's single-minded hunt of the arsonists to the saga's conclusion.[10] The distribution of the additional stanzas within the saga suggests, however, a bipartite structure, which sustains Lars Lönnroth's structural analysis of the saga, namely that *Gunnars saga was not concluded till after Þráinn Sigfússon's death.[11] The stanzas uncannily link the pivotal events from the beginning of the *Gunnars saga to its finale, drawing our attention to the most powerful and vivid scenes. The verses could serve as an index to crucial events in this part of *Njáls saga*, and we can ask ourselves if this was indeed their function; a mnemonic exercise construed to evoke key scenes in the saga by speaking the stanzas in a sequence. The first three additional stanzas belong to the opening

---

[8] POOLE 1992, 124–125. He dates *Darraðarljóð* to 919, and if his dating is correct the poem is clearly cited in the wrong historical context in *Njáls saga*.

[9] Jón Karl Helgason's study of the rewriting of *Njáls saga* was the first important attempt at elucidating this process after Einar Ól. Sveinsson's extensive research on the saga which culminated in Sveinsson's edition of the saga in 1954.

[10] EINAR ÓL. SVEINSSON 1954, cxxiii.

[11] LÖNNROTH 1976, 22–28.

section, and the last one is cited in ch. 99, only a paragraph before the narrative shifts to events abroad, signifying the change of leadership in Norway and the advent of Óláfr Tryggvason and the official arrival of Christianity in the north. Chapter 100 proclaims the beginning of the Christian era and the start of the second half of the saga, commonly called *Njáls saga, though *Kára saga would be a more fitting name, were it not for the reason that *Brennu-Njáls saga* is the name of the whole saga according to the vellum manuscripts. *Gunnars saga contains only 3 full stanzas in *Möðruvallabók*, but *Kára saga contains 17 stanzas and the poem *Darraðarljóð* in all the manuscripts. The first generations of listeners, or readers, of the saga sought to redress this imbalance between the two parts in this respect.

The main subject matter of *Gunnars saga* is the life and death of Gunnarr Hámundarson (introduced in ch. 19). The opening chapters of this part of *Njáls saga* explain the marital problems of his cousin Unnr Marðardóttir and the final section the troubles and killing of his uncle Þráinn Sigfússon. Twenty nine additional stanzas are attributed to four characters: three stanzas each to Unnr Marðardóttir and Sigmundr Lambason, thirteen to Gunnarr Hámundarson and ten to Skarpheðinn Njálsson. Their verse serves to deepen and even subtly modify the portrayal of these characters, particularly those of Gunnarr and Skarpheðinn. In a rendering of the saga before a living and appreciative audience, the verses break up the blocks of prose and draw attention to key moments in the narrative by bringing out the speaker's thoughts at that very moment.[12] These poetic outbursts are almost like monologues in a play. But which were the decisive moments in *Gunnars saga for the audience in the fourteenth century?

In an appendix to the article I have listed the narrative context of each of the twenty nine additional stanzas in *Njáls saga*. The stanzas are conveniently divided into four groups, corresponding to the four main narrative episodes of *Gunnars saga:

1. The introduction (chs. 1–18);
2. The early years of Gunnarr Hámundarson (chs. 19–32);
3. Gunnarr's marriage to Hallgerðr, his chieftaincy and his death (chs. 33–81);
4. The dealings between the Njálssynir and Þráinn Sigfússon (chs. 82–99).

Moreover, it is instructive to consider the information presented in Table 1. Only the first ten stanzas of *Gunnars saga, that is, the stanzas in the first two narrative episodes, are cited within the prose part of *Reykjabók*, but the remaining are written as marginalia or at the end of the saga. According to Einar Ól. Sveinsson's study of the manuscripts it seems that the writer of *Reykjabók* changed his exemplar at this point in the saga, that is after ch. 38 (stanza 11 is

---

[12] For a further discussion of the role of verse in the sagas of Icelanders, see BJARNI EINARSSON 1974; GUÐRÚN INGÓLFSDÓTTIR 1990; BIBIRE 1973.

cited in chapter 39), and stayed with that manuscript till chapter 116.[13] Stanzas 11–29 are merely added as marginal notes in the manuscripts, or at the end of the text, with a red sign specifying the place where they should be recited.[14] No attempt is made to adapt them to the narrative, which suggests that the verses were not in the manuscript the scribe was copying. These marginal stanzas, written at the same time as the main text of the manuscript[15] are physically on the borderline of the text. The editor of *Kálfalækjarbók* embraced all of the stanzas in his rendering of the saga. Sigmundr Lambason's libellous stanzas are not even given a marginal status in *Reykjabók*, but added at the very end of the saga; yet two of those were acceptable to the editor of the δ fragment and, of course, all three are in *Kálfalækjarbók*. The most widely preserved stanzas in the last part of *Gunnars saga are those by Skarpheðinn, suggesting perhaps the enduring appeal of this tragic figure of *Njáls saga* to its Icelandic audience; and the most popular was his mockery of Hallgerðr Hǫskuldsdóttir which will be discussed below (stanza 27).

But how important is the additional verse in *Gunnars saga for the understanding of *Njáls saga*? Do the verses add anything inventive to the interpretation of the key characters such as Gunnarr Hámundarson and Skarpheðinn Njálsson, or do they merely signal the first stage in the long-lasting relationship between the audience and the text of *Njáls saga* in Iceland?

Njáls saga opens with two references to women, Unnr Marðardóttir and Hallgerðr Hǫskuldsdóttir respectively. Both are introduced in the first chapter of the saga. Unnr is singled out as her father's only child and a fine match for any man in the Rangárvellir region in the south (*þótti sá beztr kostr á Rangárvǫllum*), and Hallgerðr portrayed as her father's favourite in a key scene where her uncle Hrútr detects her thiefing streak by looking her in the eye. Both women experience serious marital problems and at the end of the opening part of the saga they are both single again; Unnr divorced from Hrútr after a sexually unhappy marriage, destroyed by the pungent magic wrought by the third powerful woman in the introductory chapters, queen Gunnhildr, and Hallgerðr twice widowed, both husbands killed by the jealous Þjóstólfr. Their paths cross in the first chapters when Unnr marries Hallgerðr's uncle Hrútr, and later their lives will be entangled again when Hallgerðr marries Unnr's nephew Gunnarr Hámundarson, the man who had secured Unnr her dowry by challenging Hrútr to a duel. Unnr's second husband is Valgarðr grái, and their

---

[13] This part of *Reykjabók* is called R², see EINAR ÓL. SVEINSSON 1953, 120. JÓN HELGASON 1962, xiii proposed that this shift between exemplars had in fact occurred in the manuscript that the writer of *Reykjabók* is following. Moreover, the vellum manuscript called *Gullinskinna*, which was known in the seventeenth century but now lost, seems to have contained the same number of additional verses as the main text of *Reykjabók* (1–10), and this manuscript is not derived from *Reykjabók* but possibly from *Reykjabók*'s exemplar.

[14] There are two exceptions to this rule: the sign is missing (52r), or it is written in black ink (39r), see JÓN HELGASON 1962, xii.

[15] JÓN HELGASON 1962, xi.

son, Mǫrðr Valgarðsson, plays a key part in orchestrating the downfall and the killing of Gunnarr Hámundarson.

Unnr speaks three stanzas in the opening chapters of the saga, thus taking an active part in the development of the narrative, but Hallgerðr, conversely, is moulded into the most ambiguous female protagonist in the sagas. Hallgerðr is not given a poetic voice in the saga, but she is on three occasions in the poet's mind, twice in stanzas by Skarpheðinn and once in a stanza by her husband Gunnarr Hámundarson.

Unnr Marðardóttir: stanzas 1–3

Two of *Njála's* earliest manuscripts, *Reykjabók* and *Kálfalækjarbók*, preserve three stanzas by Unnr Marðardóttir recited on her second trip to her father at Alþingi, where she gives him details of her unhappy marriage.[16] The stanzas are incorporated into the narrative in *Reykjabók* and *Kálfalækjarbók* (*X* group), but are not in the *Gráskinna* fragment (*Z* group) which is also extant at this point, probably written around the same time as *Reykjabók*. *Möðruvallabók*, the only fourteenth-century representative of the *Y* group, is regrettably defective at the beginning of *Njáls saga*. The subtle difference between the two versions lies in the inclusion of Unnr's stanzas:

Reykjabók and *Kálfalækjarbók*	*Gráskinna*
Mǫrðr var á þingi, faðir hennar. Hann tók við henni allvel ok bað hana vera í búð sinni, meðan þingit væri; hon gerði svá. Mǫrðr mælti: "Hvat segir þú mér frá Hrúti, félaga þínum?" Hon kvað vísu:	Mǫrðr var á þingi, faðir hennar. Hann tók við henni allvel ok bað hana vera í búð sinni, meðan þingit væri; hon gerði svá. Mǫrðr mælti: "Hvat segir þú mér frá Hrúti, félaga þínum?"
Víst *segi ek gott frá* geystum geirhvessanda þessum, *þat er sjálfráðligt* silfra sundrhreyti *er* fundit; verð ek, því at álmr er orðinn eggþings fyrir gjǫrningum, satt er, at ek ség við spotti, segja mart eða þegja. (*Reykjabók*, 16)[17]	Hon svarar: "*Gott* má *ek frá* honum segja allt, *þat er* honum *er sjálfrátt*". (*ÍF* 12, 24)

---

[16] *ÍF* 12, ch. 7

[17] Her father Mǫrðr was at the assembly. He welcomed her warmly and invited her to stay at his booth during the thing. This she did. Mǫrðr said: "What do you have to tell me about your companion Hrútr". [*Reykjabók* and *Kálfalækjarbók*:] She recited a stanza: "I certainly have good things to report about this ambitious warrior (*geirhvessandi*) about those things as far as his (*sundurhreytir silfra*) intentions are concerned. I must either say all or nothing, because the warrior (*álmr eggþings*) has been the victim of sorcery. It is true that I am afraid of mockery." [*Gráskinna*:] She answered: "I can report nothing but good of him as far as his intentions are concerned". The edition of *Reykjabók*

The verbal echoes between the first *helmingr* in *Reykjabók* and *Kálfalækjarbók* and Unnr's answer in *Gráskinna* are printed in italics in the citation, and they indicate that the stanza may be inspired by the prose, and indeed composed after the saga was written. More specific information is added in the second *helmingr*. Unnr hints at Hrútr's fateful enchantment (*gjǫrningar* 'sorcery') by queen Gunnhildr, though she is not named in the stanza, but then the stanza closes on an uneasy note, with an acute sensitivity and wariness of mockery and gossip in her immediate community. The thrust of public opinion is a recurrent topic in *Njáls saga*, and the manuscripts containing these three powerful stanzas in the opening chapters throw into relief two crucial issues in the saga, ambiguous sexual relationships and slander in small communities.[18] The next two stanzas are opened by a short introduction:

Reykjabók and *Kálfalækjarbók*	*Gráskinna*
Mǫrðr varð hljóðr við ok mælti: "Þat býr þér nú í skapi, dóttir, at þú villt at engi viti nema ek, ok munt þú trúa mér bezt til órráða um þitt mál." Þá gengu þau á tal, þar er engir menn heyrðu þeira viðrmæli. Þá mælti Mǫrðr til dóttur sinnar: "Seg þú mér nú allt þat, er á meðal ykkar er, ok lát þér þat ekki í augu vaxa." "Svá mun vera verða," segir hon, ok kvað vísu:	Mǫrðr varð hljóðr við. "Hvat býr þér í skapi, dóttir?" segir hann, "því at ek sé, at þú villt, at engi viti nema ek, ok munt þú trúa mér bezt til órráða um þitt mál." Þá gengu þau á tal, þar er engir menn heyrðu þeira viðrmæli. Þá mælti Mǫrðr til dóttur sinnar: "Seg þú mér nú allt þat, er á meðal ykkar er, ok lát þér þat ekki í augu vaxa." "Svá mun vera verða," segir hon.

Víst hefir hringa hristir,
Hrútr, líkama þrútinn,
eitrs þá er línbeðs leitar
lundýgr munuð drýgja;
Leita ek með ýti
undlinna þá finna
yndi okkars vanda
aldræðr boði skaldar!

Ok enn kvað hon vísu:

Þó veit ek hitt, at hreytir
handfúrs, jǫkuls spannar
meiðr! er jafnt sem aðrir

---

is in Modern Icelandic. The reference to the edition are in a normalized spelling in this paper to make a comparison with the *ÍF*-edition easier.

[18] On the effective use of slander as a narrative technique in *Njáls saga*, see KRESS 1991; and on the importance of sexual themes in the saga see DRONKE 1982 and ÁRMANN JAKOBSSON 2000. See also SVERRIR TÓMASSON 2002, 74–75 who suggests that verses were used to cloak the message in words not immediately clear to everyone in the audience, such as the children.

ýtendr boga nýtir;
vilda ek við ǫldu
jókennanda þenna –
rjóðr, lít þú orð ok íðir,
undleggs! – *skilit segja*.
(*Reykjabók*, 16–17)[19]

"*Ek vilda segja skilit við* Hrút, ok
má ek segja þér, hverja sǫk ek má
helzt gefa honum. Hann má ekki hjú-
skaparfar eiga við mik, svá at ek mega
njóta hans, en hann er at allri nátt-
úru sinni annarri sem inir vǫskustu
menn." (*ÍF* 12, 24)

There are few verbal echoes between the prose of *Gráskinna* and the verse
in this section of *Reykjabók* and *Kálfalækjarbók*; the most obvious being: *Ek
vilda segja skilit við Hrút* or *ǫldu jókennanda* ('the seafarer'). The *eitr* ('poison')
is a reiteration of the *gjǫrningar* ('sorcery') in Unnr's first stanza, explaining
how Hrútr's body (*líkami*), or more precisely his sexual organ, is poisoned
when he eagerly (*lundýgr*) seeks pleasure (*munuð*) in the marital bed (*línbeð*).
The manuscript readings are *linnbeðs* (*Kálfalækjarbók*) and *línbeðs* (*Reykjabók*).
Einar Ól. Sveinsson and Finnur Jónsson prefer the former reading, but the
latter is more suggestive and delicately fits the context. *Línbeð* cleverly refers
to the marital bed, succinctly evoking the bridal dress, the *lín* worn by Unnr
on the wedding night. The listener is reminded of the fact that their relations
never developed beyond their first night together; their marriage was never
consummated and therefore Unnr is still an untouched bride. Unnr uses the
engaging verb *leita* (to seek, search) for both husband and wife: for Hrútr when
he passionately (*lundýgr*) leitar 'seeks' his sexual pleasures, and for her own
longing for marital bliss (*yndi*). Both are left wanting. The stanza is filled with
deep sadness which is missing in the prose in *Gráskinna*. However, Unnr's third
and final stanza is more abrupt. She depicts Hrútr in elegant, yet strikingly
cold and distant kennings. The frosty reference to a glacier (*jǫkull*) in the
first kenning for Hrútr (*meiðr spannar jǫkuls*) would not have been lost on an
Icelandic audience. Hrútr's wealth is evoked by an image of icy silver, and the
reference to jewellery has the hint of the feminine; bringing home the stark
realities of their relationship. In the last kenning Hrútr is seen from afar, as
the swift seafarer, the traveller to foreign lands, where another woman wielded
those magical powers over him.

---

[19] Mǫrðr became silent and said: "You have something on your mind, daughter, which you don't want
anyone else to know but myself, from whom you can best expect help in your troubles." Then they
went aside where no one could her them talk. Then Mǫrðr spoke to his daughter: "Now tell me
everything about you two and don't be afraid to tell me the whole story." "So it shall be", she says,
[*Reykjabók* and *Kálfalækjarbók*:] and recited a stanza: "Hrútr, the wealthy man (*hristir hringa*), has
a swollen penis because of poisoning when he eagerly comes to the soft bed to enjoy pleasure. I
try to find a way to have pleasure with him (*ýtir undlinna*), you old warrior (*boði skjaldar*). Yet I
know, warrior (*meiðr spannar jǫkuls*), that the generous man (*hreytir handfúrs*) is like other good
men (*ýtendr boga*). I want to divorce this man (*kennandi ǫldu jós*); you (*rjóðr undleggs*) observe
the facts of the matter." [*Gráskinna*:] "I would like to be divorced from Hrútr, and I can tell you
what particular reason I have for it. He is not able to have marital intercourse with me in any such
manner that I can enjoy. In all other respects he hast he ways of other excellent men."

Both manuscript groups agree on the closing of the discussion between the father and daughter, when Unnr describes her marital troubles in plain words:

"Hversu má svá vera?", segir Mǫrðr, "ok seg enn gørr." Hon svarar: "Þegar hann kemur við mik, þá er hǫrund hans svá mikit, at hann má ekki eptirlæti hafa við mik, en þó hǫfum vit bæði breytni til þess á alla vega, at vit mættim njótask, en þat verðr ekki. En þó áðr, vit skilim, sýnir hann þat af sér, at hann er í œði sínu rétt sem aðrir menn." (ÍF 12, 24)[20]

Unnr may offer the same information in the verse and in the prose, but in *Reykjabók* the message is developed elegantly in powerful images which linger on in the listener's mind, and then they are reiterated in the plain language of the prose. The presentation of Unnr as the poetess also deepens her portrayal in the saga. It is rare to find verses spoken by women in the skaldic corpus, and none are as explicit in their sexual longing as these three by Unnr Marðardóttir.

Three stanzas about Hallgerðr Hǫskuldsdóttir: stanzas 17, 24 and 27

The portrayal of Hallgerðr Hǫskuldsdóttir in *Njáls saga* has sparkled more debate within the audience of the sagas than that of any other character in the sagas of Icelanders. Is Hallgerðr vilified by the author? Is she an independently-minded woman in a male society who never stood a chance, or does she live up to Hrútr's prediction of the untruthful woman? The first readers and users of *Njáls saga* did not seek to soften the negative portrayal of Hallgerðr in the saga by giving her a chance to explain her actions in verse, on the contrary, they chose to bring more attention to some of her most disreputable moments. Three of the additional stanzas in *Gunnars saga* focus on Hallgerðr's actions, and these stanzas register the apprehension with which her portrayal had distilled in the audience in the early fourteenth century. Two are by Skarpheðinn Njálsson, the first spoken after the killing of Sigmundr Lambason (verse 17) and the other at Hallgerðr's last sighting in the saga at Grjótá (verse 29), and one by Gunnarr Hámundarson when she flatly refuses to give him a lock of her hair (ch. 24).

Sigmundr Lambason is introduced into the saga in chapter 41, when he comes to stay with his kinsman, Gunnarr Hámundarson at Hlíðarendi. He is described as a *skáld gott ok at flestum íþróttum vel búinn, hávaðamaðr mikill, spottsamr ok ódæll* 'a good poet and skilled in most sports; he was boisterous, sarcastic and overbearing';[21] qualities which anticipate the action to come. Hallgerðr eggs Sigmundr to avenge the killing of her kinsman Brynjólfr who had been killed by Þórðr leysingjasonr, the fosterfather of the sons of Njáll, in the escalating dispute between Bergþóra Skarpheðinsdóttir and Hallgerðr. Njáll

---

[20] "I don't quite understand?" said Mǫrðr, "be more specific. She answered: "Whenever he touches me his member is so large that he cannot gratify himself with me; and yet we have tried all ways to have intercourse, but it is not to be. Yet before we part he shows that he is in all other respects has the ways of other men."

[21] ÍF 12, 105. Transl. Cook 2001, 68.

accepts Gunnarr's offer of compensation after the slaying, but slander in the district leads to Hallgerðr's insulting remarks about Njáll and his sons, upon which she eggs Sigmundr to compose verses of the men at Bergþórshváll. These stanzas are not cited in *Möðruvallabók*, and they probably did not belong to the saga originally, but the omission of the stanzas clearly invited a response from a creative and appreciative audience. The stanzas take their cue from Hallgerðr's derogatory comments.[22] The writer of *Reykjabók* does not integrate the stanzas in the narrative, but cites them at the very end of the saga. All three are incorporated into the narrative in *Kálfalækjarbók*, only two in the δ fragment. The defamatory stanzas sparkle the wrath of Bergþóra, and spur the sons of Njáll to action. A fight between Sigmundr and the sons of Njáll swiftly follows, where Sigmundr is killed. Skarpheðinn speaks two stanza in relation to the killing of Sigmundr, and these are not in the δ fragment. The second one is spoken after he has beheaded Sigmundr, and his words are directed at Hallgerðr.[23] The inclusion of this stanza in *Kálfalækjarbók* is typical for those instances where the editors make room for the stanza in the narrative by cutting the equivalent prose, which probably inspired the composition of the stanza in the first place, in order to avoid repetition.

Kálfalækjarbók	*Möðruvallabók* and *Gráskinna*
Skarpheðinn sá smalamann Hallgerðar; þá hafði hann hǫggvit hǫfuð af Sigmundi; hann seldi smalamanni í hendr hǫfuðit, ok kvað vísu:	Skarpheðinn sá smalamann Hallgerðar; þá hafði hann hǫggvit hǫfuð af Sigmundi; hann seldi smalamanni í hendr hǫfuðit ok bað hann *færa* Hallgerði ok kvað hana kenna mundu, *hvárt þat hǫfuð hefði* kveðit *níð* um þá.
Hǫfuð þetta skaltú, hrotta hljómstærandi! *færa*, – kom þú eldskerðir orðum Álfs ferðar, – *Hallgerði.* Hykk, at þǫll muni þekkja Þynjar logs ok skynja, þýð, *hvárt þat hafi* smíðat þungt *níð*, boði skíða!	
Smalamaðr kastaði niðr hǫfðinu, þegar þeir skilðu, því at hann þorði eigi, meðan þeir váru við. (*Reykjabók*, 76)[24]	Smalamaðr kastaði niðr hǫfðinu, þegar þeir skilðu, því at hann þorði eigi, meðan þeir váru við. (*ÍF* 12, 117)

---

[22] *ÍF* 12, 113.

[23] Written in the lower margin of fol. 24v in *Reykjabók*.

[24] Skarpheðinn saw Hallgerðr's shepherd; then he had beheaded Sigmundr; he handed the shepherd the head, [*Kálfalækjabók*:] and recited a stanza: "Give, man (*hljómstærandi hrotta*), this head to Hallgerðr; convey, man (*eldskerðir Álfs ferða*), these words: 'I think, workman (*boði skíða*), that the gentle woman (*Þynjar logs þǫll*), will recognize whether this head has composed serious mockery.'" [*Möðruvallabók* and *Gráskinna*:] And he told him to take it to Hallgerðr. He said that she would recognize the head as the one which had composed mockery about them. [All:] The shepherd

There is a greater sense of urgency in the stanza than in the prose. Skarph-eðinn asks the *smali* in the prose in the *Möðruvallabók*, but in the stanza he instructs him (*skaltú*) to bring the severed head to Hallgerðr. Even though the stanza carries the same message as the prose, it is brought home in a more forceful manner in the reflective and incisive imagery of the stanza. The choice of imagery for the smali is not appropriate: *hljómstærandi hrotta* ('the increaser of the sound of the sword', i.e., warrior); it would however, be very apt for Sigmundr. The depiction of the resounding sword evokes the image of the tongue, which can strike as forcefully as a sharp-edged weapon. This is exactly what happened in *Njáls saga*; Sigmundr's stanzas cut through the reconciliation reached by Gunnarr and Njáll. The last two lines in each *helmingr* contain the same consonant clusters in the internal rhyme (-*rð*-). In the first *helmingr* the internal rhyme leads up to a climax when speaking Hallgerðr's name:

(line 3) -*skerð*- / *orð*-
(line 4) *ferð*- / -*gerð*-

Skarpheðinn may have killed Sigmundr for his verses, but the blame for the deed rested ultimately with her. The effect of assonance, of repeating or near-repeating the same rhyme, is also at play in the second *helmingr* where *Hallgerðr* is again in the poet's mind. She is depicted deceptively tenderly as the *Þynjar logs Þǫll*, but then the kenning is upset by the unexpected adjective *þýð* ('gentle'). Such a description of Hallgerðr by Skarpheðinn is clearly ironic, succinctly evoking her favours towards Sigmundr which made him fulfil her wishes. The rhyming pattern gives us a further clue to the unlocking of the poet's word game:

(line 7) *þýð* / *smíð*-
(line 8) *níð* / *skíð*-

The repetition in the rhyming syllables has the effect of marrying Hallgerðr's gentle (*þýð*) disposition towards Sigmundr, to the destructive insult instigated by her. The adjective *þungt* applies equally to the *níð* and to Sigmundr's head. This technique of repetition may suggest oral performance of the kind we find in Old English vernacular poetry,[25] but it could equally be a rhetorical device. When Skarpheðinn has spoken the stanza he disappears from the scene, leaving the terrified *smali* with the heavy burden of taking the head to Hallgerðr.

Gunnarr Hámundarson's ten stanzas are spoken in relation to his disputes and battles at home or abroad, stringing together his courageous actions and bravery in the saga. The last stanza is no exception. Gunnarr recites the stanza when he is defending himself against his enemies in his farm at Hlíðarendi. The stanza is not intended as a comment on his brave deeds, but as his farewell to Hallgerðr, following her last gesture towards him:

---

dropped the head to the ground as soon as the sons of Njáll had departed; he had not dared to do so while they were still there.

[25] See ORCHARD 1997, 102–103, and his references there.

Kálfalœkjarbók and *Reykjabók*
"Þá skal ek nú," segir hon, "muna þér kinnhestinn ok hirði ek aldri hvárt þú verr þik lengr eða skemr." Gunnarr kvað þá:

Hverr hefir dreyrgra darra
dómreynir *til*, sóma
niður drepr sveigar Sága,
síns ágætis, mínum.
øngr *skal lítils lengi*
liðs ráðandi *biðja*;
fús verður fagurmjǫls dísi
Fenju hǫnd á venju.

"*Hefir hverr til síns ágætis* nǫkkut,"
segir Gunnarr, "ok *skal* þik þessa eigi
lengi biðja."
(*Reykjabók*, 123)[26]

Mǫðruvallabók
"Þá skal ek nú," segir hon, " muna þér kinnhestinn, ok hirði ek aldri, hvárt þú verr þik lengr eða skemr."

"*Hefir hverr til síns ágætis* nǫkkut,"
segir Gunnarr, "ok *skal* þik þessa eigi
lengi biðja."
(*ÍF* 12, 189)

The editors of *Reykjabók* and *Kálfalœkjarbók* do not integrate the stanza in the prose narrative; it is merely added after Hallgerðr's famous rejection of Gunnarr's request.[27] The stanza precedes his answer. The verbal echo between verse and prose is resounding, and yet again we detect the subtle effect of the repetition, of the power of reflecting on the implications of a scene. The inclusion of the stanza gives Gunnarr a possibility of depicting his wife in two glorious, if dispassionate and mythical, images: he sees her wearing a headdress (*sveigar Sága*), and then as *Fenju fagrmjǫls dís*. She is the object of his eye, just as she was at their first meeting at Alþingi.

After Gunnarr's killing, Hallgerðr goes to live with her daughter Þorgerðr and her son-in-law Þráinn Sigfússon at Grjótá. The saga notes that Rannveig, Gunnarr's mother, blamed her for Gunnarr's killing and Hallgerðr believed that she would indeed kill her. Rumours arose in the district that Hallgerðr was sexually involved with Hrappr, the enemy of the sons of Njáll, who is also staying with Þráinn. They pay him a visit at Grjótá:

Reykjabók and *Kálfalœkjarbók*
Hallgerðr stóð í anddyrinu ok hafði talat hljótt við Hrapp. Hon mælti: „Þat mun engi mæla sá er fyrir er,

Mǫðruvallabók
Hallgerðr stóð í anddyrinu ok hafði talat hljótt við Hrapp. Hon mælti: "Þat mun engi mæla, sá er fyrir er, at

[26] Then I will remind you of the slap you gave me in the face, and I don't care whether you last for a long or a short time. [*Kálfalœkjabók* and *Reykjabók*:] Then Gunnarr recited: "Every man (*dómreynir darra*) has good qualities; the woman (*Sága sveigs*) devalues my honour. No man (*liðs ráðandi*) shall ask for a small favour for a long time; the woman (*dís Fenju fagramjǫls*) is true to her habits." [All:] "Each one obtains fame in his own way", says Gunnarr, and I will not ask you again.
[27] Written in the lower margin of fol. 39r in *Reykjabók*.

at þér séð velkomnir. "Skarphéðinn
kvað vísu:

Auk munu elda síka,
orð þín mega skorða,
gjarn séð ek úlf ok ǫrnu,
ekki þessum rekkum;
hornkerling ert, Hernar
hrings víðs freka skíða
Baldr semr Óðins ǫldu,
útigangs eða púta.

Skarpheðinn mælti: „*Ekki* munu
mega orð þín því at þú *ert* annathvárt
hornkerling eða púta"
(*Reykjabók*, 148–9)[28]

þér séð velkomnir."

Skarpheðinn mælti: "*Ekki* munu
mega orð þín, því at þú *ert* annathvárt
hornkerling eða púta."
(*ÍF* 12, 228)

The third stanza about Hallgerðr is in stark contrast with the first two; she
is depicted in brutal words as an outsider in society, as a *hornkerling*, a term
evoking a scene much earlier in the saga when Bergþóra's seating arrangements
at Bergþórshváll offend Hallgerðr.[29] This stanza highlights an instance in the
text where the audience felt a stanza was missing, or where it was appropriate to
reiterate the message, such as in the above example where Skarpheðinn's views
on Hallgerðr are ruthlessly brought home. The editors of *Reykjabók* and *Kálfalækjarbók* do not edit the accompanying prose,[30] and indeed it may have been
their intention to repeat the cruel evaluation of Hallgerðr's social degradation
after Gunnarr's death. We are here at the borderline between oral and literary
traditions.

Skaldic verse carries a symbolic meaning in the sagas of Icelanders. The mere
citation of a skaldic stanza conjures up several historical and cultural connotations to an audience in the fourteenth century, when skaldic verse was still
actively composed in the community. A stanza attributed to a known historical
character pretends to be spoken by a person from the past, from the time of
the events themselves. At that moment the speaker, whether he is Gunnarr or
Skarpheðinn, becomes the centre of attention. We have noticed in the examples
above, how the pace of the narrative slows down when a verse is cited and the

[28] Hallgerðr was standing on the porch, and had whispered something to Hrappr. She said: "No man
standing here will say that you are welcome here". [*Reykjabók* and *Kálfalækjabók*:] Skarpheðinn
spoke a verse: "Your words, woman (*elda skorða síka*), will not count much to these men; I am eager
to feed the wolf and eagle (femine). You are either a cast-off hag or a whore. The man (*Baldr víðs
Hernar hrings skorða*) composes verse (*Óðins alda*)." [All:] Skarpheðinn spoke: "Your words don't
count, for you're either a cast-off hag or a whore". The translation of the prose here is taken from
Cook's translation of *Njal's saga* 2001: 155.
[29] *ÍF* 12, 91.
[30] Written in the lower margin of fol. 47v. in *Reykjabók*.

scene is set for a reflective moment. The stanzas in *Gunnars saga were probably composed late, most likely in the thirteenth century,[31] and for this reason the additional verses have been considered secondary in relation to others in *Njáls saga*. The dating of the stanzas is, however, less significant than the actual citation of the verse in the early manuscripts. In fact, the dating of the stanzas is of little consequence to the authors of the sagas of Icelanders, only their applicability in the narrative. The original text of *Njáls saga* remains elusive, yet it seems that the wording of some of the additional stanzas is lifted from the prose text and thus the stanzas must be composed after the prose was written. It is unlikely that it happened the other way around;[32] even though we cannot be certain.

It is striking that the additional verses punctuate important events in the saga, and draw us closer to the two tragic heroes of *Gunnars saga, Skarpheðinn and Gunnarr. The poetic speech of Gunnarr and Skarpheðinn, copied by some writers of the manuscripts of the *X* group, bring to life the active reception of the audience of *Njáls saga* and moreover make almost visible the borderline between the oral and literary in the early fourteenth century. The commanding voice of Skarpheðinn, the only one of the brothers to speak in verse, needed to be heard and the audience gave him a chance to speak his mind. Gunnarr and Skarpheðinn rejoice in their killings; Gunnarr's battle stanzas are at odds with the well-known utterance of Gunnarr, *mér þykkir meira fyrir en ǫðrum mǫnnum at vega menn* 'killing other men troubles me more than others'.[33] Only two stanzas by Gunnarr and Skarpheðinn are cited in *Möðruvallabók*: Gunnarr's verse in the mound and Skarpheðinn's stanza heard from within the burning farm at Bergþórshváll. Both are spoken by ghosts from a distant world; their verses belong literally to the afterworld, to the past and an old social order. By contrast, it is Kári, the Christian hero of the second part of *Njáls saga* who speaks repeatedly in verse in this version of the saga, lamenting his fate, the only proper poet of the saga in *Möðruvallabók*.

The editors of *Njáls saga* have struggled with the multifaceted and versatile textual transmission of *Njáls saga*. Both Konráð Gíslason and Finnur Jónsson based their editions on *Reykjabók*.[34] Konráð included all the additional stanzas (also the two by Skarpheðinn that are only in *Kálfalækjarbók*, Table 1, sts. 11–12); Finnur, on the other hand, omits all the additional verse. Einar Ól. Sveinsson in his 1954 edition of *Njáls saga* chose *Möðruvallabók* as his main text and therefore the additional verse was omitted but printed in an appendix. Subsequent editors have followed his practice of omitting this verse. The additional stanzas of the *X* group have consequently been absent in *Njáls saga*'s editions in the last fifty years, even though they clearly belong to the first stage in the transmission of *Njáls saga*. The only exception is a new edition of the

---

[31] Einar Ól. Sveinsson 1954, xliv; Jón Helgason 1962, xi–xii. See also Finnur Jónsson 1904.

[32] Jón Helgason 1962, xi: "There can be no doubt that the manuscripts which do not have them [the verses] represent in this respect the original form of the saga".

[33] ÍF 12, 139.

[34] Konráð Gíslason 1875–1889; Finnur Jónsson 1908.

Reykjabók which appeared in a modern Icelandic edition in 2003. The example of *Njáls saga* lays bare the problems of rendering the complex text of *Njáls saga* in a modern edition, and of how to bring to life the changes made to the saga, which originated in a period of fertile and constant interaction between the written text and its audience.

Bibliography

Primary sources

ÍF 12 – *Brennu-Njáls saga*, ed. EINAR ÓL. SVEINSSON, *Íslenzk fornrit* 12. Reykjavík.

Reykjabók, ed. SVEINN YNGVI EGILSSON, *Brennu-Njáls saga: Texti Reykjabókar*. Reykjavík 2003.

Secondary sources

ÁRMANN JAKOBSSON 2000: "Ekki kosta munur: Kynjasaga frá 13. öld." *Skírnir*, 174 21–48.

BIBIRE, Paul 1973: "Verses in the Íslendingasögur." In *Fyrirlestrar 1*, alþjóðlegt fornasagnaþing, Reykjavík 2.–8. ágúst 1973, 28 pages.

BJARNI EINARSSON 1974: "On the rôle of verse in saga-literature." *Mediaeval Scandinavia*, 7 118–125.

COOK, Robert 2001: *Njal's saga*. London, transl.

DRONKE, Ursula 1982: *On the Role of Sexual Themes in* Njáls saga. *The Dorothea Coke Memorial Lecture in Northern Studies delivered at University College London 27 May 1981*. London.

EINAR ÓL. SVEINSSON 1953: *Studies in the Manuscript Tradition of Njálssaga*, *Studia Islandica*, vol. 13. Reykjavík.

EINAR ÓL. SVEINSSON (ed.) 1954: *Brennu-Njáls saga*, *Íslenzk fornrit*, vol. 12. Reykjavík.

FINNUR JÓNSSON 1904: "Om Njála." *ANOH*, p. 89–166.

FINNUR JÓNSSON (ed.) 1908: *Brennu-Njáls saga*. Altnordische Sagabibliothek, Halle.

GUÐRÚN INGÓLFSDÓTTIR 1990: "Um hlutverk vísna í Íslendinga sögum." *Skáldskaparmál*, 1 226–240.

JÓN HELGASON (ed.) 1962: *Njáls Saga: The Arna-Magnæan Manuscript 468 4to (Reykjabók)*, *Manuscripta Islandica*, vol. 6. Copenhagen.

JÓN KARL HELGASON 1999: *The Rewriting of Njáls Saga: Translation, Ideology and Icelandic Sagas*, *Topics in Translation*, vol. 16. Clevedon.

KONRÁÐ GÍSLASON (ed.) 1875–1889: *Njála udgivet efter gamle håndskrifter*. Copenhagen.

KRESS, Helga 1991: "Staðlausir stafir: Um slúður sem uppsprettu frásagnar í Íslendingasögum." *Skírnir*, 165 130–156.

LÖNNROTH, Lars 1976: *Njáls saga: A Critical Introduction*. Berkeley, Los Angeles.

NORDAL, Guðrún 2005: "'Attraction of Opposites': Skaldic Verse in *Njáls saga*." In Pernille Hermann (ed.) *Literacy in Medieval and Early Modern Scandinavian Culture*, Viking Collection in Northern Studies, p. 211–236, Odense.

ORCHARD, Andy 1997: "Oral traditions." In Katherine O'Brien O'Keeffe (ed.) *Reading Old English Texts*, p. 101–123, Cambridge.

POOLE, Russell G. 1992: *Viking Poems on War and Peace. A Study in Skaldic Narrative*. Toronto.

SVERRIR TÓMASSON 2002: "Endursköpun bókmenntagreina í handritum." In Gísli Sigurðsson & Vésteinn Ólason (eds.) *Handritin. Ritgerðir um íslensk miðaldahandrit, sögu þeirra og áhrif*, p. 73–80.

Appendix 1:
The additional verses and their prose context

1. *The opening section* (chs. 1–18)

   Sts. 1–3 Unnr Marðardóttir relates her marital problems to her father at Alþingi.

2. *Part I*: Gunnarr's life before marrying Hallgerðr (chs. 19–32)

   Sts. 4–5 Gunnarr, in his disguise as Kaupa-Heðinn, speaks two stanzas to Hrútr about Mǫrðr gígja and his unsuccessful dealings with Hrútr.

   St. 6 Gunnarr speaks a stanza at Alþingi where he challenges Hrútr to a duel.

   St. 7 Gunnarr speaks a stanza when Hrútr agrees to repay Unnr's dowry.

   St. 8 Gunnarr speaks a stanza in the battle on Gautelfr against Karl and Vandill.

   St. 9 Gunnarr speaks a stanza before a battle in Estonia (Rafala).

   St. 10 Gunnarr speaks a verse when he obtains the *atgeirr* from Hallgrímr.

3. *Part II*: Gunnarr's troubles as a chieftain in Iceland; the *Húskarlavíg*, and Gunnarr's dispute with his neighbours, leading to his death (chs. 33–81).

   St. 11 Skarpheðinn speaks a stanza when Þórðr leysingjasonr has killed Brynjólfr.

   St. 12 Skarpheðinn speaks a stanza after Þórðr leysingjasonr has been killed, and before he is avenged.

   Sts. 13–15 Sigmundr Lambason's defamatory stanzas about Njáll and his sons.

   St. 16 Skarpheðinn composes a stanza when they leave Bergþórshváll to kill Sigmundr.

   St. 17 Skarpheðinn composes a stanza after he has beheaded Sigmundr.

   St. 18 Gunnarr speaks a stanza in the middle of the fight where he kills Skammkell.

   St. 19 Skarpheðinn composes a stanza at a horse fight, where tensions arose between Þorgeirr Starkaðsson and Gunnarr Hámundarson.

St. 20 Gunnarr speaks a stanza after he has his dream before the fight at Knafarhólar.

St. 21 Gunnarr speaks a stanza in the battle at Knafarhólar.

Sts. 22–23 Gunnarr speaks two stanzas in a conversation with Kolskeggr after the killing of Þorgeirr Otkelsson when Kolskeggr tells him to kill Þorgeirr Starkaðarson as well.

St. 24 Gunnarr speaks a stanza when Hallgerðr denies him a lock of her hair in his final battle.

St. 25 Þormóðr's eulogy for Gunnarr.

4. *The final section* (chs. 82–99) The dispute between Þráinn Sigfússon and the sons of Njáll

St. 26 Skarpheðinn speaks a stanza to Mǫrðr Valgarðsson when he and Hǫgni have avenged Gunnarr by slaying four of his killers.

St. 27 Skarpheðinn speaks a stanza about Hallgerðr at Grjótá.

Sts. 28–29 Skarpheðinn speaks two stanzas after he has killed Þráinn Sigfússon inciting the others to kill Hrappr.

St. 30 Skarpheðinn composes a stanza after Hǫskuldr Þráinsson and Njáll Þorgeirsson have settled the killings of Hǫskuldr Njálsson and Lýtingr's brothers (whom the sons of Njáll killed in revenge for the death of their half-brother Hǫskuldr).

Mixing *oratio recta* and *oratio obliqua*: A Sign of Literacy or Orality?

Ljubiša Rajić

A N OLD DISCUSSION, the Homeric problem of the transition of the oral into written form,[1] arose again during 1980s in the form of a general discussion on the relations between oral and written language, dealing both with medieval and modern times (and has been alive ever since). Being primarily a language historian, I know far from enough about that discussion, so my ambition is only to point out one difference in interpretation of a single style element in oral and written literature.

In his well-known work *Studier i Heimskringlas stil* [Studies in the style of *Heimskringla*] from 1936, Hallvard Lie introduces a literary term called "halvreplikk", which perhaps could be translated in English as "mixing of *oratio recta* and *oratio obliqua*". This style phenomenon can be described as a sentence where less important parts of a monologue are in *oratio obliqua* and where the most important part of a monologue is told in *oratio recta*. He gives the following example: "Then he says to the king that they are prepared to leave, and that their horses are saddled outside – "Now I would like to know" – said Bjorn – "what is the errand I have to travel for or what is the plan you made for us".

For Lie this type of stylistic variation is typical for literary tradition, a sign of literacy of a high individual quality in medieval written saga tradition.

In 1969 the Croatian folklorist Maja Bošković-Stulli – in her also well-known article "O rečenici usmenog pripovjedača" [On the Sentence of Oral Story-teller] – drew attention to the same type of stylistic variation (among other syntactic characteristics) and named it "free non-direct speech", often combined with a characteristic omission of *verbum dicendi*. She gives a few examples, but here I will quote instead a passage from a famous folk story, *Tsar Trojan Has Got Goat Ears*, about a barber who shaves tsar Trojan and discovers that the tsar has goats ears. But the barber cannot tell that to anyone because he is afraid of a death penalty:

---

[1] A short and very instructive overview is given by HOLBEK 1984.

> The master notices that and starts asking him whether something
> is going on with him, and he answers at last – after a lot of question
> making – that he has got something on his heart, not to be told to
> anyone, "and if I could", he says, "tell that to anyone, I would be
> immediately relieved. . . "

Contrary to Hallvard Lie, however, Maja Bošković-Stulli classifies this phenomenon as being typical oral tradition: "The extreme of ease of switching
between direct and indirect speech is characteristic oral story-telling".[2] If we
analyze syntax in standard editions of folk-stories in both Balkan and Scandinavian areas, we find several examples such as this. Furthermore I have found
similar syntactic elements in urban stories that I have heard in Belgrade among
students during the last two decades.[3] All of this supports Bošković-Stulli's
conclusion.

Common to Lie and Bošković-Stulli is that they see the reason for mixing
oratio recta and *oratio obliqua* as the story-teller's need to keep the audience's
attention by shifting over to direct speech whenever the story is especially
exciting. And there is a lot of evidence for that phenomenon.

If switching between *oratio recta* and *oratio obliqua* is a sign of literacy, then
we have to classify that phenomenon as an element of genuine medieval literary
style of secular literature. If that assumption is right, such elements in oral
literature do not initially belong to oral literature, but to the transition from
oral to written form. In that case the written form of an oral story would be
a "better" variant than the original form; a person who wrote down an oral
story used his or her own literary style, moving the oral story to a higher literary
level that is under the influence of literary tradition in the nineteenth century
and later.[4] Such a conclusion is not unrealistic: medieval written literature is a
product of the upper-class and oral literature has survived in a lower-class, but it
has been written down by middle-class intellectuals. Both medieval upper-class
and the early nineteenth-century middle-class share a tendency to refine this
simple folk product.

But if that switch is a sign of high oral quality, the situation is rather
the opposite: the oral story-teller has instead been a model for later written
literature; Snorri Sturluson imitates his oral literary ancestors, and so do later
literary writers. They simply use typical oral style elements in a written literature.

We can also take a look at transforming the written but heard story into a
pure oral story. In his experiment with the re-telling of a heard story Hirvonen
points out the following conclusions as differences between the written and
spoken versions:[5]

---

[2] Bošković-Stulli 1969, 270.
[3] See also Bošković-Stulli 1988 for some examples from her research.
[4] Elias Lönnroth's compilation of *Kalevala* is an excellent example of creating written literature out of
an oral tradition.
[5] Hirvonen 1978, 38.

1. The more dramatic points of the anecdotes, especially the punch lines, are rendered predominantly in direct speech.
2. Information that is important for the development of the story but not particularly dramatic tends to be rendered in either indirect or paraphrased speech.
3. Information that is peripheral to the development of the story is mostly omitted but is sometimes given in direct speech to add vividness to the narrative.

Even if an oral storyteller is familiar with *oratio tecta* and *observatio tecta*, as Polanyi points out, these forms are seldom used in everyday storytelling because the oral storyteller does not see any special stylistic value in using them.[6] And – as far as I can see – *oratio tecta* and *observatio tecta* are also less present in saga literature.

If we take a look at other syntactical elements specific to folk stories, as occurrences of reduplication and with a high degree of parataxis,[7] we can see that they also can be found in saga literature.

It seems clear to me that oral literature generally, and medieval secular Scandinavian saga literature especially, share some common syntactic characteristics when reporting speech.[8]

Do we have this type of syntactic usage in other texts? The switching between *oratio recta* and *oratio obliqua* and the use of other syntactical characteristics of folk-stories can be found in Scandinavian medieval laws;[9] that again means in literature with some connections to oral tradition. But we do not find those characteristics in *Landslagen* of Magnus Eriksson and *Stadslagen*, neither in the law of Magnús lagabøtir. Diplomatic material also shows examples of switching between *oratio recta* and *oratio obliqua*, especially in crime reports which are often formed into short criminal stories.

There are some infrequent occurrences of such elements in translated so-called court literature in Scandinavia and in the South-Slavic tradition, for example, Scandinavian and Serbian version of *Story of Troy* and *Story of Alexander*, but these texts are far from oral tradition, and nearly no examples of switching between *oratio recta* and *oratio obliqua* in the few of Serbian and Scandinavian medieval religious texts I have looked into, such as *Maríu saga*. Practically speaking, religious writers use only *oratio recta* as a systematic mean of expression. It is not necessary to mention that religious literature is on the opposite side of oral literature.[10]

---

[6] Polanyi 1982.

[7] Bošković-Stulli 1988, 258, 260.

[8] Why medieval studies and oral literature studies to a high degree share subjects of similar character but do not share the experience under many decades – for example Holbek 1978 does not mention Hallvard Lie's work in his bibliography "Formal and Structural Studies of Oral Narratives" – is also an interesting question but out of the focus of this article.

[9] See e.g. texts in Ståhle & Tigerstedt 1968.

[10] I have used standard Scandinavian and Serbian editions of this literature, so I do not give any special references to them.

I will not try to discuss in detail the relation between invention of a story, telling a story, spatial and temporal spreading of a story, and writing it down by a folklorist; it is much wider and controversial field than my knowledge reaches.[11] I will only point out that there are clear parallels between Lord's[12] explanation of mixing central and secondary themes in oral literature, Old-Norse *setja saman* for saga-telling, and the notion of Sturla Þórðarson's re-telling of *Hulda saga* as better than the others. All of that belongs to main structures of oral storytelling. But inside the structuring of the story, the singer of oral epic forms changes the form from time to time[13] as a part of rearranging and modifying both the central and peripheral elements to a much greater extent than musicians interpreting a composition.

To say that the difference between oral and written text has to do with the type of presentation is not new:[14] The oral story-teller has to draw attention to the performance by making strong points and *oratio recta* is very suitable, just as in daily conversation.[15] Oral performance depends on the right form of interaction between story-teller and audience. If we listen to story-telling, we can often receive both direct paralinguistic and non-verbal elements from the story-teller and his or her reproduction of paralinguistic and non-verbal elements used in different actions taken by persons he or she is telling about as if he or she is an actor playing all of the roles in the story. Those elements of oral performance must be omitted in the written reproduction of oral performance, but they can be described, or "textualised" in the written text. Switching between *oratio recta* and *oratio obliqua* has the opposite stylistic function that retardation in the form of skaldic verses in sagas has: retardation should slow down,[16] *oratio recta* should speed up. It is like a jam session: jazz performance has many similarities with oral story-telling in stressing main points or using improvisation as a counter-response to the response of audience.

The differences between oral and written literature should be understood more the way that Schier defines: "Mündliche Tradition und literarische Über-lieferung – das wurde oben schon hervorgehoben – sind nicht zwei scharf voneinander getrennte Informationsströme, die einer jeweils nur für eine Art gültigen Eigengesetzlichkeiten unterliegen".[17]

Personally I would rather support Bošković-Stulli's view instead of Lie's, but in a modified formulation: switching between *oratio recta* and *oratio obliqua* is more typical for speech than writing, and it occurs more frequently in texts closer to an oral tradition and less in texts closer to a written tradition.

---

[11] Sometimes I have impression that controversies are not always as fruitful as they seem to be; for example the big debate between "collective tradition" and "individual creativity" among Russian folklorists has to a large degree been a debate between extreme positions. For a short overview see VESTERHOLT 1973.

[12] LORD 1988.

[13] SERTIĆ 1962.

[14] See for example SHAFE 1982.

[15] See MØLLER 1993 on general research on oral telling and for a general discussion of oral versus written in ONG 1982.

[16] On retardation see, for example, MAGERØY 1991.

[17] SCHIER 1977, 112.

Bibliography

Bošković-Stulli, Maja 1969: "O rečenici usmenog pripovjedača." *Umjetnost riječi*, XIII (4) 255–272.

———— 1988: "Tradicijsko pričanje u gradu." In Svetozar Petrović (ed.) *Usmeno i pisano/pismeno u književnosti i kulturi*, pp. 169–182, Novi Sad.

Hirvonen, Pekka 1978: *Direct and Indirect Speech in Spoken and Written Story-Telling in English*. Joensuu.

Holbek, Bengt 1978: "Formal and structural studies of oral narratives." *UNI-FOL*, pp. 149–194.

———— 1984: "Formelhaftigkeit, Formeltheorie." In *Enzyklopedie des Märchens*, pp. 1415–1439, Berlin.

Lie, Hallvard 1937: *Studier i Heimskringlas stil: Dialogene og talene, Skrifter utgitt av Det Norske Videnskaps-Akademi i Oslo. II Hist.-Filos. Klasse 1936*, vol. 5. Oslo.

Lord, Albert B. 1988: "Some characteristics of oral-traditional poetics." In Svetozar Petrović (ed.) *Usmeno i pisano/pismeno u književnosti i kulturi*, pp. 15–29, Novi Sad.

Magerøy, Hallvard 1991: "Skaldestrofer som retardasjonsmiddel i islendinge-sogene." In Eyvind Fjeld Halvorsen, Finn Hødnebø, Else Mundal & Vésteinn Ólason (eds.) *Norroena et Islandica: Festskrift til Hallvard Magerøy på 75-årsdagen den 15. januar 1991*, pp. 137–150, Øvre Ervik.

Møller, Erik 1993: *Mundtlig fortælling – fortællingens struktur og funktion i uformel tale*. København.

Ong, Walter 1982: *Orality and Literacy: The Technologizing of the Word*. London.

Polanyi, Livia 1982: "Literary complexity in everyday storytelling." In E. Tannen (ed.) *Spoken and Written Language: Exploring Orality and Literacy*, pp. 155–170, New Jersey.

Schier, Kurt 1977: "Einige metodische Überlegungen zum Problem mündlicher und literarischer Tradition im Norden." In Hans Bekker-Nielsen, Peter Foote, Andreas Haarder & Hans Frede Nielsen (eds.) *Oral Tradition – Literary Tradition*, pp. 98–115, Odense.

Sertić, Mira 1962: "Problemi usmene predaje u narodnoj pjesmi." *Filologija*, 3 141–158.

Shafe, Wallace L. 1982: "Integration and involvements in speaking, writing, and oral literature." In E. Tannen (ed.) *Spoken and Written Language: Exploring Orality and Literacy*, pp. 35–53, New Jersey.

Ståhle, Carl Ivar & Tigerstedt, E. N. 1968: *Medeltidens och reformationstidens litteratur, Sveriges litteratur*, vol. 1. Stockholm.

Vesterholt, Ole 1973: *Tradition and Individuality: A Study in Slavonic Oral Epic Poetry*. Copenhagen.

Oral or Scribal Variation in *Vǫluspá*: A Case Study in Old Norse Poetry

ELSE MUNDAL

THE MOST FAMOUS of all the Old Norse Eddic poems, *Vǫluspá*, is preserved both in *Codex Regius* (from about 1275) and in *Hauksbók* (from the 1330s or perhaps some years later); half of the poem is also quoted in Snorri's *Edda*. It is not possible to draw absolute conclusions about the composition of the version of *Vǫluspá* which Snorri knew and quoted since he only quoted parts of the poem and he did not quote the stanzas in chronological order. What we can say is that the version Snorri quoted can hardly have included much – if any – material in addition to what is known from the two other versions. Snorri's stanzas have some lines which are different from the other versions, and a few additional lines – in the recounting of names of dwarfs – but he never quotes a whole stanza which is not found in at least one of the two other versions. These facts are a strong argument against the theories that some important parts of the poem have been lost if we assume that the three versions of *Vǫluspá* are the result of three separate acts of transcription from oral tradition.

The *Codex Regius* version and the *Hauksbók* version of the poem differ from each other where composition and order of stanzas are concerned, especially in the middle part of the poem. The differences in composition are shown in Figure 1 and the differences in the placement of the *stef* stanzas (refrains) in Figure 2.

The differences in wording within the individual stanzas between the two versions of the poem must be characterized as relatively small compared to the differences in composition. However, both types of differences are of interest in regards to the question of oral or scribal variation.

It has been, and still is a matter of discussion whether the poem was written down from oral tradition once, twice or three times. I am not going to give a full overview of who believed what and why, but I will mention a few of the scholars whose views on the question of oral or scribal variation in *Vǫluspá* have been most influential. Sophus Bugge was convinced that the *Codex Regius* version and the *Hauksbók* version of the poem were both written down from

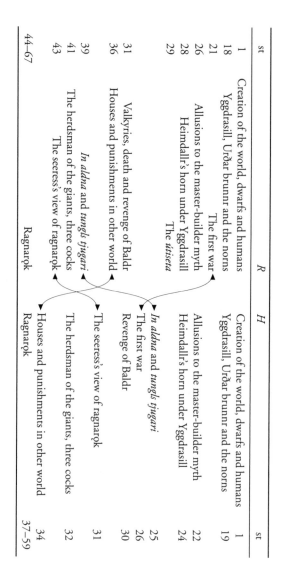

Figure 1: The composition of the two versions of *Vǫluspá*. The figure does not show all minor differences in composition between the two versions. From stanza *R* 44/*H* 37 the stanzas and their order are with a few exceptions substantially the same. One difference is that the second but last stanza in *H* about the mighty one coming from above is not found in *R*.

Þá gengu regin ǫll á rǫkstólar		Vituð ér enn, eða hvat?		Geyr (nú) Garmr mjǫk...	
R	H	R	H	R	H
6,1	6,1	28,8	24,8		31,1–4
9,1	9,1		25,16	43,1–4	
24,1		29,14			36
26,1	22,1		30,8	46	42
	28,1	34,8			47
		35,8		55	51
		38,10	35,10		
		40,8			
		59,8	55,8		
		60,6	56,6		

Figure 2: The placement of the three *stef.* Entries that are placed on the same line in the table appear in the text in similar contexts.

oral tradition independently of each other.[1] In his opinion the version quoted in Snorri's *Edda* was a third independent version. The *Codex Regius* version and the *Hauksbók* version are, according to Bugge, closer to each other than either of them is to Snorri's version.

According to R. C. Boer, the *Hauksbók* version and the stanzas quoted by Snorri could be traced back to a common written text, while the *Codex Regius* version and the *Hauksbók* version were independent of each other. The text was consequently written down twice.[2]

According to Sigurður Nordal it is impossible that the *Codex Regius* version and the *Hauksbók* version could be traced back to a common written text. In his opinion the *Codex Regius* text was first written down some time after Snorri wrote his *Edda*, and Snorri therefore quoted his verses from oral tradition. Nordal discussed the possibility that the *Hauksbók* version could go back to the written *Codex Regius* version through a "second" oral tradition, but his conclusion was that the three versions were all independent.[3]

Andreas Heusler held the opinion that Snorri's verses and the *Codex Regius* version of the poem could be traced back to a common written text, which was the first written version of the poem. The *Hauksbók* version, on the other hand, could not simply be derived from the *Codex Regius* version or from the common source of this version and Snorri's text, "since its middle portion used oral sources anew".[4]

In his introduction to *Vǫluspá* Jón Helgason stated that the *Vǫluspá* text in *Codex Regius*, *Hauksbók* and Snorri's *Edda* were all independent of each other, the result of three transcriptions from oral tradition.[5] His statement put an end to the discussion of this problem for a long time.

---

[1] BUGGE 1867, XXIIIf.
[2] BOER 1904.
[3] NORDAL 1923, 2f.
[4] HEUSLER 1937, 33.
[5] JÓN HELGASON 1951, viii.

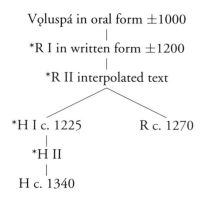

Vǫluspá in oral form ±1000

*R I in written form ±1200

*R II interpolated text

*H I c. 1225   R c. 1270

*H II

H c. 1340

Figure 3: Dronke's stemma (redrawn)

Recently Ursula Dronke, in her critical edition of *The Poetic Edda* which includes her edition of *Vǫluspá*, has argued that all three versions of the poem go back to one and the same manuscript.[6] Her stemma is shown in Figure 3. Ursula Dronke does not actually provide many arguments in favour of her view, seeming to take it more or less for granted that the variation between the different versions of *Vǫluspá* is the result of scribal variation. Some of the examples of what she regards as common faults could indicate scribal variations of some sort. Other differences between the versions are, in my opinion, more likely to be the result of oral variation. And as we have seen, over time the majority of scholars have been inclined to regard the differences as oral variations.

In the following, I will discuss the problem of oral or scribal variation in *Vǫluspá* by way of examples of variants and differences at different textual levels of the poem. I will start with the composition, the different order of stanzas in *Codex Regius* and *Hauksbók*. Thereafter I will discuss some textual differences between stanzas which are found both in the *Codex Regius* version and the *Hauksbók* version of the poem in order to decide whether these particular differences are likely to be the result of oral variation or of scribal variation.

When discussing variants on the level of composition it may be important to try to imagine how an Eddic poem was orally performed in the Old Norse society. This is of course a matter about which definite conclusions cannot be drawn.

One question with relevance both to the view of the stability of composition and the textual stability of the individual stanzas is where the Eddic poems fit in between improvisation and memorization. Although this is an important topic within the study of Eddic poetry only a few scholars have studied this

---

[6] DRONKE 1997. Karl G. JOHANSSON 2000 has since supported the view of Ursula Dronke.

question in depth.[7] I will only touch on these problems here since my concern instead is the question of whether the different texts of *Vǫluspá* are the result of oral or scribal variation. However, this is a question which cannot be separated from the question of how stable or fluent this poetry was on the oral stage. Therefore I will start this discussion with some reflections on oral Eddic poetry and how it is possible to investigate this subject to which we have no direct access. The view of Eddic poetry as improvised is closely connected to the oral-formulaic theory as developed in the works of Milman Parry and Albert B. Lord. According to this theory oral poetry is characterized by formulaic language. The use of formulas helped the poets to improvise. Parry defined a formula as "a word or group of words regularly employed under the same metrical conditions to express a given essential idea".[8] During oral transmission it was the formulas, structured phrases and lines which were remembered rather than a fixed text, and improvisations would therefore play an important part both during composition and transmission.

Concerning Eddic poetry it is important to ask whether there really are many formulas to be found in the poetic language of this genre. In spite of Parry's definition, it is not always easy to decide what is a formula and what is not. This may also be the reason why some scholars term the poetic language of Eddic poetry as formulaic, while the majority of scholars would hesitate to use that characterization even though they would not deny that some formulas may be found.

In Old Norse poetic language, especially in the skaldic poetry, there are stereotypes of many kinds to be found, the majority of which are connected to the use of *kenningar* and stock phrases and cannot be characterized as formulas. But all kinds of stereotypes, stock phrases, type-scenes, repetitions – whether formulas or not – would make some sort of improvisation expected. However, regarding Old Norse poetry, we should perhaps distinguish between

---

[7] Robert KELLOGG introduced the theories of Parry and Lord and tried to make them applicable to Eddic poetry in a chapter titled "The Oral Heritage of Written Narratives" in the book *The Nature of Narrative* which he wrote together with Robert SCHOLES in 1966. Here he argued that both Eddic poetry and saga literature have their origin in older epics more similar to the Serbian and Homeric type. KELLOGG 1990; 1991 has since defended this opinion. Kellogg's theory of Eddic poetry as formulaic and improvised is discussed by Lars LÖNNROTH 1971 in his article "Hjálmar's Death-Song and the Delivery of Eddic Poetry". Lönnroth is rather critical of using formulas as an argument in favour of the view that Eddic poetry is characterized by oral formulaic improvisations. In a later article, however, he argued that even though Eddic poems as we know them must be characterized as predominately memorized poetry, this must have been otherwise earlier. They must have been more like Anglo-Saxon verse, "more loosely structured and more formulaic in style; easier to improvise, more difficult to memorize" (LÖNNROTH 1971, 312; see also LÖNNROTH 1978 and 1979). Another scholar who is critical of applying the oral-formulaic theory to Eddic poetry is Joseph Harris. He argues that a theory developed on the basis of one culture cannot necessarily be made applicable to another culture. According to HARRIS 1985, 112 the "major task is to determine the specific nature of each tradition" (see also HARRIS 1983). GÍSLI SIGURÐSSON 1988; 1990a; 1990b; 1998, on the other hand, has argued strongly in favour of applying the oral formulaic theory to Eddic poetry. He has been equally strongly rejected by EINAR MÁR JÓNSSON 1988; 1990a; 1990b. According to him Eddic poetry must be seen in connection with the skaldic tradition in Old Norse society. A work devoted to the discussion of formulas in Eddic poetry is GUREVIC 1986.

[8] PARRY 1930, 80.

improvisation connected to the creation of stanzas and improvisation connected to the transmission of stanzas. The making of a skaldic stanza can in one way be regarded as a sort of improvisation, since the skald could model his stanza on older stanzas by reusing or varying older *kenningar*, stock phrases and so on. However, in the oral transmission of skaldic stanzas there would certainly not have been many opportunities to improvise. In the making of an Eddic poem there would be fewer chances to compose stanzas by help of improvisation on the basis of models of different kinds, since this genre is less stereotypical than skaldic poetry. On the other hand, during the oral transmission there would be more space for improvisation within the Eddic transmission than within the skaldic transmission. However regarding improvisation it may have been easier to improvise during the oral transmission of some poems than others. The poems I have in mind are poems such as *Alvíssmál* and *Vafþrúðnismál*, poems which consist of questions and answers. It would be relatively easy to improvise new stanzas by asking new questions. *Vǫluspá* is, however, not a poem of this type.

If Eddic poetry, and especially a poem like *Vǫluspá*, can be characterized as memorized poetry, another important question is: did the idea of a "correct" oral Eddic poem exist, a poem which consisted of a certain number of stanzas which were expected to be performed in the same order every time? Or, is it possible that the person who performed an oral Eddic poem would sometimes – or even normally? – quote only some stanzas and perhaps retell the contents of others in prose?

It would perhaps be useful to compare the performance of oral Eddic poetry with the performance of skaldic poetry and of oral saga-telling, of which we know a little bit more.

We do not find anything in the medieval written sources about the performance of Eddic poetry, except for the short piece of information in *Þorgils saga ok Hafliða* about the wedding at Reykjahólar where Hrólfr af Skálmarnesi told sagas, probably of the fornaldarsaga type – *ok margar vísur með* 'together with many stanzas'. Stanzas in fornaldarsagas are, with few exceptions, stanzas of the Eddic type, and this text seems to fit in with the picture we get from the written fornaldarsagas, namely that stanzas were sometimes included in oral performance of prose narratives. This may be of some relevance to our understanding of the performance of heroic narrative poems, which in written form are often found in a prose framework and include prose passages. Some of the mythological poems are also found in a prose framework, but in these poems there are only a few examples of short prose passages within a poem.

The prose passages in poems have sometimes been explained as substitutes for "lost" or "forgotten" stanzas. I would prefer to see this mixing of prose and stanzas in Eddic poetry in connection with the same mixing in the fornaldarsagas. In these two types of literature we have prose without stanzas, prose with stanzas, stanzas with prose and stanzas without prose. As Carol Clover has pointed out in the article "The Long Prose Form", the mixing of prose and poetry was common within many oral cultures.[9] The interesting question concerning the oral performance of these mixed genres is how much of a story was told with the help of stanzas and how much was told in prose varied from time to time. Unfortunately we are not able to answer this question since we have no parallel text of this kind independently written down from oral tradition. But the fact that Eddic poetry is in principle a mixed genre, as we have the texts in written form, makes it necessary to take into consideration that the "whole story" could be told without quoting all the stanzas. An interesting question here is whether prose passages which connected stanzas and scenes within a poem, in poems which normally had a mixed form, were seen as more or less obligatory, or whether the connecting and explaining prose could sometimes be left out because the context was assumed to be known to the audience. Another question is whether a person who performed an Eddic poem always recited all the stanzas he or she knew, or whether parts of a poem could sometimes be omitted. Could the length of the quiz (or question-and-answer-session) in poems like *Alvíssmál* vary from time to time, and could a few stanzas sometimes represent the whole quiz?

Eddic poems differ in style. The mixing of prose and stanzas is typical of poems with a full epic or epic/scenic form. In *Vǫluspá* there is not a single prose line to be found in the poem. But this poem does not retell a full and continuous story. Instead we could say that the stanzas evoke associations with myths behind the poem which are assumed to be known. This is therefore not a poem of a type where, as I see it, we would expect a blend of prose and stanzas. Prose passages which would connect blocks of stanzas to each other would more or less comprise the whole of Old Norse mythology. *Vǫluspá* is probably also not a poem where some stanzas could easily be left out and assumed to be known. It would not disturb the textual context if, for instance, some names of dwarfs were left out. But I suppose that it is rather disturbing that the stanza about the killing of Baldr is left out in *Hauksbók* – or, does the fact that the revenge on one of Baldr's killers, Loki, is mentioned, tell us that the killing of Baldr is actually part of the mythological background on which the poem is to be understood?

Some poems – including some of those within which there are no prose passages – are, as we have them, placed in a prose framework. The prose framework is in other words more common than the mixing of stanzas and prose passages. In *Vǫluspá* we have no prose framework either in *Codex Regius* or *Hauksbók*. A sort of frame is included in the poem itself, in the first stanza and in the ending of the last stanza. The *útiseta*-scene, where Óðinn turns to the *vǫlva* to get knowledge about the future, is closely connected to the framework. But in *Hauksbók* the stanzas which tell about the *útiseta* are missing. When these stanzas are left out in *Hauksbók*, is this scene really missing, or is the scene part of a frame which is assumed to be known?

Concerning the question of whether the idea of a "correct" form of an Eddic poem existed, it could perhaps be fruitful to compare this concept on the one

---

[9] Clover 1986.

hand with Carol Clover's theory of the so-called immanent saga and on the other with what we know about performance of skaldic poetry. According to Clover's theory, any part of an orally performed story would evoke the rest of the story in the audience's memory – or the rest of the story that they knew. The idea of the immanent saga is related to prose narratives, not to Eddic poetry. However, the fact that in an oral society the oral literature which was performed was seldom unknown to the audience, has the same consequences for poems as for prose narratives: part of the story would evoke memories of the rest. Therefore it is relevant to question what it actually meant to the understanding of the poem that some stanzas were left out in an oral performance either deliberately or because the performer did not remember them there and then.

Performance of skaldic poetry is quite often mentioned in Old Norse literary sources. Here we get the impression that a poem was normally performed from the first to the last stanza without interruptions of any kind. As far as a *drápa* is concerned, with its use of *stef* at fixed intervals, the artistry of the poem would be damaged if stanzas were left out. On the other hand, a reciter could of course forget one or more stanzas of a poem or recite only a few stanzas of a poem when it was appropriate. But the question is whether this would affect the *idea* of a "correct" form of a skaldic poem.

There is, however, one example of a skaldic poem which seems to have existed in both long and shorter forms. In *Orkneyinga saga*, ch. 81, it is told that when Rǫgnvaldr Kali Kolsson and Hallr Þórarinsson composed *Háttalykill* they composed five stanzas in each metre; but this was thought to make the poem too long, and now, the saga says, two stanzas are recited in each metre. There was also a manuscript which recited three stanzas.[10] Here it is more difficult to say whether the shorter forms of the poem are regarded as variants of the poem, or whether the original long form is still seen as the full and "correct" form even though all stanzas were never recited, and many perhaps forgotten. It is, however, important to note that the potential variation of a skaldic poem from one performance to another concerning how much of a poem was recited – or perhaps the order in which stanzas were given – is in principle a different issue than a variation in words, forms and meaning *within* a skaldic stanza.

Eddic poems could possibly be in an intermediate position between texts which had a "correct" form and texts which could be changed from one per-formance to another. But perhaps some Eddic poems are closer to the skaldic poems in this respect than others, and *Vǫluspá* may be an Eddic poem of the more skaldic type.

A last point I want to mention before we return to the text of the poem is that a comparison with Old Norse prose narratives and skaldic poetry tells us that there seems to be a nearly unbroken rule among all Old Norse genres that episodes follow in chronological order. This rule has consequences for our judgement of the *Hauksbók* text.

The different order of stanzas in the middle part of the poem in *Codex Regius* and *Hauksbók* must either be the result of a conscious rewriting of the poem, or

---

[10] Jón Helgason & Holtsmark 1941, 6–7.

the result of oral variation. In the first case we should expect that a plan or an idea behind the rewriting of the poem would be possible to deduce from the new arrangement of the stanzas themselves. That is hardly the case. In the opinion of most scholars it is hard to find any meaning in the arrangement of the stanzas in *Hauksbók*. I, too, find the arrangement of stanzas in *Hauksbók* to be rather strange, especially if the arrangement here is to be seen as a rearrangement of stanzas which existed more or less in the same order as in *Codex Regius*. Some of the scenes which are fundamental to the understanding of the whole poem are left out in *Hauksbók*. As we have seen, the *útiseta* and the killing of Baldr are missing, but as I have discussed, the question is whether they are really missing, or deliberately left out and assumed to be known by the audience. Perhaps the scribe or his informant knew them, but left them out by mistake.

How a poem was understood or interpreted is not only a question of how the text sounded. Different persons could interpret the same text in different ways. As Judy Quinn has pointed out, the *Hauksbók* text is in many ways more dramatic than the *Codex Regius* text. There is, for instance, more use of the present tense, and the refrain *Geyr nú Garmr mjǫk* is used more often, and earlier, than in *Codex Regius*.[11] This version of the poem was probably shaped by a person on whom Ragnarǫk had made an enormous impression. The rearrangement of the stanzas in the middle part of the poem could also, at least partly, be explained by the focus on Ragnarǫk. The arrangement of the different blocks of stanzas is, however, not in an orderly and logical manner. The rule of chronological order is broken at least once. The so-called masterbuilder-myth occurs very early in the *Hauksbók* text, and before the stanzas about the first war. But Freyja, whom the giant masterbuilder wanted as a reward from the gods for his building of the stronghold around Ásgarðr, came to the *æsir*-family as a hostage after the first war. Here the chronology of mythic time is not in order.

Is then the different order of stanzas in the middle part of the poem most easily explained as oral or scribal variation?

- The different number of stanzas in two versions of a poem is most easily explained as oral variation.
- The different order of stanzas could be the result of a conscious rewriting, but it could also be the result of oral variation.
- An interpretation of the poem which focused on Ragnarǫk – as the *Hauksbók* text does – could cause the rearrangement of stanzas which moved the first foreboding of Ragnarǫk forward (to st. 25), and back in mythic time. This could easily happen at the oral stage, especially if the oral tradition at this point in time was falling apart. A written text would probably keep the stanzas in place in spite of a new interpretation.
- The dissolution of a text into text blocks out of order, which we have in the *Hauksbók* version of *Vǫluspá*, is rather similar, I think, to what happened within the oral tradition of ballads at a late stage when they were known only by a few people. The text of the individual stanzas in

[11] Quinn 1990.

Hauksbók is, however, not in worse shape than the text in *Codex Regius*. Here, too, we may find a parallel in the oral ballad tradition. It seems that it is not the text, but the context, that first falls apart.

– The differences which we have between the text in *Codex Regius* and in *Hauksbók* – different number of stanzas, different order of stanzas, some stanzas are found in one manuscript and not in the other – are differences of a kind which are not found in the variants between poems which we have both in *Codex Regius* and its sister manuscript AM 748 4to. AM 748 4to contains many of the same mythological poems as *Codex Regius*, but not *Vǫluspá*. Here we know that we have scribal variation.

We will now go on to look at some differences at a textual level between the two versions of the poem.

Commentaries to st. 1 (*Codex Regius* 1, *Hauksbók* 1)

Codex Regius	*Hauksbók*
1. Hliods bið ec	1. Hlioðs bið ek allar
allar kindir	helgar kind*ir*
meiri *oc* mi*n*i	meiri ok min*n*i
mavgo heimdallar	mǫgu hei*m*dallar
vilðo at ec ualfavð*r*	villtu at ek vafǫdrs
uel fyr telia	vel fram telia
forn spioll fíra	forn spiǫll fíra
þav *er* fremst u*m* man.[12]	þau er ek fremz v*m* man.

We find different sorts of variations in this stanza. The word *helgar* is missing in the second line in *Codex Regius*. This must be a scribal variation. The rhyme lies in the word *helgar*, and the line is defective without it.

The two texts also differ from each other in the fifth line. *Codex Regius* has the nominative form *ualfavþr* and *Hauksbók* has the genitive form *vafǫdrs*. In *Codex Regius valfǫðr* is a term of address for Óðinn and *vafǫdrs* is a name of Óðinn as well. If the *Codex Regius* form is original, as most scholars think, the *Hauksbók* text could have been brought about by the fact that the *útiseta* scene is missing, and to address Óðinn is therefore less natural than in the *Codex Regius* version of the poem.

However, it is the two variants of line 6 which I find most interesting to the discussion of oral or scribal variation. The *Codex Regius* text has the form *fyr telia*, *Hauksbók* the form *fram telia*. The meaning is in both cases 'to tell/to recite'. It is difficult to see how one of the scribes could misread one of the

[12] The meaning of the text is in many cases disputed and the translations are only meant as a help for readers who does not understand Old Norse. The translation follows *R* but readings from *H* are added in parentheses: "I ask for attention from all beings (*H*: sacred beings) Heimdallr's greater and lesser offspring. You wished, Óðinn, that I should recite well (*H*: you wished that I should recite Óðinn's cunning acts), the ancient stories of living beings, the first I remember."

forms for the other – but perhaps this is an explanation for the existence of two different forms? It is even more difficult to understand why one of the scribes should consciously want to change one of the forms to the other since the meaning would be more or less the same. Variants where one word/one phrase are replaced by another *with the same meaning* are in my opinion most easily explained as the result of oral variation. (A combination of oral and scribal variation could also be possible if a scribe knew another version of the poem than the version in the manuscript in front of him.)

Commentaries to st. 3 (*Codex Regius 3, Hauksbók 3*)

Codex Regius	*Hauksbók*
3. Ar uar alda	3. Aar uar allda
þar er ymir bygði	þar er ymir bygði
vara sandr nę sęr	vara sandr ne sior
ne sualar unir	ne svalar unnir
iorð fanz ęva	iǫrð fannz ęfa
ne upp himin	ne vpp himinn
gap uar ginvnga	gap var ginnvnga
en gras hvergi[13]	enn gras ekki.

In the last line of the third stanza we have a very good example of the same phenomenon that occurs in *fyr telja* and *fram telja*. In *Codex Regius* we have the line *en gras hvergi*. In *Hauksbók* the same line reads as: *enn gras ekki*. It is impossible to misread the word *ekki* for *hvergi*, or vice versa. It is also difficult to see why a scribe should want to replace one of the words with the other since the meaning would not change. Again the two variants are most easily explained as oral variation; we have variations where word or phrases differ, but not the meaning.

Commentaries to st. 9–10 (*Codex Regius 9–10, Hauksbók 9–10*)

Codex Regius	*Hauksbók*
9. Þa g. r. a. ar.	9. Þa gengu regin ǫll
hverr scyldi duerga	aa rǫkstola
drotin scepia	ginnheilug goð
or brimis bloði	ok vm þat giættuz
oc or blam leGiom.	hverer skylldu duergar
	drottir skepia
	or brimi bloðgv
	ok or blains leggium.

---

[13] It was in the beginning of time where Ymir lived; there was no sand, no sea, no cool waves; earth did not exist, not heaven above, Ginnunga-gap was there, but grass nowhere (*H*: not grass).

10. Þar motsogn*ir*	10. Þar u*ar* modsogn*ir*
m*o*ztr v*m* orðin*n*	m*e*ztr of orðin*n*
dv*e*rga allra	d*u*erga allra
e*n* dvri*n* a*n*a*r*	en*n* durin*n* an*n*a*r*
þe*i*r manlicon	þe*i*r manlikan
m*o*rg v*m* gorðo	m*o*rg of giorðv
dv*e*rgar or iorðo	d*u*erga i i*o*rðu
sem dvri*n* sagdi.[14]	se*m* durin*n* sagði.

In st. 9 and 10 we have examples of more complicated variants which perhaps do not differ from each other when it comes to content. In stanza 9 it could be a matter of discussion whether the subject is *hverr*, 'who', or *hverr duerga*, 'which of the dwarfs'. In the *Hauksbók* text the subject is *hverer duergar*, 'what dwarfs'. Some scholars have taken *hverr* alone to be the subject. In that case *hverr* could be anyone, even the gods. But if we see the two versions in connection, the most logical reading of the *Codex Regius* text is the reading which gives the same meaning as the only possible reading of the *Hauksbók* text. According to this reading the creators of *drottir/drotin*, 'people' (pl. in the first case, definite form in the last case), which in this context must mean 'dwarfs', are the dwarfs themselves. Two of these dwarfs, Motsognir and Durinn, are mentioned in the next stanza. The word *þeir*, the first word in the last half-stanza of stanza 10, must stand for these dwarfs. The seventh line of stanza 10 has the form *dvergar or iorðu* in *Codex Regius* and the form *duerga i iorðu* in *Hauksbók*. In the first case the line stands in apposition to the subject, *þeir*, 'they' (*dvergar* is the nominative form). In the last case the line stands in apposition to the object *manlikan*, 'humanlike beings', which in this context must stand for the dwarfs (*duerga* is the accusative form).

I see it as impossible that all the small differences – both those I have commented on and others in these two stanzas – are the result of unconscious scribal errors. It is very unlikely that a number of unconscious scribal errors would result in a new text without grammatical mistakes. A conscious rewriting is not, in my opinion, a good explanation of the variants either, because the meaning is very much the same in the two variants – if the opinion in Old Norse society was that the dwarfs themselves created more dwarfs. On the other hand, if this was in fact the opinion in Old Norse society, the variants in these two stanzas are easily explained as oral variants. If the dwarfs were both subject and object, both creators and created beings, it would not matter, and it would not change the meaning, whether the seventh line stood in apposition to the subject or the object. Of the two forms of the subject in st. 9, *hverr dverga* and

[14] 9. Then all the powers of order went to their judges' thrones, the sacrosanct gods, and considered this: Who should create the people of dwarfs, *or*: who among the dwarfs should create the (dwarf) people (*H*: what dwarfs should create (dwarf) people) out of Brimir's blood and Bláinn's legs (*H*: out of bloody sea and Bláinn's legs). 10. There Motsognir had become the greatest of all the dwarfs, and Durinn another; they, dwarfs of earth, made many manlike figures (*H*: they made many manlike figures, dwarfs in the earth), as Durinn recounted.

hverir dvergar, one was as good as the other, and could perhaps change from one oral performance to the other.

Commentaries to st. 45–47 (*Codex Regius 44–45, Hauksbók 37–40*)

Codex Regius

44. Broþr mvno beriaz
oc at bavnom verþa
mvno systrvngar
sifiom spilla
hárt er i heimi
hór domr micill
sceᴳavld scalm avld
scildir ro klofnir
vindavld vargavld
aþr verold steypiz
mvn engi maþr
oðrom þyrma.

45. Leica mims synir
eɴ miotvðr kyndiz
at en galla
giallar horni
hatt blęss heimdallr
horn er alopti
męlir oðiɴ
við mims havfuþ
ymr iþ aldna tre
eɴ iótvɴ losnar
scelfr yᴳdrasils
ascr standandi.[15]

Hauksbók

37. Bræðr munu beriaz
ok at bǫnum verðaz
munu systrungar
sifium spilla
hart er i heimi
hordomr mikill
skeggǫll skaalmǫlld
skilldir klofnir.

38. Vind ǫlld vargǫlld
aaðr verǫlld steypiz
grundir gialla
gifr fliugandi
man eingi maðr
ǫðrum þyrma.

39. Leika mims synir
enn miǫtvǫr kyndiz
at hínv gamla
giallar horni
haatt blęss heimdallr
horn er aa lopti
męler oðinn
við mims hǫfut.

40. Skelfr yggdrasils
askr standandi
ymr hid alldna tre
enn iǫtunn losnar
hrædaz allir
aa helvegum
aaðr surtar þann
sevi of gleypir.

[15] 44. Brothers will fight each other, and one will be the killer of the other. Children of sisters will violate the bond of kinship; it is hard in the world, much adultery, axe-age, sword-age, shields are cleft, wind-age, wolf-age, before the world goes under; (*H* adds: The lands ring out, flying giantesses) no man will spare another. 45. The sons of Mímr are playing at the shrill (*H*: old) Gjallar-horn, and the world tree catches fire (Or: The sons of Mímr are playing, but fate was stirred up by the shrill Gjallar-horn). Heimdallr blows loudly, the horn is in the air; Óðinn speaks with

If we compare the text of these stanzas in the *Codex Regius* version and in the *Hauksbók* version, we find many differences at a textual level between the level of composition (meaning in the order of stanzas) and the verbal level – where we find differences of words and phrases.

As we can see, where the stanzas begin and end differs. What is one stanza in *Codex Regius* (R 44) is two stanzas in *Hauksbók* (H 37 and 38). The stanza, which in both versions begins with the line *Leika Mims synir*, is longer in *Codex Regius* than in *Hauksbók*. The last four lines in *Codex Regius* are found in the next stanza in *Hauksbók*. Such variants can both be oral and scribal. The beginning of a new stanza is not always clearly marked in the manuscripts, and scribal variations could therefore be expected. On the other hand, oral variation is equally good an explanation as scribal variation.

Stanza 38 in *Hauksbók* incorporates two lines before the lines which are the last two lines in stanza 44 in *Codex Regius*, and the last half-stanza of st. 40 in *Hauksbók* is not to be found in *Codex Regius*. These extra lines in *Hauksbók* are not easily explained as scribal variation, but there is of course the possibility that the scribe has interpolated his text with extra material which he knew from oral tradition.

The last four lines in st. 45 in *Codex Regius* are found as the first half-stanza in stanza 40 in *Hauksbók*, but the two long lines (that is, two lines linked by rhyme) have changed place. This replacement of long lines is not easy to explain as scribal variation. One possible explanation could be that a scribe first passed over two lines (a long line), saw his error, and corrected his mistake by exchanging the long lines. The *Hauksbók* text has, in my opinion, the best order of these two long lines. Here the world tree is named in the first long line, and then we know that *it aldna tre* in the second long line is Yggdrasill. Therefore the order of long lines in *Hauksbók* is hardly the result of a scribal mistake. The text in *Codex Regius* could, however, be the result of a mistake. Here the text from *ymr* to *scelfr* is in fact written twice, and the first text (from *ymr* to *scelfr*), erased. But since the word *scelfr* in the erased text follows the word *losnar*, the word order must have been the same in the manuscript which the scribe of *Codex Regius* copied as it is in *Codex Regius*.

The types of differences I have mentioned here – where stanzas begin and end, extra lines and half-stanzas in one version and not the other and exchange of lines – are all more easily explained as oral variation than as scribal variation. These discrepancies are again of a kind which are not found in the variants between poems which we have both in *Codex Regius* and in AM 748 4to.

There are of course also arguments in favour of the view that the differences between the *Codex Regius* text and the *Hauksbók* text of *Vǫluspá* are the result of scribal variation. Ursula Dronke's conclusion that all the three known variants of *Vǫluspá* are the result of scribal variation is based on the fact that all variants

---

Mímr's head, the old tree groans and the giant becomes free; the ash of Yggdrasill trembles standing upright (*H* 40,5–8: All are frightened in the realm of Hel before Surtr's kin (the fire) swallows it (the ash?) up).

of the poem have what she calls common interpolations, the names of dwarfs being the largest of these. But if we have common interpolations, are they necessarily interpolations made by a scribe? Is it not possible that an oral poem was interpolated during the oral stage, and that the new stanzas were accepted and became part of the oral tradition? And can we be sure that the stanzas which consist of names of dwarfs are in fact interpolations?

If we can argue that the *Codex Regius* and the *Hauksbók* texts have common faults/scribal errors, this would greatly strengthen the arguments in favour of the view that the two versions of the poem, in spite of their differences, belong to the same manuscript tradition. Among Dronke's examples of "common faults" is one line which is found in both versions of the poem and which seems to support her view strongly. This line which is the first line of the second *stef* (refrain) is found in stanza 43 in *Codex Regius* and in stanza 31 in *Hauksbók*:

Codex Regius	*Hauksbók*
43. Geyr garmr mioc	31. Geyr garmr miǫk
fyr gnipa helli	*fyrir* gnupa helli
festr mvn slitna	festr man slitna
e*n* freki re*n*a	en*n* freki ren*n*a
fiolþ veit ho*n* frǫða	fram*m* se ek lengr
fram se ec leng*ra*	fiǫlð kan*n* ek segia
v*m* ragna ravc	um ragna rǫk
ravm sigtyva.[16]	rǫm*m* sigtiva.

As we can see, the word *nú* is "missing" in both versions. The *stef* has the form *Geyr nú Garmr mjǫk* every time it is used except here. Dronke explains this as a scribal error in *R II which is inherited both in *Codex Regius* and in *Hauksbók*. That seems to be a good explanation. On the other hand, the last half-stanza is different in the two manuscripts, and this difference is more likely to be the result of oral variation than of scribal variation. The stanza is found in different contexts in the two manuscripts, a fact which is a complicating factor if we want to explain the missing *nú* as a common fault. It is also possible that the line *geyr (nú) Garmr mjǫk* could have variants, with or without *nú*, in the oral tradition. One version is as acceptable as the other. Dronke has a strong argument in this line, but her argument would be more convincing if the "common fault" was meaningless.

One underlying argument against the view that the different versions of *Vǫluspá* could be the result of three independent acts of transcription from oral tradition seems to be that the differences are too small, smaller than they usually are when compared with oral traditions in other cultures. Even so, the question is to what extent can we draw conclusions about one oral culture on the basis of material from another oral culture. The anthropological approach, by which we

---

[16] Garmr barks loudly before the Gnipa-cave, the bond will break and the aggressive one run free; she knows much of wisdom, I see further ahead to the strong victorious gods' ragnarǫk (*H*: I see further ahead, I can say much, to the strong victorious gods' ragnarǫk).

try to shed light on one phenomenon in one culture by comparison with other comparable cultures, may of course be very useful. But it is an open question how similar one oral culture really is to other oral cultures. It is difficult to ascertain to what extent oral tradition, in prose or verse, in different cultures shares certain distinctive features which can be defined as hallmarks of orality. These hallmarks may also differ from genre to genre within one and the same culture, but knowledge about one oral genre in a certain culture may also shed light on other oral genres in the same culture.

Regarding Eddic poems and the different versions of *Vǫluspá*, the fact that some stanzas in one version are lacking in the other version, and vice versa, most probably shows that stanzas could be forgotten during the oral transmission, and new stanzas could be added or perhaps replace stanzas which had been omitted. However, the lack of a stanza does not necessarily mean that the stanza has been lost forever. The next time the poem was performed orally a stanza which had been left out at a previous performance could pop up in the memory of the performer. Shorter or longer versions of an Eddic poem should also be seen in connection with "the immanent saga" theory. Even though this theory primarily claims to shed light on oral tradition in epic prose, it could have some relevance to all kinds of oral tradition because all oral genres share the quality that they are assumed to be known by the audience beforehand. However, the "immanent saga" theory would probably be more relevant to Eddic poems with a more typical epic style than *Vǫluspá*. But when judging different versions of an Eddic poem, we should bear in mind that a written transcription of an oral poem would in all likelihood in every stage be one of several possible versions. Even if a performer had planned to recite all the stanzas he knew – and we must assume that he would have wanted to recite them all if the poem was to be transcribed – he would probably forget a few stanzas, at least where long poems are concerned.

In the Old Norse society skaldic poetry in oral tradition existed side by side with Eddic poetry in oral tradition, probably often performed by the same people. Nobody doubts that skaldic poetry changed very little in oral tradition. For scholars who have argued that Eddic poetry is memorized poetry, the coexistence of skaldic and Eddic poetry in the same culture is strong evidence. Scholars who have argued that Eddic poetry is improvised poetry have stressed the differences between Eddic and skaldic art and looked upon the two types of poetry as very different genres following different rules. If we compare Eddic poetry with skaldic poetry there are great differences when contrasting Eddic poetry with the most typical skaldic metres such as *dróttkvætt*. However, some skaldic metres, like *kviðuháttr*, come close to Eddic metres, and skalds could also use Eddic metres in skaldic poems. It is in fact very difficult to draw a sharp line between Eddic and skaldic poetry. That should be a complicating factor for scholars who want to argue that one type of Old Norse poetry is memorized poetry, the other type improvised. A culture could of course have both forms. However, the existence of skaldic poetry which was memorized and in many cases much more complicated and probably more difficult to remember than

Eddic poetry, tells us that memorizing Eddic poetry should not be above the level of ability in the Old Norse culture.

As to whether the different versions of *Vǫluspá* are the result of oral or scribal variation, it is difficult to draw any firm conclusions. The types of variants I have focused upon here point, in my opinion, in the direction of oral variation. However, I would not disregard the possibility that the different versions of *Vǫluspá* as we have them are the result of some sort of a mix of oral and scribal variation. It is impossible to rule out the possibility that the *Hauksbók* version could be derived from the *Codex Regius* version through "a second" oral tradition. The differences between the different versions of *Vǫluspá* – especially if we compare the wording of individual stanzas – are in actuality small, and much smaller than those between oral variants within most other genres and cultures. This is, however, not necessarily an argument that the variants of *Vǫluspá* must then be the result of scribal variation. The variants of *Vǫluspá* could also be a reminder that the characteristics of oral literature may vary from one culture to another, and that even the main characteristic of oral literature according to the oral-formulaic theory, namely the formulas, is characteristic of this oral literature only to a certain degree.

Bibliography

Primary sources

Orkneyinga saga, ed. Finnbogi Guðmundsson. Íslenzk fornrit 34. Reykjavík.

Vǫluspá (Codex Regius), ed. Sophus Bugge in *Norrœn fornkvæði, Islandsk Samling af folkelige Oldtidsdigte om Nordens Guder og Heroer almindelig kaldet Sæmundar Edda hins fróða*: 12–18. Christania 1867.

Vǫluspá (Hauksbók), ed. Sophus Bugge in *Norrœn fornkvæði, Islandsk Samling af folkelige Oldtidsdigte om Nordens Guder og Heroer almindelig kaldet Sæmundar Edda hins fróða*: 19–26. Christania 1867.

Secondary sources

Boer, R. C. 1904: "Kritik der Völuspá." *Zeitschrift für deutsche Philologie*, XXXVI.

Bugge, Sophus (ed.) 1867: *Norrœn fornkvæði, Islandsk Samling af folkelige Oldtidsdigte om Nordens Guder og Heroer almindelig kaldet Sæmundar Edda hins fróða*. Christania.

Clover, Carol J. 1986: "The long prose form." *Arkiv för nordisk filologi*, 101.

Dronke, Ursula (ed.) 1997: *Mythological Poems, The Poetic Edda*, vol. II. Oxford.

Einar Már Jónsson 1988: "Góður veðurviti." *Timarít máls og menningar*, 88 (3), review of Gísli Sigurðsson's *Hávamál og Völuspá*, Reykjavík 1987.

——— 1990a: "Heilsurækt fræðanna. Munnleg geymd og eddukvæði." *Timarít máls og menningar*, 90 (1).

——— 1990b: "Heilsurækt fræðanna. Munnleg geymd og eddukvæði – niður-lag." *Timarít máls og menningar*, 90 (2).

GÍSLI SIGURÐSSON 1988: "Ádrepur: Fordómar fáfræðinnar." *Timarít máls og menningar*, 88 (4).

——— 1990a: "Munnmenntir og staða fræðanna." *Timarít máls og menningar*, 90 (2).

——— 1990b: "On the classification of Eddic heroic poetry in view of the oral theory." In *The Seventh International Saga Conference: Poetry in Scandinavian Middle Ages, Spoleto 4–10 Septembre 1988*, Spoleto, preprint 1988.

GÍSLI SIGURÐSSON (ed.) 1998: *Eddukvæði*. Reykjavík.

GUREVIC, Elena A. 1986: "The formulaic pair in Eddic Poetry: An experimental analysis." In John Lindow, Lars Lönnroth & Gerd Wolfgang Weber (eds.) *Structure and Meaning in Old Norse Literature: New Approaches to Textual Analysis and Literary Criticism*, Odense.

HARRIS, Joseph 1983: "Eddic Poetry as oral poetry: The evidence of parallel passages in the Helgi poems for questions of composition and performance." In Robert J. Glendinnig & Haraldur Bessason (eds.) *Edda: A Collection of Essays*, Winnipeg.

——— 1985: "Eddic Poetry." In Carol J. Clover & John Lindow (eds.) *Old Norse-Icelandic Literature: A Critical Guide, Islandica*, vol. XLV.

HEUSLER, Andreas (ed.) 1937: *Codex regius of the Elder Edda: MS no. 2365 4to in the Old Royal collection in the Royal Library of Copenhagen, Corpus Codicum Islandicorum Medii Aevi*, vol. 10. København.

JOHANSSON, Karl G. 2000: "Vǫluspá – muntlig og skriftlig tradisjon. En diskus-sion om skärningspunkten mellan filologi och litteraturvetenskap." In Krist-inn Jóhannesson, Karl G. Johansson & Lars Lönnroth (eds.) *Den fornnordiska texten i filologisk och litteraturvetenskaplig belysning, Gotenburg Old Norse Stud-ies*, vol. 2, Göteborg.

JÓN HELGASON (ed.) 1951: *Vǫluspá Hávamál, Eddadigte*, vol. I. København.

JÓN HELGASON & HOLTSMARK, Anne (eds.) 1941: *Háttalykill enn forni, Biblio-theca Arnamagnæana*, vol. 1. København.

KELLOGG, Robert 1990: "The prehistory of Eddic Poetry." In *The Seventh Inter-national Saga Conference, Spoleto 4–10 sept 1988. Poetry in the Scandinavian Middle Ages*, Spoleto, preprints 1988.

——— 1991: "Literacy and orality in the Poetic Edda." In A. N. Doane & Carol Braun Pasternack (eds.) *Vox Intexta: Orality and Textuality in the Middle Ages*, pp. 89–101, Madison, Wisconsin.

LÖNNROTH, Lars 1971: "Hjálmar's death-song and the delivery of Eddic Poetry." *Speculum: A Journal of Medieval Studies*, XLVI (1).

——— 1978: *Den dubbla scenen: Muntlig diktning från Eddan til ABBA*. Stock-holm.

——— 1979: "The double scene of Arrow-Odd's drinking contest." In Hans Bekker-Nielsen (ed.) *Medieval Narrative: A Symposium*, Odense.

NORDAL, Sigurður 1923: *Völuspá*. Reykjavík.

PARRY, Milman 1930: "Studies in the epic technique of oral verse-making. I. Homer and Homeric style." *Harvard Studies in Classical Philology*, 41.

QUINN, Judy 1990: "*Vǫluspá* and the composition of Eddic verse." In *The Seventh International Saga Conference, Spoleto 4–10 sept 1988. Poetry in the Scandinavian Middle Ages*, Spoleto, preprints 1988.

SCHOLES, Robert & KELLOGG, Robert 1966: *The Nature of Narrative*. New York.

Index

Zeta, 98
Zmaj Despot Vuk, *see* Vuk
     Branković
Zmajognjeni Vuk, *see* Vuk
     Branković
Zumthor, Paul, 71

Þiðriks saga, 131
Þjóðólfr Arnórsson, 171, 183
Þjóðólfr ór Hvini, 168, 171, 177,
     178, 183
Þjóstólfr, 190
Þórðar saga kakala, 14
Þórdís Súrsdóttir, 31, 38
Þórðr leysingjasonr, 194, 201
Þorgeirr Hávarsson, 10
Þorgeirr Otkelsson, 202
Þorgeirr Starkaðsson, 201, 202
Þorgils saga ok Hafliða, 9, 12, 14,
     156, 214
Þorgils saga skarða, 14
Þorgrímr nefr, 35–37
Þorgrímr Þórsteinsson, 32–37
Þórir hundsfótr, 159
Þorkell Súrsson, 31–34, 36, 37
Þormóðr Bersason, 10
Þormóðr Óláfsson, 186–188, 202
Þorsteinn Egilsson, 15
Þorsteinn Þorkelsson, 35
Þórður Ingi Guðjónsson, 30
Þráinn Sigfússon, 188, 189, 197,
     202

Øxarflokkr, 183

Aarmote, Hæge, 143
Aase, maiden, 127

Ǫrlygsstaðir, 11